Lakes and Fells
of the English Lake District
The Art of Jennifer Buxton RMS HS

by Tom Buxton

Copyright

For more information please visit

www.JenniferBuxton.uk

Map Copyright

Acknowledgements

Author
Tom Buxton

Illustrations
Jennifer Buxton

Cover Design
Tom Buxton

Editor
Susan Johnson

Technical Review
Henry Buxton
Brenda Griffin

Photographs
Tom Buxton
Barrow News - www.nwemail.co.uk
Westmorland Gazette - www.thewestmorlandgazette.co.uk
Others (unknown)

Maps
Ashworth Maps and Interpretation Ltd
www.ashworthmaps.co.uk

OpenStreetMap contributors
www.openstreetmap.org

First Published in 2021
Manuscript: v 4.2
ISBN: 978-1-7777939-1-3

in loving memory of
Jennifer Mary Buxton
1937 - 2017

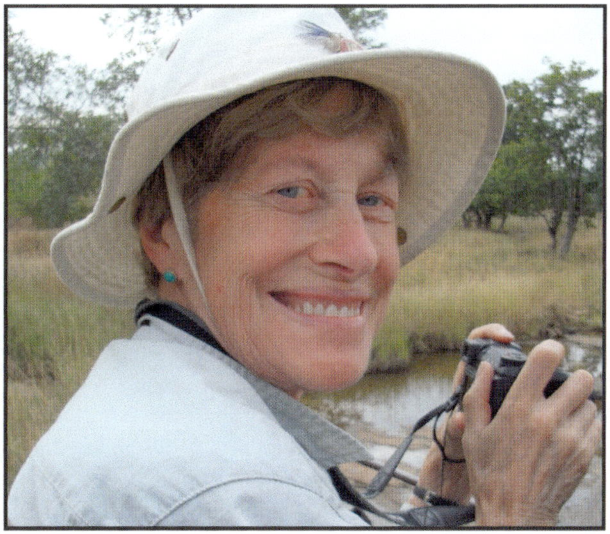

Jennifer

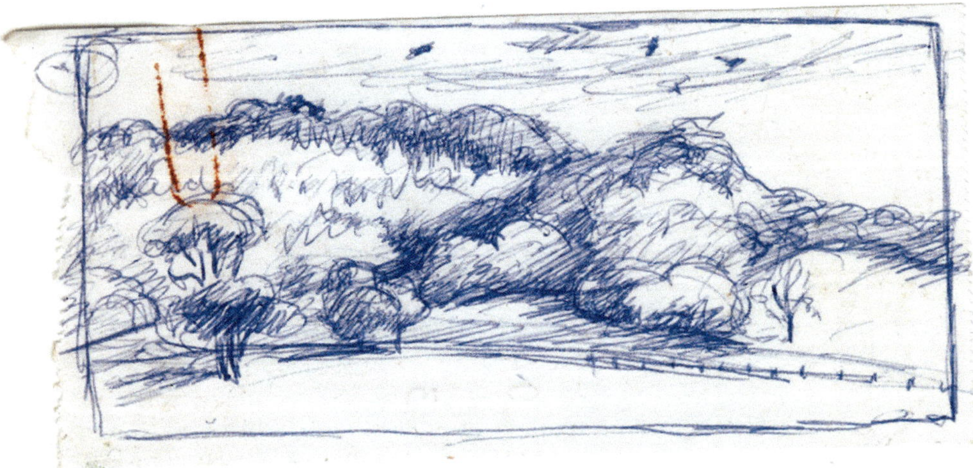

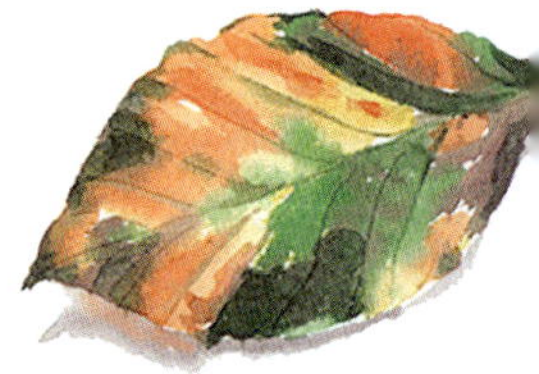

Jennifer was wont to sketch on anything that happened to be available. I think this is the back of an envelope; you can see the outline of a rusty paperclip that must have been attached to it at one point.

Wetherlam from East of Lake, Coniston Water

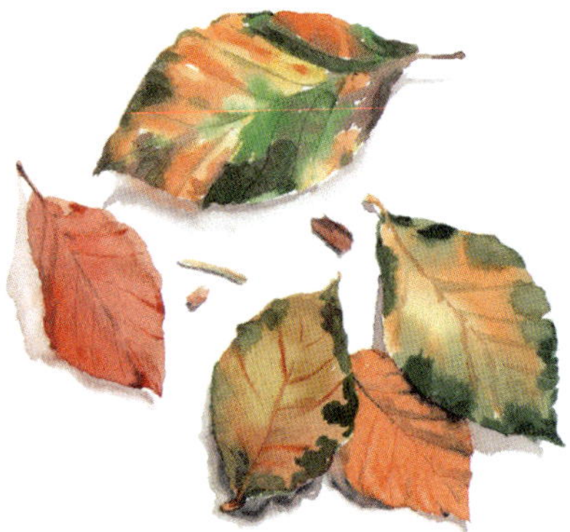

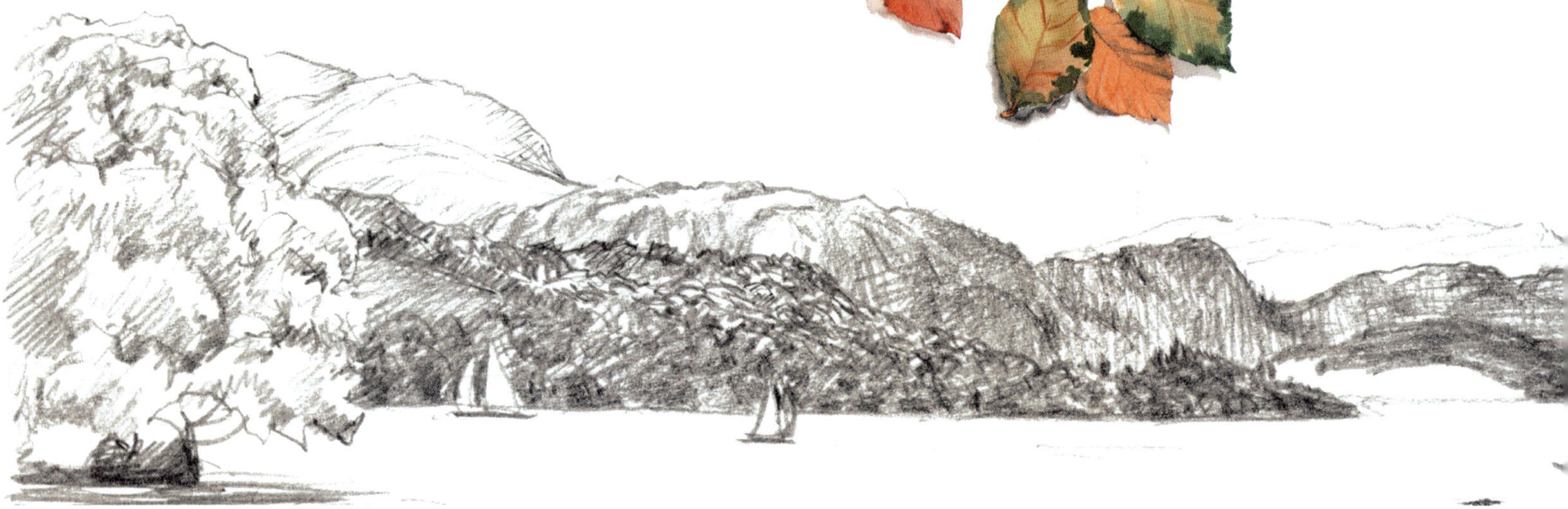

Index

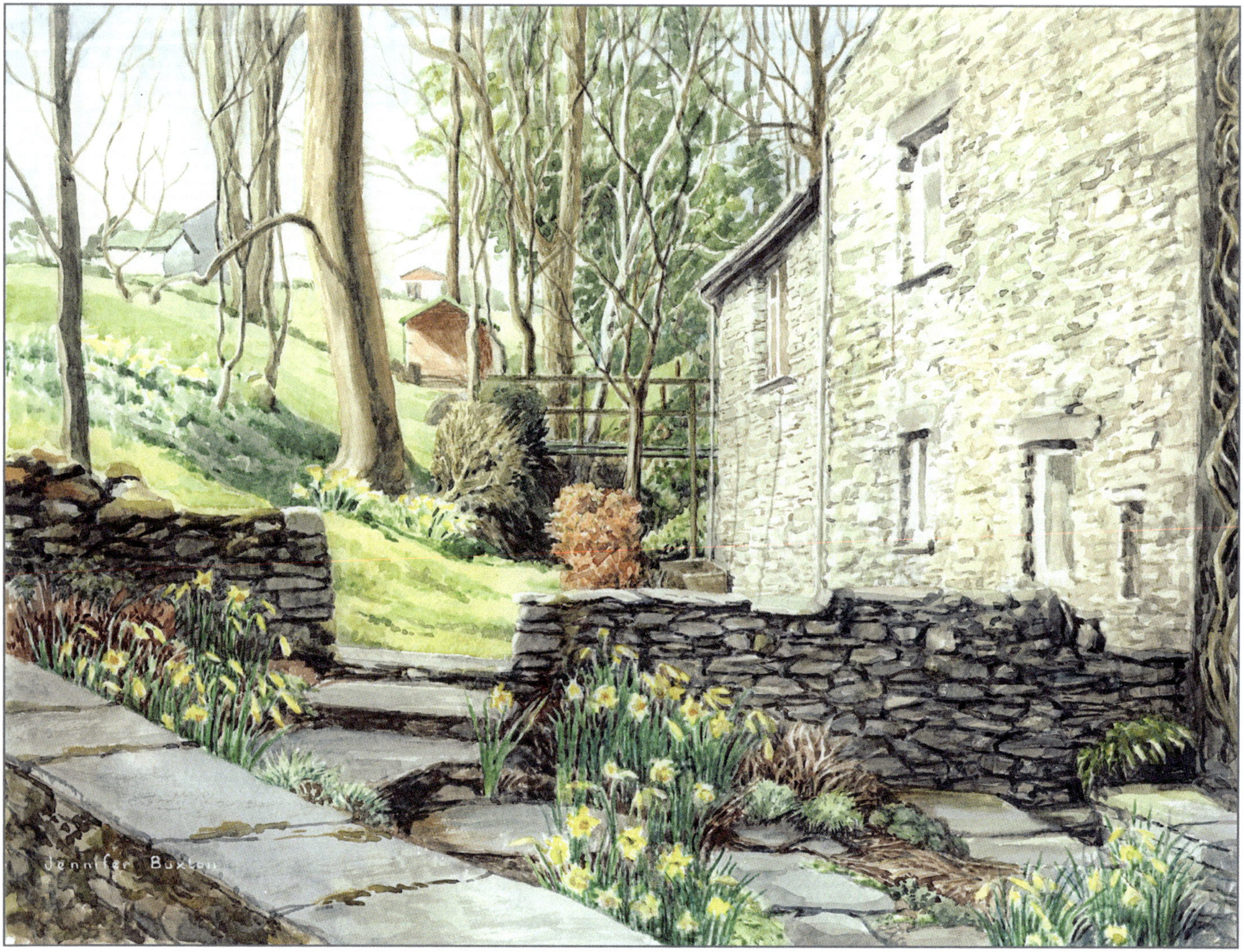

A typical Lakeland farmhouse

Forward by Tom Buxton

My mother, Jennifer Buxton, was one of the United Kingdom's foremost miniature portrait painters. Even as a young girl growing up during the second world war, Jennifer displayed an amazing talent for drawing and painting. She could capture a true likeness regardless of whether she was drawing a person, an animal, or a landscape, and this was coupled with an incredible curiosity and attention to detail. Throughout her life she would draw attention to the colours and shapes of things in the world around her that most of us have become oblivious to, and then capture their spirit in the drawings and paintings that were her driving force.

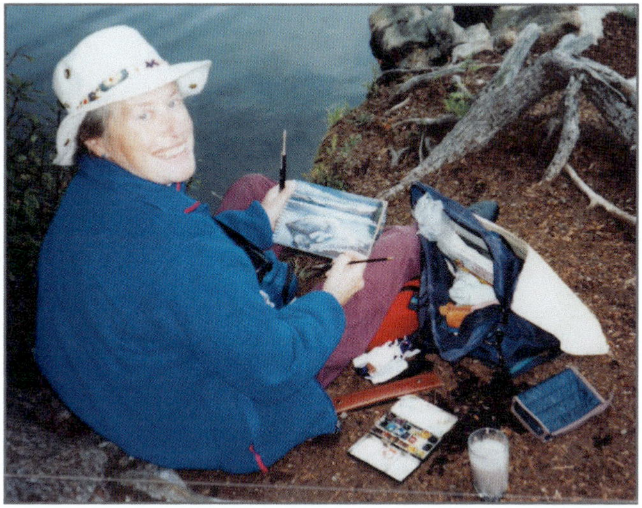

Jennifer painting in Canada...

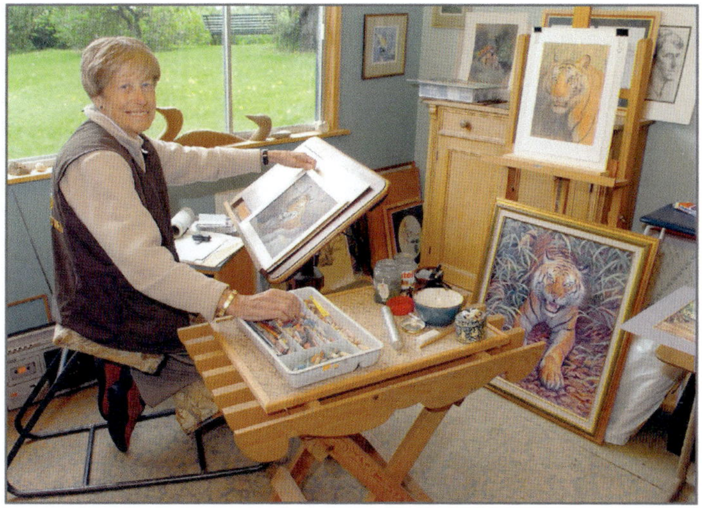

...and in her studio (© Newsquest Cumbria)

Jennifer was a free spirit, an inspirational soul. I count myself forever fortunate to have been able to share in some of her many adventures. Sometimes alone, but often together with my father Vic, I've experienced the world through her eyes in such places as the north of Scotland, Canada and the national parks of Madhya Pradesh, India.

On elephant rides into the jungle in search of tigers, and road trips to Tofino on the west coast of Vancouver Island, always with Jennifer settled in a seat with her sketchbook on her lap and her camera around her neck, recording the sites around us as they unfolded. Our friends Bill and Dora, also frequent companions on these trips, would joke that the journey was a waste if she hadn't filled at least five pages of her sketchbook by the time we arrived at our destination!

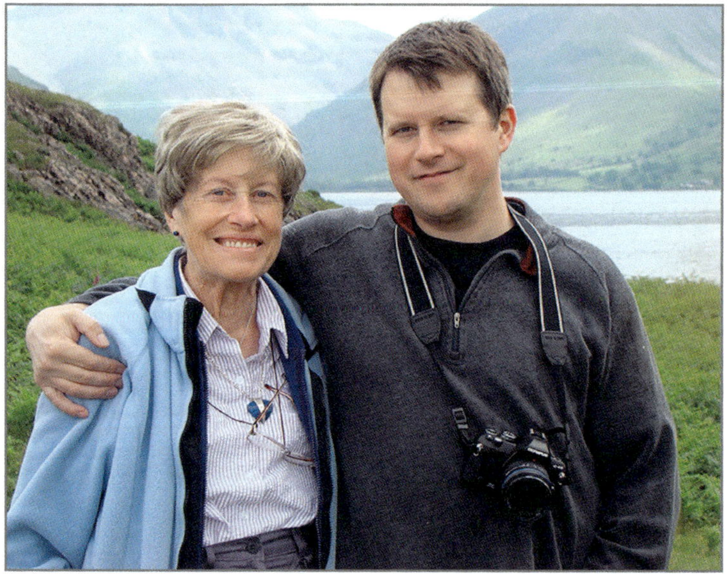

Jennifer and I
by Wastwater, June 2007

Over the years, Jennifer and I had talked about combining the pictures and stories from some of these adventures into a book, but it wasn't until after her death in 2017 that the letters she'd written to her godchildren in Tasmania would provide Vic and I with the basis to start making that happen.

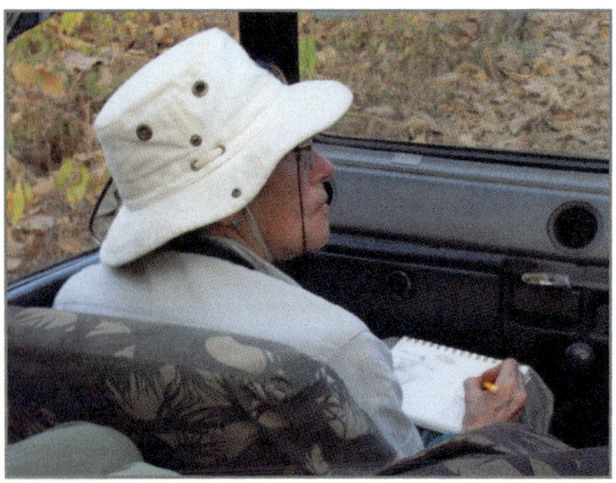

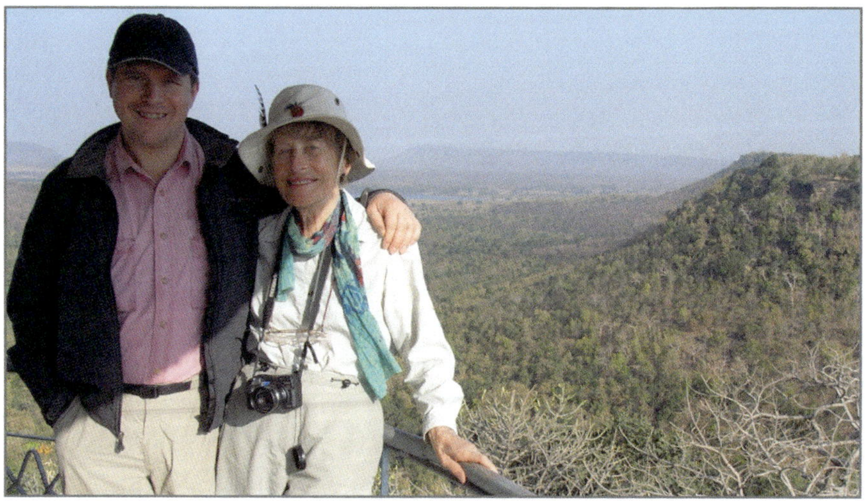

With Jennifer in Panna Tiger Reserve, India, in 2006

We began with a website to showcase a selection of her art, **www.JenniferBuxton.uk**, and then started to work on three books that would tell the story of her trips to India looking for tigers. The first book was published just prior to Vic's death in 2018, but the process of creating and proofing the first of those books had opened our eyes to the impact of seeing her drawings and paintings presented together, rather than scattered among galleries and private collections in isolation. This is the motivation behind this book, and the others that are still to come.

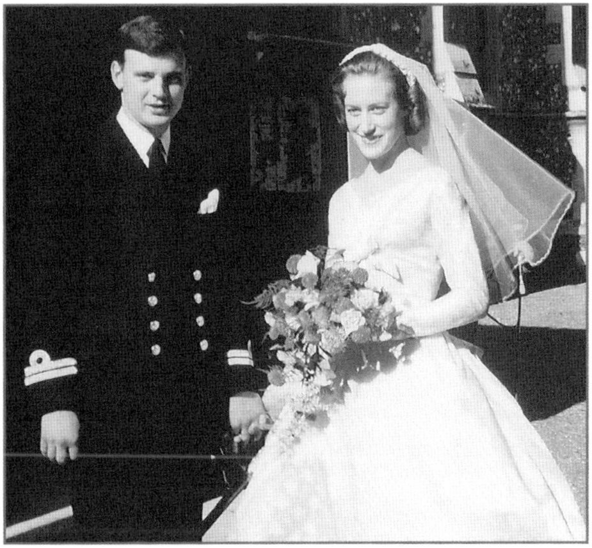

Vic and Jennifer,
6 September 1958

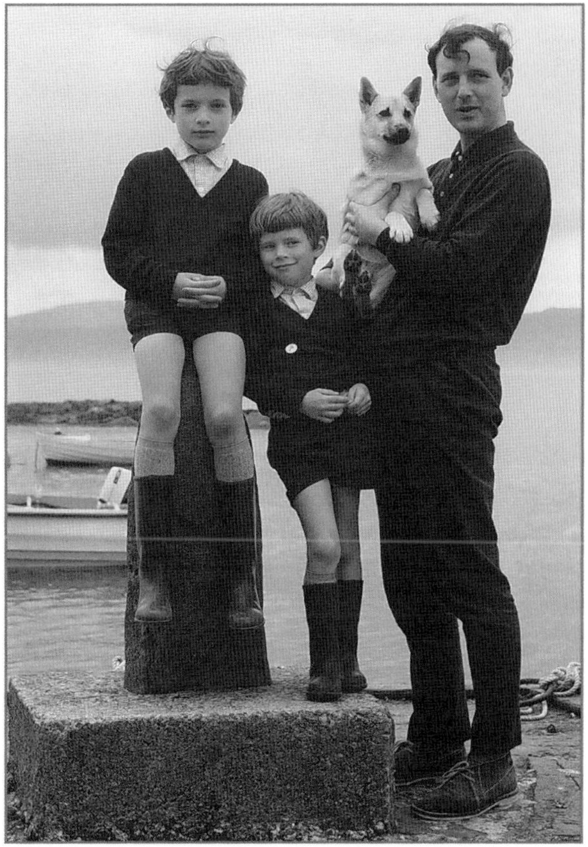

Henry, Tom, Vic, and Mutley the dog

The subject of this book came naturally out of the process of cataloging the nearly 3000 paintings and drawings that Jennifer has left behind as part of her personal collection. The Lake District had been a huge part of her life; firstly during the period in the 1960's when Vic, at the time a young naval officer, was involved in the commissioning of the submarine HMS Valiant at Barrow-in-Furness; then later during school holidays when we stayed in a cottage we owned in Baycliff just south of Ulverston; and finally after Vic retired from the navy in 1987, when he and Jennifer moved back to the area, and lived there for the remainder of their lives apart from a brief sojourn in Thurso, Caithness.

Throughout this long association with the area, Jennifer loved to paint the Lakeland fells and lakes, and as a result there was a rich collection of watercolours and pencil sketches to select from, created over a period of nearly 50 years. I sought to illustrate this unique region of the UK through Jennifer's art and eye for the dramatic. I sincerely hope you enjoy seeing the Lake District as she saw it, and come to love it as she did, if you don't already.

Tom Buxton, May 2021

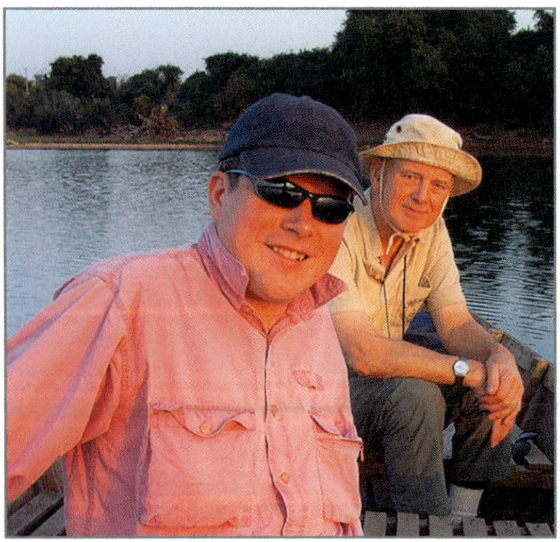

With my father Vic, in India in 2006, taking a break after a number of days searching for tigers in nearby Panna National Park.

Jennifer had opted not to take a rest day, and as was so often the case, her luck at being in the right place at the right time meant that she saw a leopard in the park that same afternoon. Vic and I were out in a wooden boat with a local fisherman, but true to my usual form, we didn't catch anything!

Introduction

Jennifer was born in 1937 in Hemel Hempstead, North London. She started to draw people and animals when she was very young, and by the age of 10 she was taking weekly lessons with Marguerite Frobisher at her School of Animal Painting in Bushey, Hertfordshire. At 18, she gained a scholarship to the Byam Shaw School in Kensington, where she won the head painting prize in her final year.

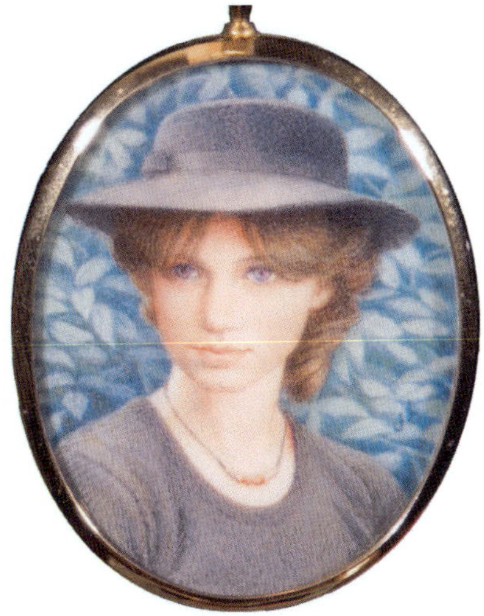

Cousin Rebecca

She initially worked with oils and pastels, but after marrying a young naval officer, Victor Buxton, in 1958 and, while bringing up her young family, she started to paint miniature portraits in watercolor, being inspired by an elderly professional miniaturist, Boyd Waters. Her talent for recreating a likeness was prodigious, and after a period of experimentation she perfected her own method of painting tiny portraits on ivory and vellum. Over a number of years she became acclaimed as one of the UK's best miniature portrait painters.

Jennifer was elected into the Royal Society of Miniature Painters, Sculptors and Engravers (RMS) in 1969, served as the society's honorary secretary for nine years, and was on the board of governors of the Federation of British Artists. In 1985 she was awarded the Royal Miniature Society's Gold Bowl in its inaugural year for the best miniature portrait in an exhibition of over 700 works. She won the Bell Award for the best miniature portrait in the Hilliard Society Exhibition in 1986, and the Mundy Sovereign Award for the best portrait in the RMS Exhibition in 1987. She exhibited work all over the UK, as well as in France, Canada and the USA where she won the prize for best portrait at the Miniature Society of Florida exhibition in 1993.

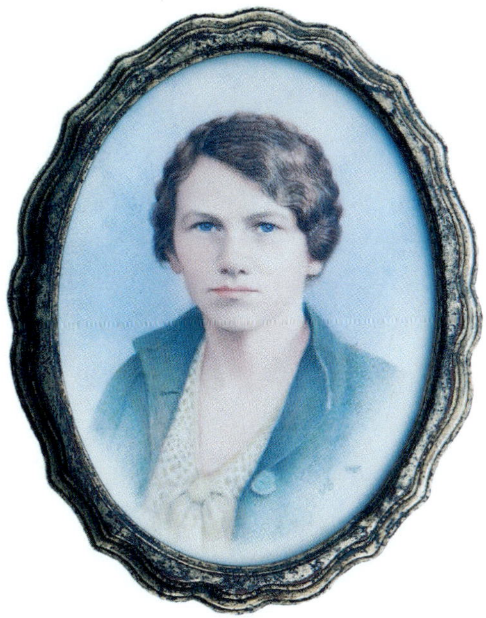

Winner of the 1985
RMS Gold Bowl

In 1988 Jennifer retired from the Royal Miniature Society to concentrate on painting and drawing in larger formats. Over the ensuing years she continued to build a large collection of work including landscapes of her beloved Lake District, other locations in the UK, Canada, France and Australia, portraits of tigers, horses, dogs, cats, and other animals, and also Her Majesty's submarines.

From 1991 to 1994 she was chairman of the Ulverston Society of Artists, and for many years taught portrait painting in Bardsea and Ulverston.

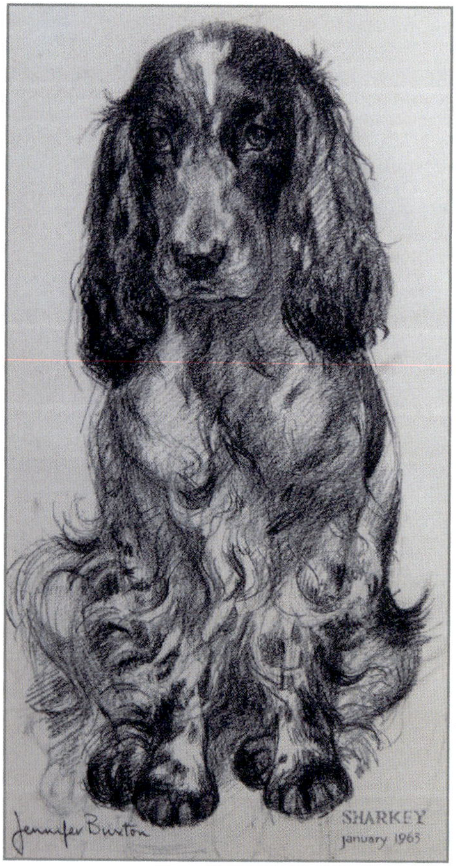

Sharkey in a rare moment of contrition

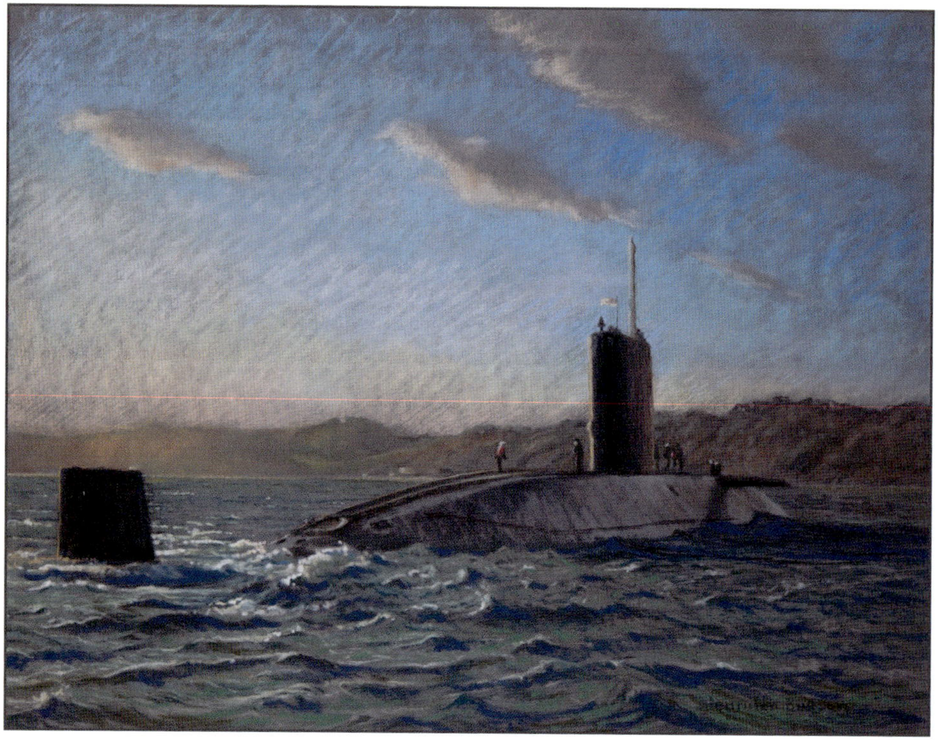

HMS Valiant

Jennifer was in great demand on the Women's Institute lecture circuit as a speaker on such diverse topics as miniature portrait painting, the adventures of a naval captain's wife, and her ever popular cooking disasters.

After an initial visit to India in 2004, Jennifer spent the last years of her life raising money and awareness for preserving wild tigers within the Panna and Bandhavgarh National Parks in Madhya Pradesh in central India. With her financial assistance, the school in Madla Village outside the Panna Tiger Reserve was rebuilt and expanded, and the children taken on trips into the park to help them understand how tigers and their natural habitat contribute to the local economy.

Jennifer first moved to the English Lake District around 1960 with her husband Victor who was working in Barrow-in-Furness at the time on the commissioning of HMS Valiant. This was the start of her love of the region which continued throughout her life. When the young family moved away to Bath they still returned for the school holidays, and while the rest of the family walked on the fells or fished in the lakes, Jennifer sketched and painted the landscapes of this beautiful part of England. After Vic retired from the navy they returned to the area and lived there for the remainder of their lives.

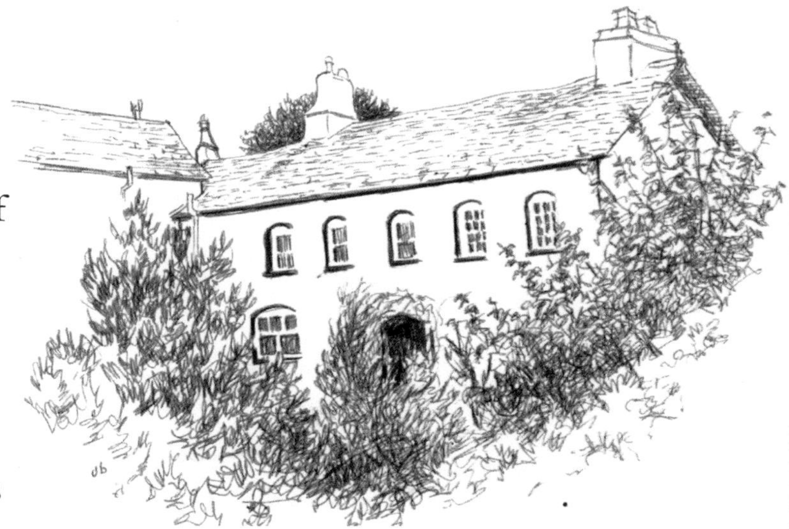

Windy Ash, Osmotherley, where Jennifer lived from 1986

After an illness lasting several years, Jennifer passed away on January 17, 2017 at the age of 79. She left a personal legacy of over 3000 pictures and sculptures in many media, as well as portraits and landscapes painted on commission in private collections all over the world.

The English Lake District

Covering 912 square miles (2,362 square km) in Cumbria, north west England, the Lake District National Park is a UNESCO World Heritage Site that has been home to the likes of William Wordsworth, Beatrix Potter and John Ruskin.

The area has a rich history with influences from Roman, Viking, Old and Middle English settlers, reflected in local names such as beck, fell, mere and grange.

The park contains 16 lakes: Windermere, Coniston Water, Esthwaite Water, Elterwater, Grasmere, Rydal Water, Thirlmere, Haweswater, Ullswater, Wastwater, Ennerdale Water, Derwent Water, Loweswater, Buttermere, Crummock Water, and Bassenthwaite Lake.

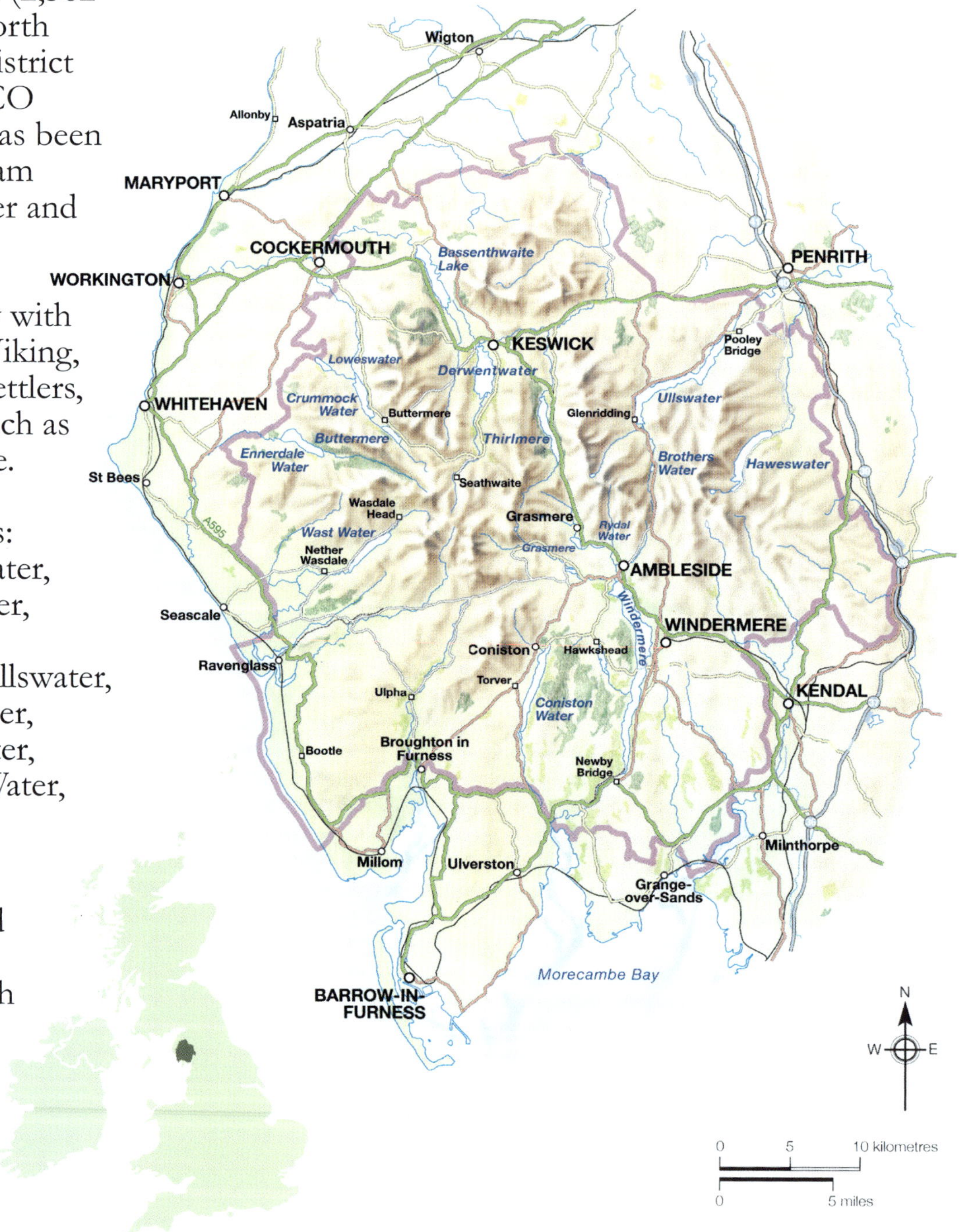

The Lake District's rugged fells and sweeping lakes make it a popular spot with artists and photographers. The vistas evolve from rolling moorland in the south to higher fells and remote lakes in the north.

Approach from the M6

I chose to start our journey with the drive into the South Lakes and the Furness Peninsular from Junction 36 of the M6 motorway on the eastern boarders of the Lake District.

It's about a 40 minute drive on the A590, and provides an impressive view of the imposing bulk of Whitbarrow Scar. On a clear day there are views north to the southern fells of the Lake District National Park.

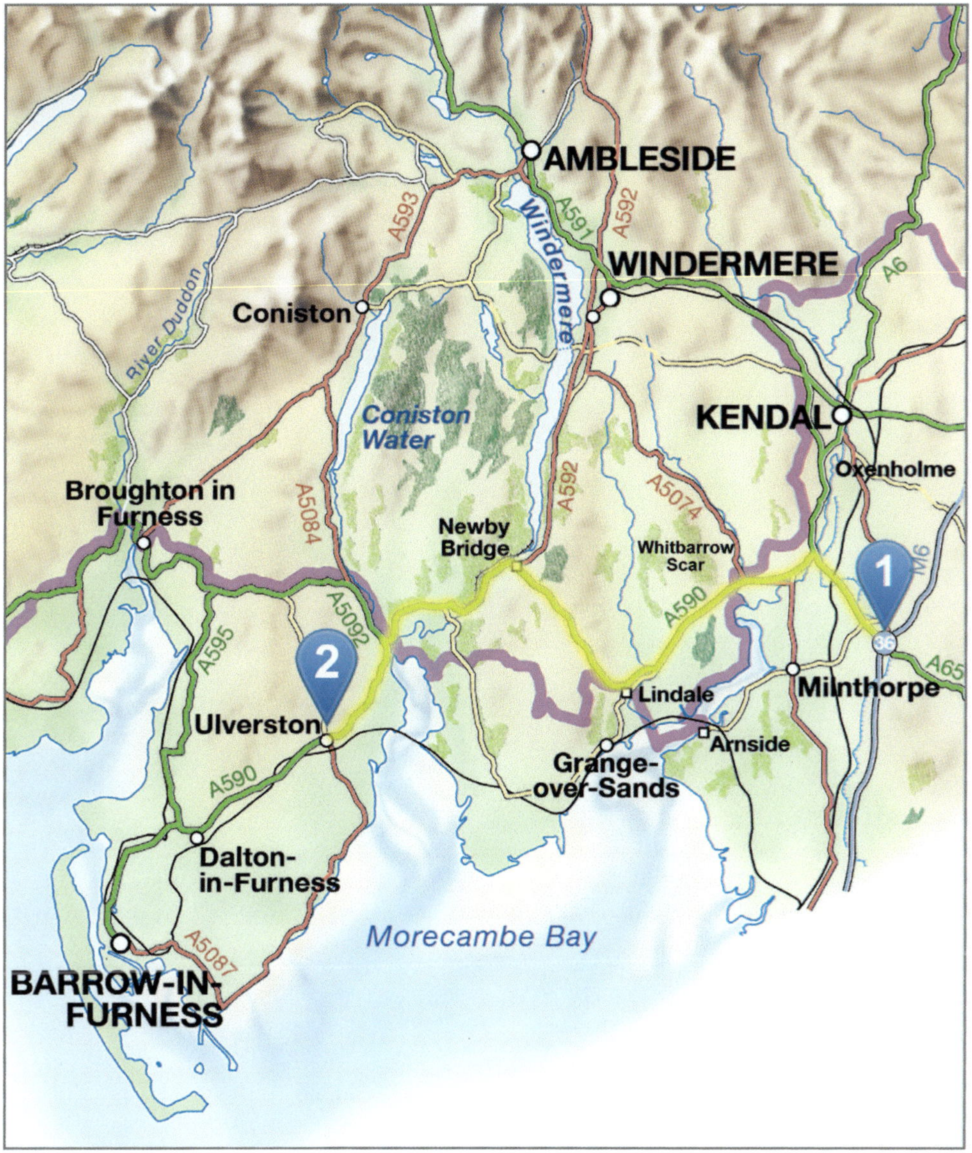

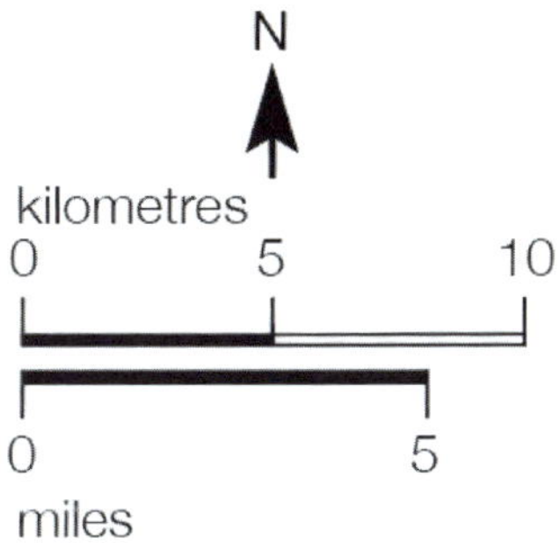

Map Locations

1. M6 Junction 36
2. Ulverston

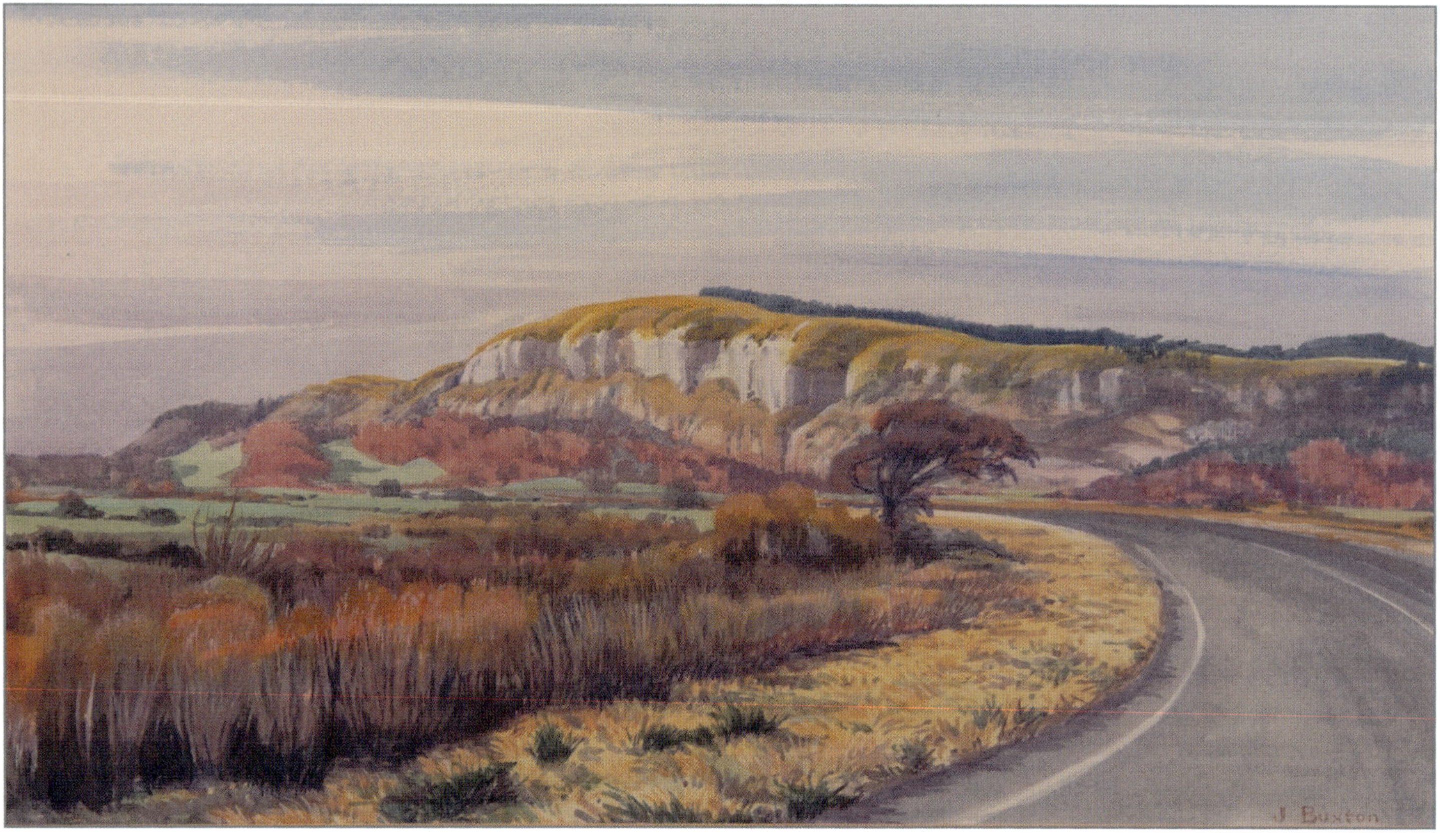

While she painted this watercolor of Whitbarrow Scar in her studio, Jennifer painted many of the landscapes in this book "in the field". Though she could create an impression of a scene in minutes, in most cases a painting would take her an hour or two to complete and this could lead to some challenging situations. I remember one time when I was very young, being attacked by red ants and trying to get my mother's attention but failing dismally to distract her from the painting she was working on. Often autumn and winter sketches would end up with smudges from rain or ice damage from freezing paint, an occupational hazard when working with watercolours outside!

Whitbarrow Scar from close to Arnside

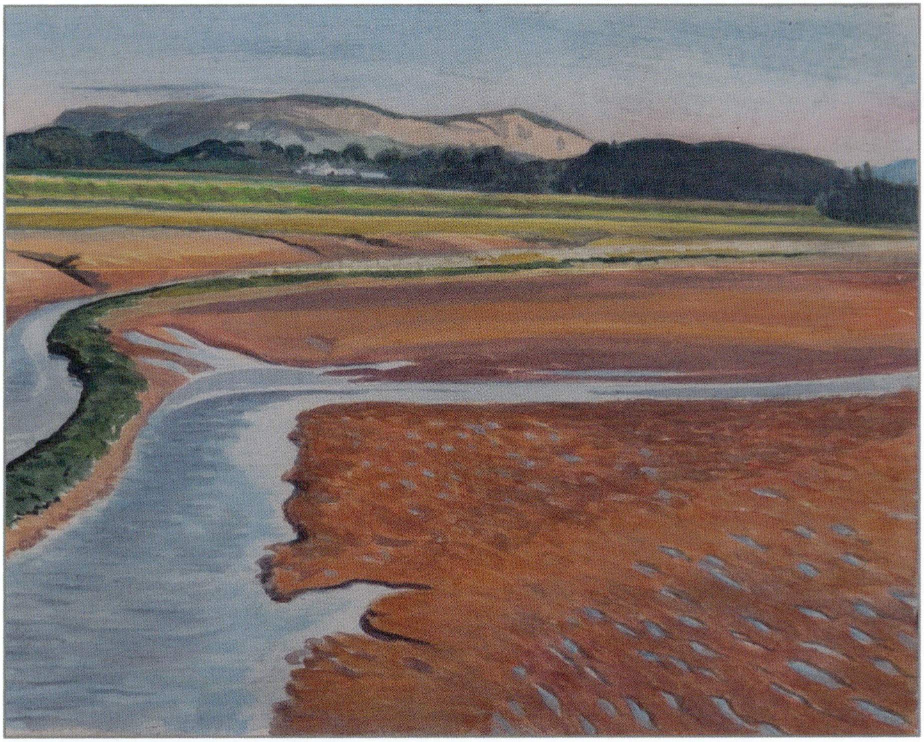

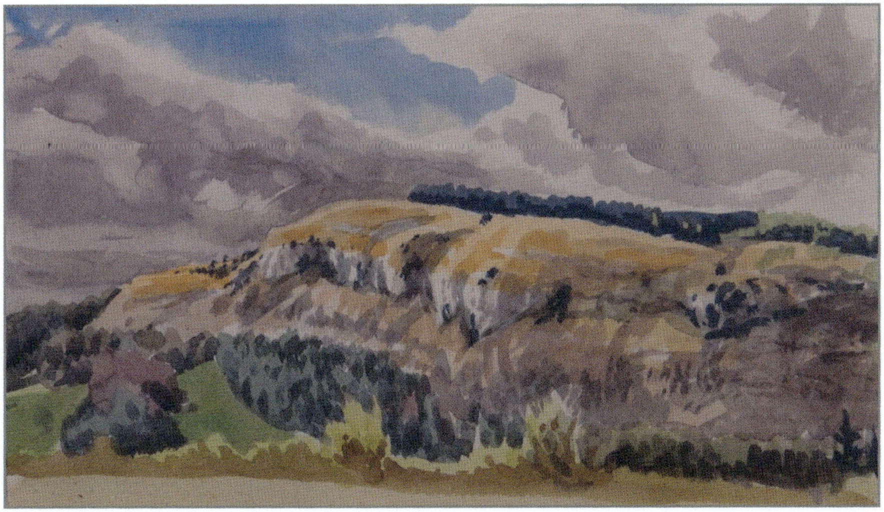

Jennifer mourned the loss of the crest of trees which proudly brushed the skyline along the back of Whitbarrow Scar. This painting was done shortly before the trees were cut down.

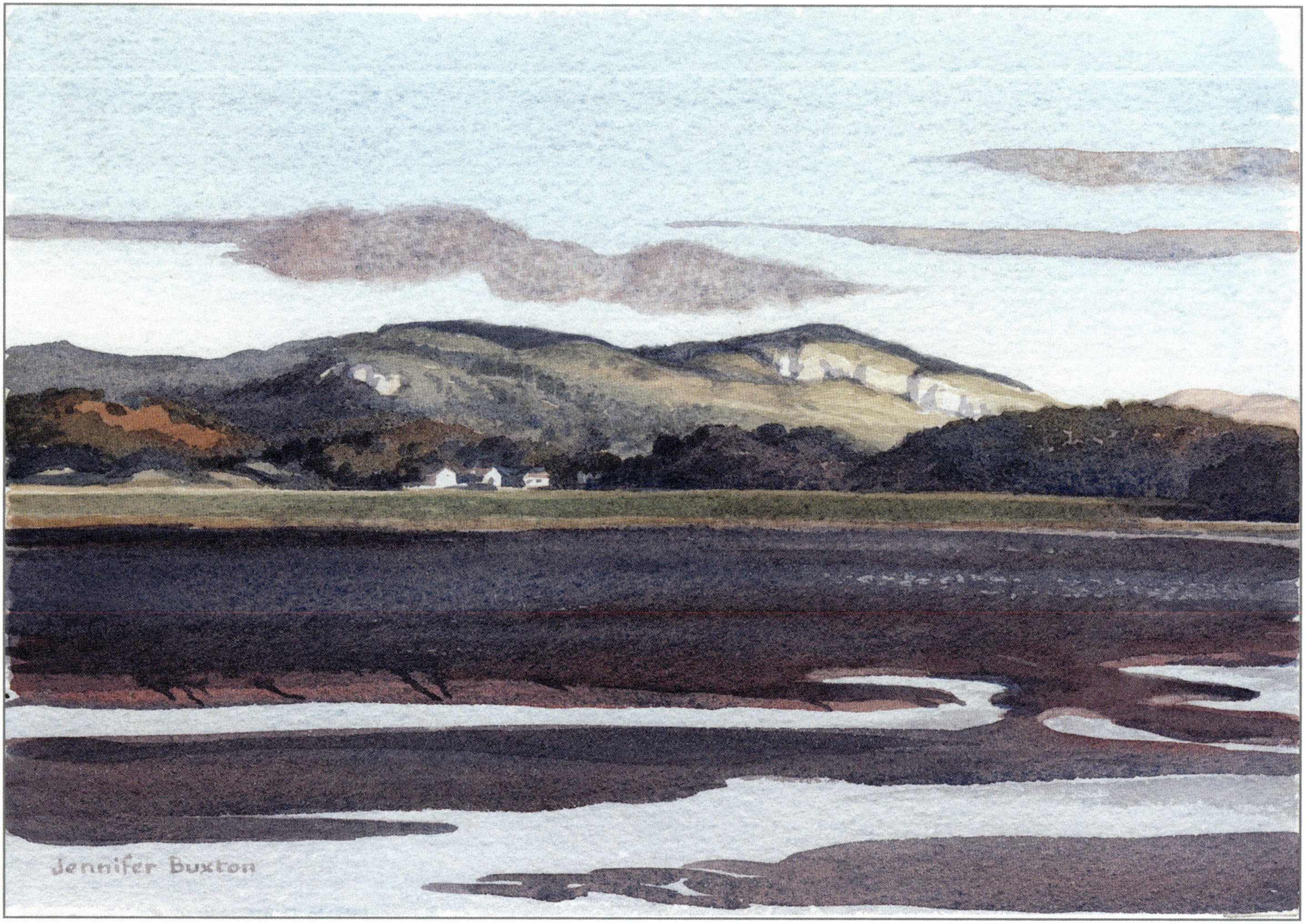

Towards Whitbarrow National Nature Reserve and
Whitbarrow Scar, from across the River Kent

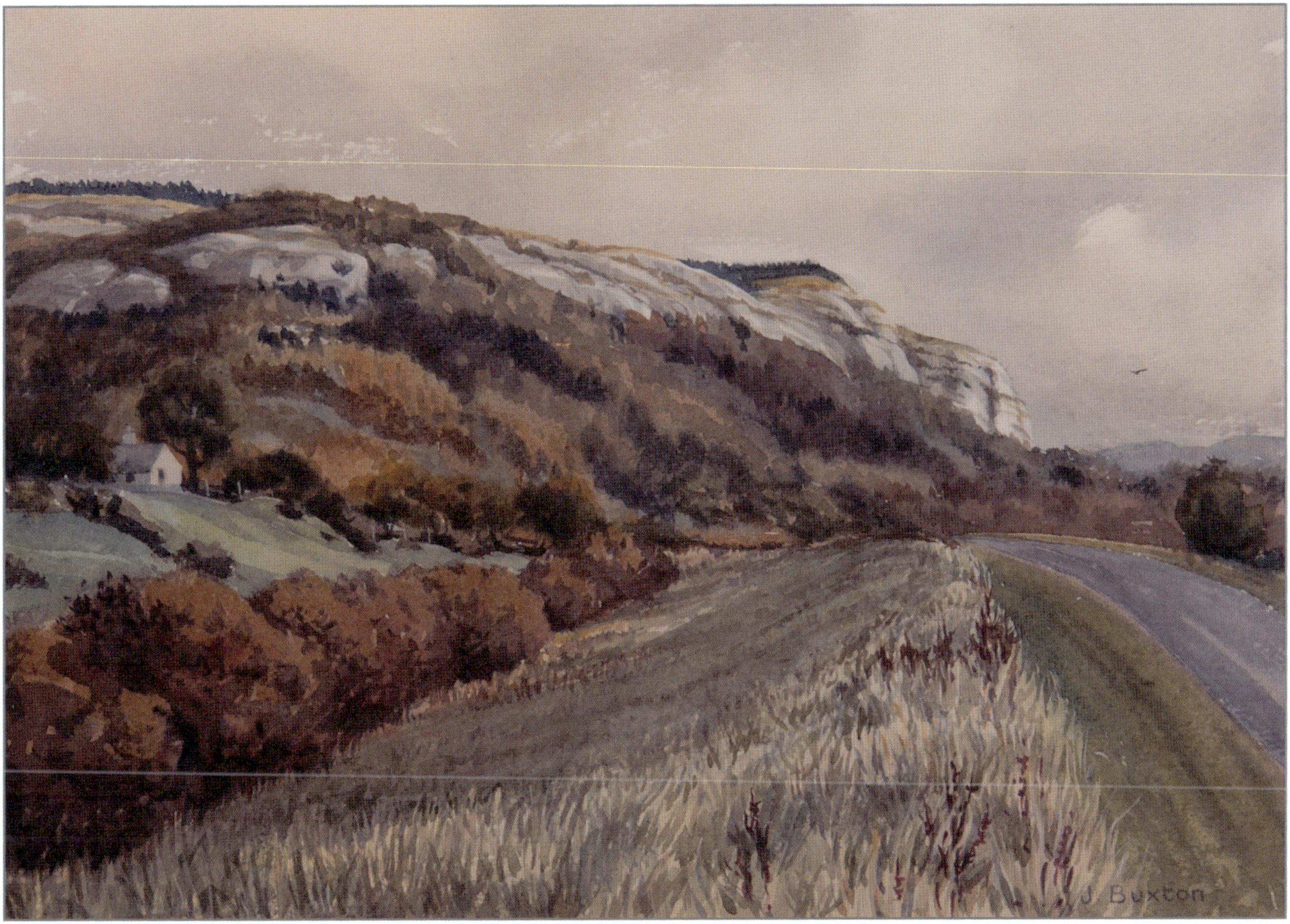

I think this painting was done from a photo taken before the dual carriageway was added to this section of the A590. Sometimes we'd stop in some rather precarious spots to allow Jennifer to take a quick photograph of a view that caught her eye!

Jennifer was a keen photographer and used to develop and print her own black-and-white photos when we were younger. Taking photographs to work from later was an important part of her process, however she would also paint or sketch in the moment, sometimes adding notes to herself to remind her of the colours or some detail in the clouds.

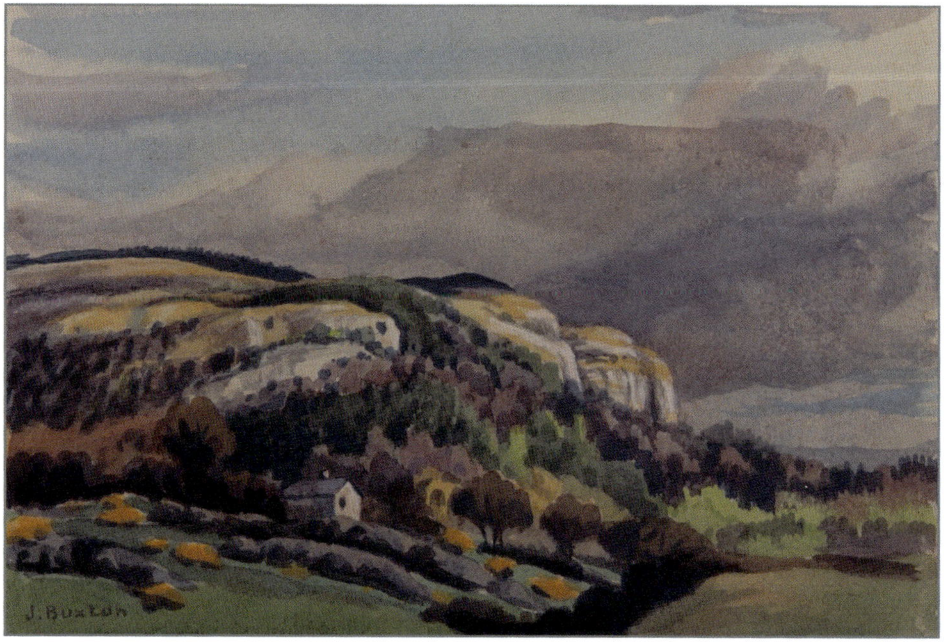

Field notes, sketches and the finished artwork

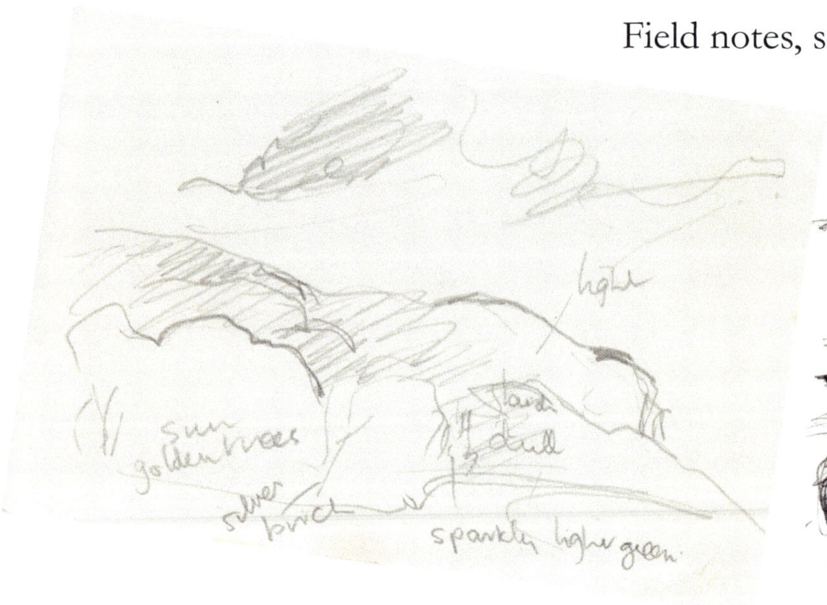

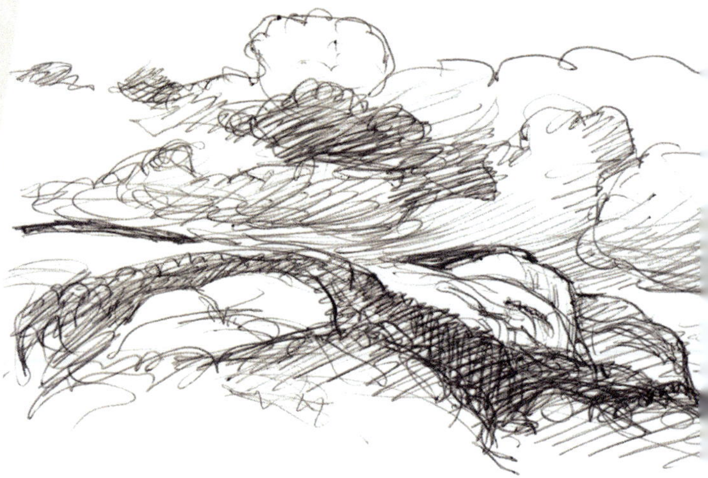

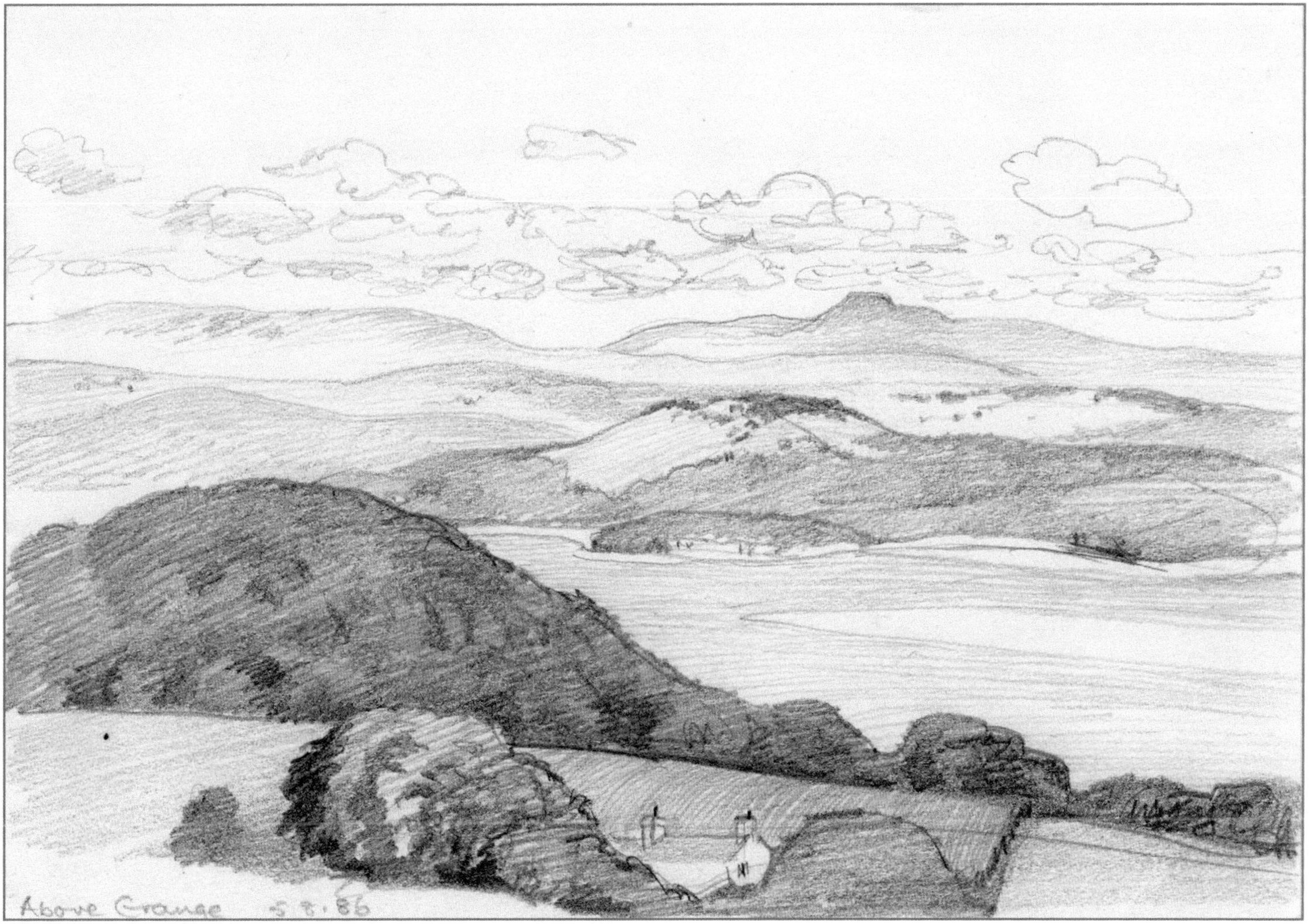

The A590 bypasses a number of small towns along the shore of Morecambe Bay such as Silverdale, Arnside and Grange-over-Sands, but they are all delights to explore in their own right when you have time. My brother Henry and I used to go climbing on some of the crags and disused quarries around Silverdale after Henry got his driving license.

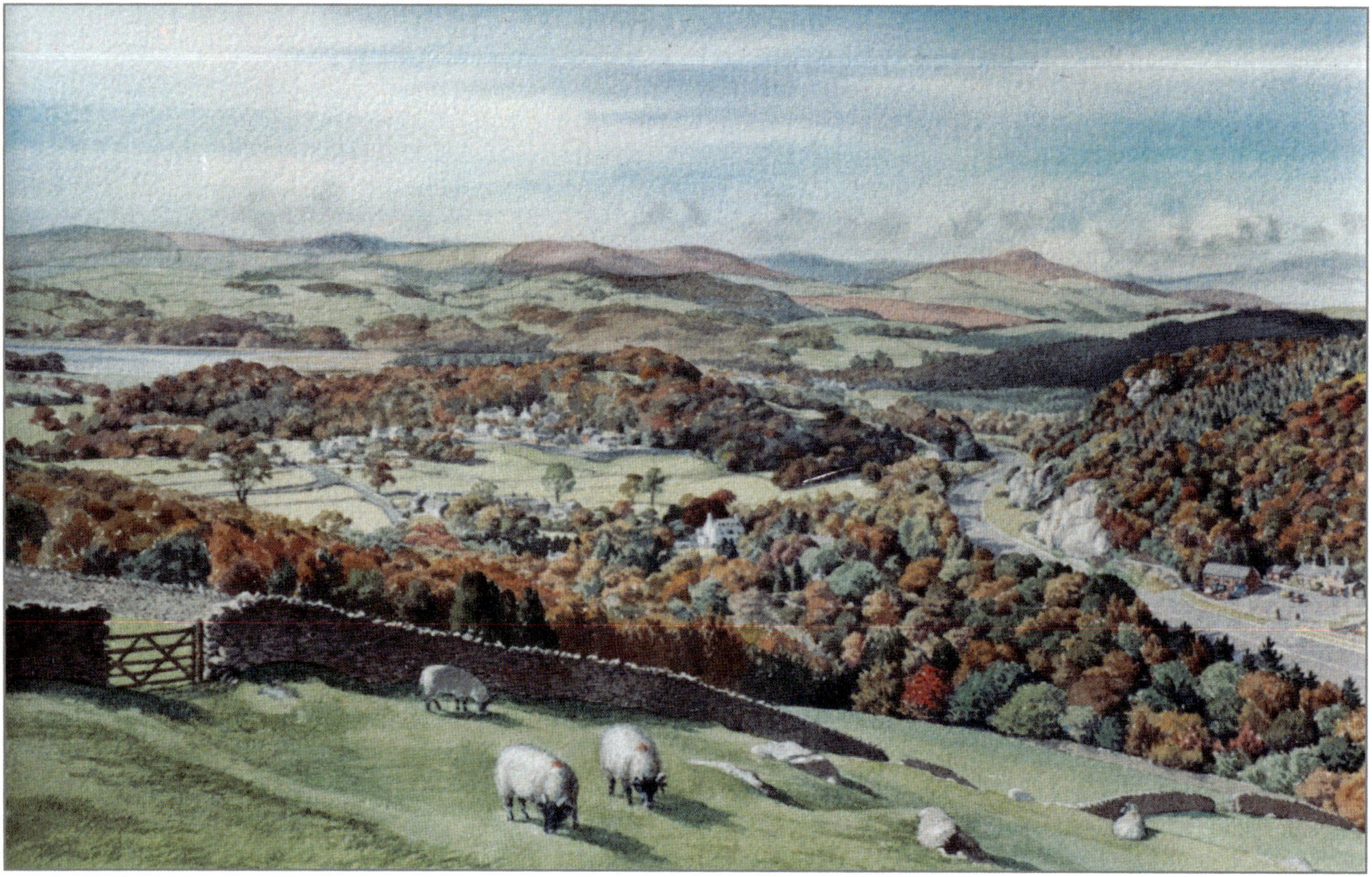

Approaching Morecambe Bay

This was painted from photographs taken above the A590 at Backbarrow, looking towards Greenodd. Ulverston is to the left, which is south-west; Coniston Old Man and the Central Lakeland fells are out of sight to the right.

Ulverston and Osmotherley

Ulverston is a small market town of about 12,000 people, situated around ten miles from Barrow-in-Furness and the Vickers Shipyards (now BAE Systems) which had originally brought my parents to the area in the 1960s.

Both my brother and I were born here in the Ulverston cottage hospital, and when my father Vic retired in 1987 he and Jennifer moved back to the area and lived at Windy Ash in the parish of Osmotherley for the remainder of their lives.

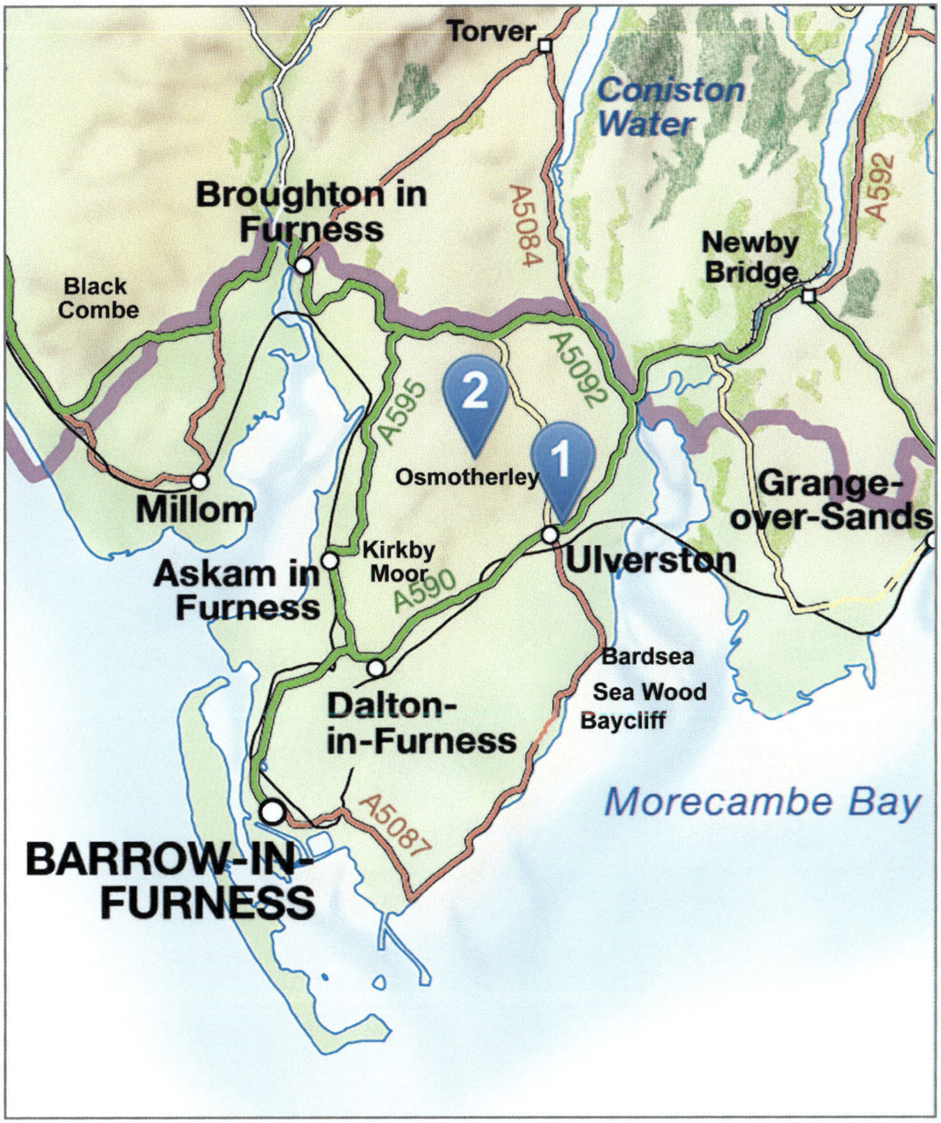

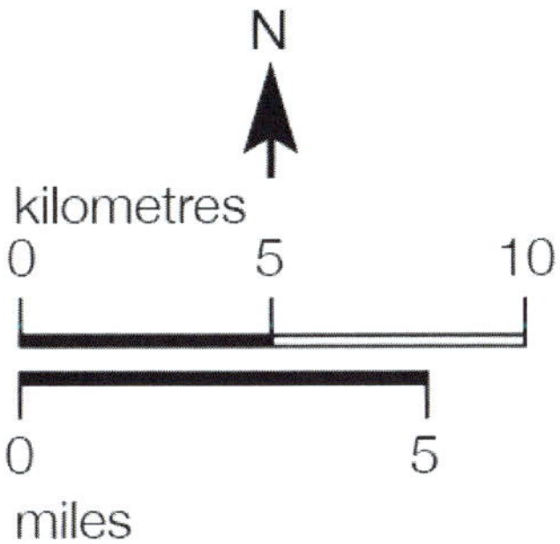

Map Locations
1. Ulverston
2. Osmotherley

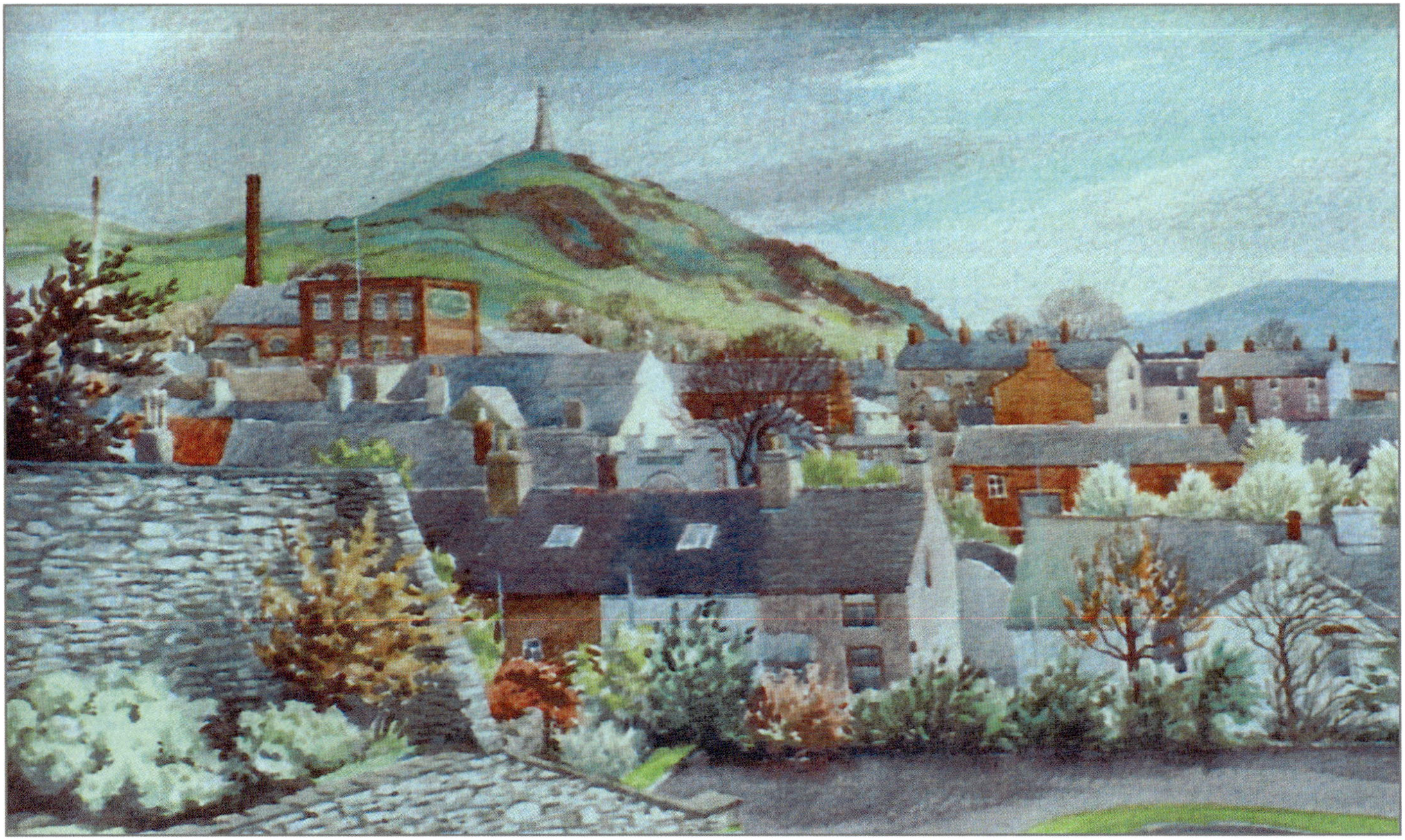

Known as the Festival Town, Ulverston has a thriving market square that blossoms with stalls on Thursdays and Saturdays. Overlooked by Hoad Monument, built in 1850 to commemorate Sir John Barrow, Ulverston was the birthplace of Stan Laurel, of Laurel and Hardy fame. As a boy I remember a myriad of fascinating shops, like Smith and Harrison's the local ironmonger where my father Vic would buy wrought iron nails measured out on a scale by the pound. There's the Stan Laurel Museum to visit, and more recently the town has become popular for its Dickensian Festival held each year in November.

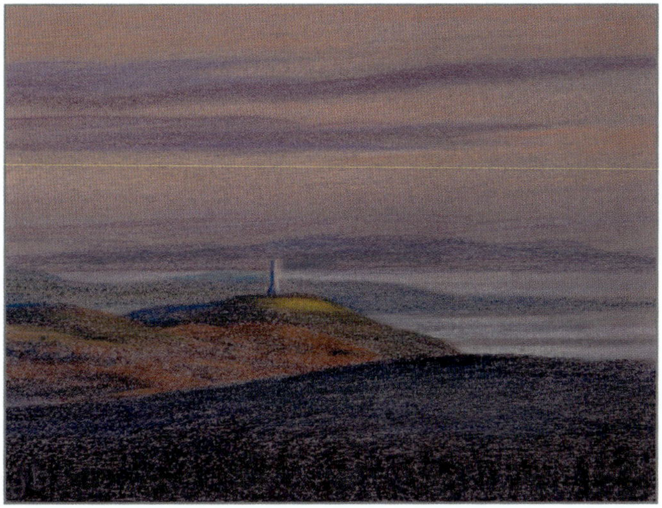

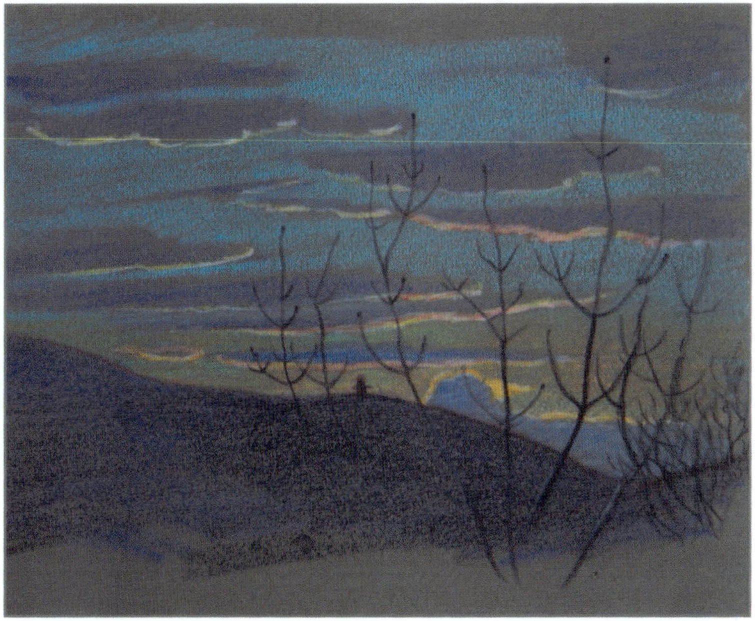

These pictures are all from around Windy Ash in Osmotherley

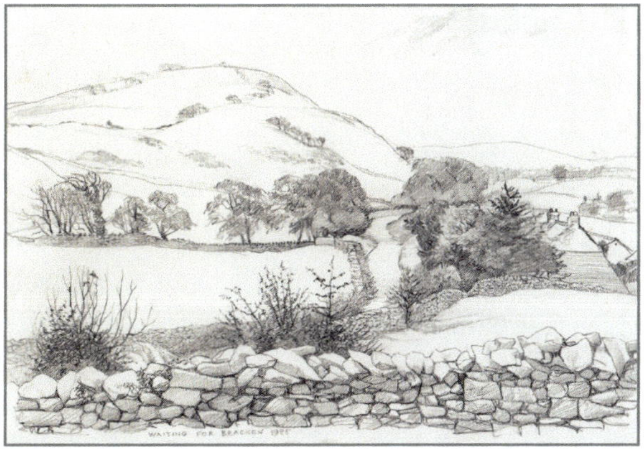

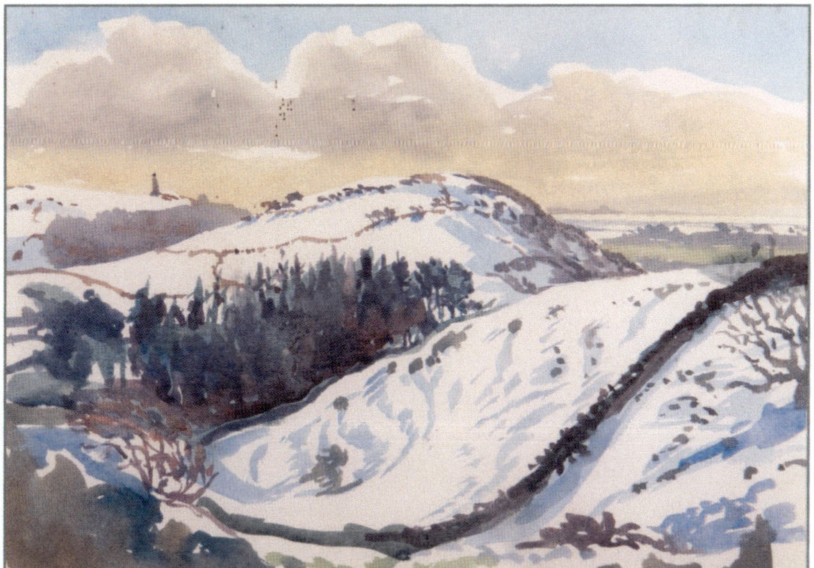

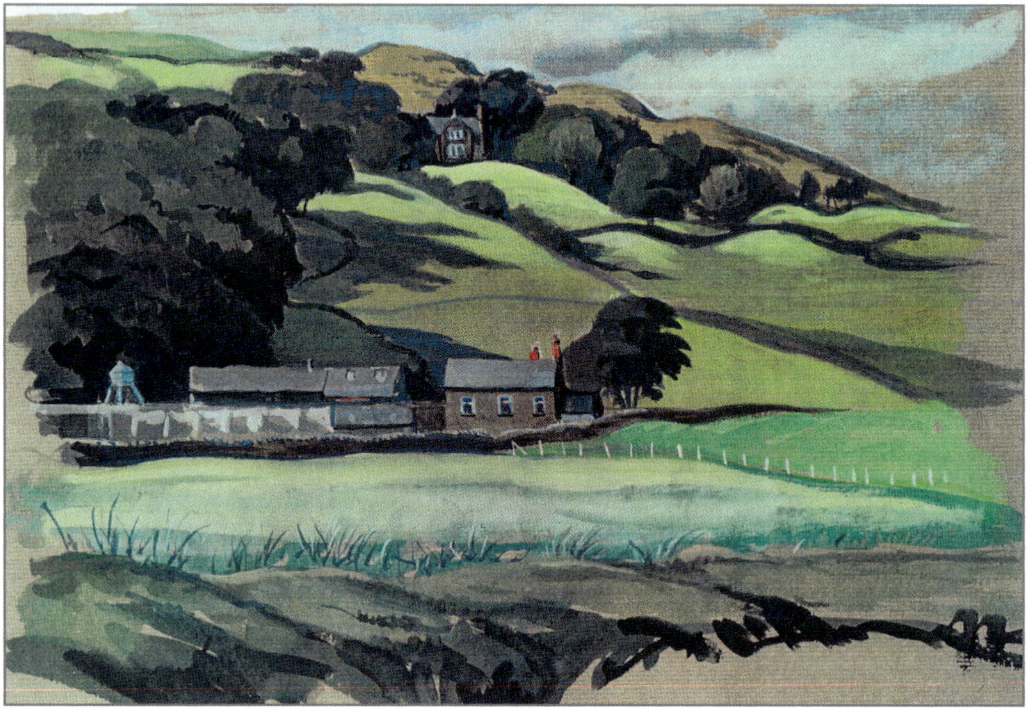

These are the hills around Windy Ash in Osmotherley where Jennifer and Vic lived from 1986. The area includes a number of dairy farms, an alpaca farm that produces wool, and St. John's Church.

Old Hall Farm and Bortree Stile. Windy Ash is out of sight to the right

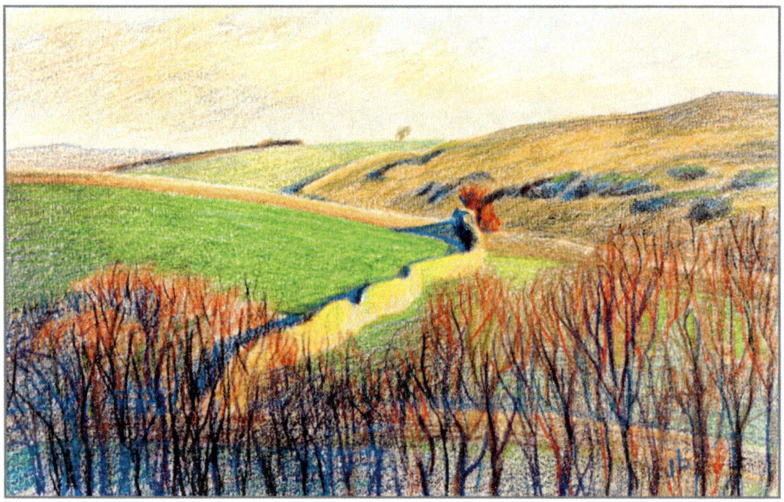

The Crooked Wall

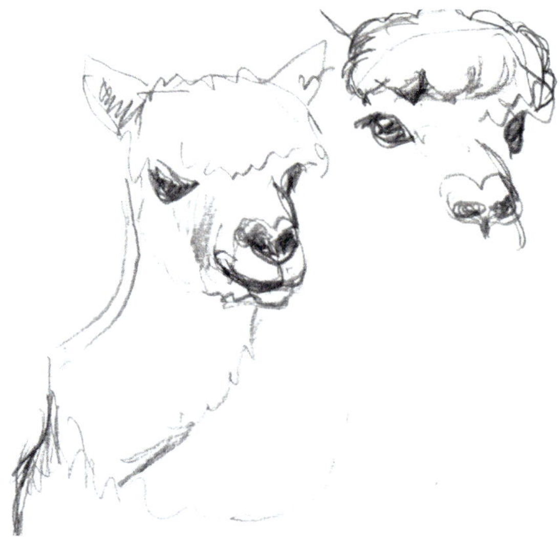

Windy Ash

This is Windy Ash drawn from the B5281 Broughton Beck road. The wood to the left and the fields to the immediate front belonged to the house. The road winds steeply up the hill to Knottallow Tarn and Kirkby Moor.

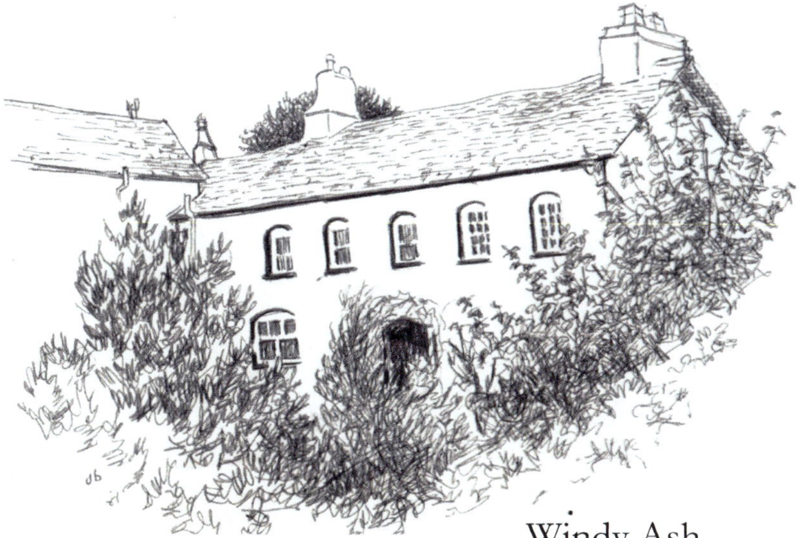

Windy Ash,
Osmotherley

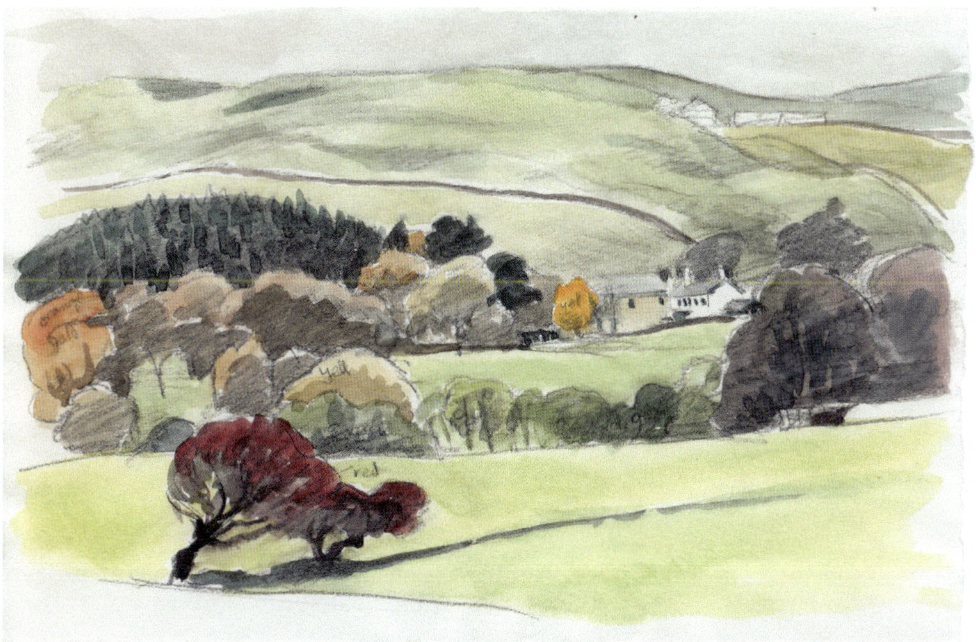

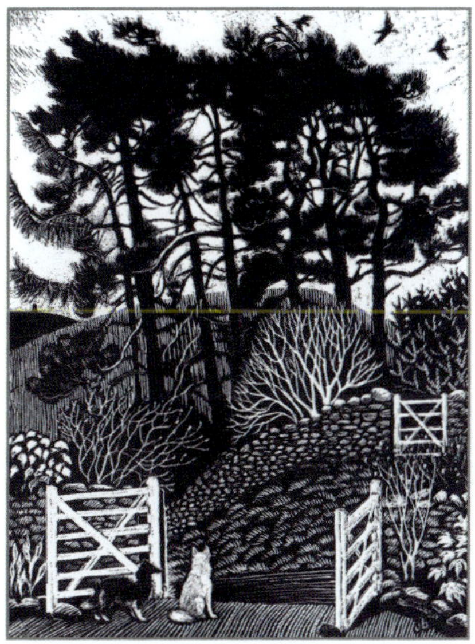

Caspian and Chimo
wait by the gates

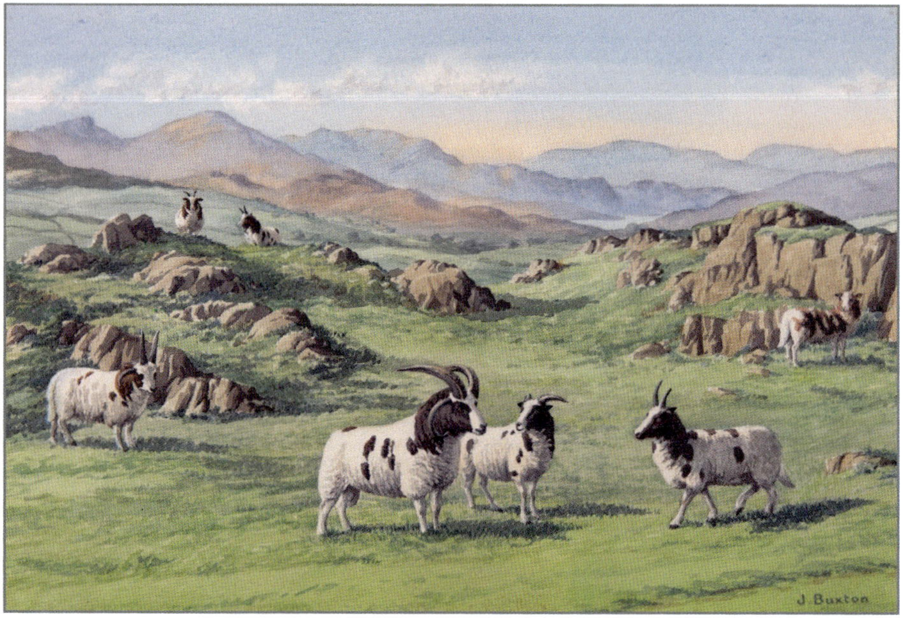

Jacobs Sheep belonging to our friend Clive. Dow Crag, Coniston Old Man and Wetherlam behind.

For a few years Jennifer and Vic kept sheep at Windy Ash. Jennifer even had to develop some skills as a mid-wife to their little flock during lambing season, never seeming to mind the nightly vigils in the stable.

Over the course of their lives Jennifer and Vic kept dogs, ponies, sheep, chickens, cats, and a particularly noisy goat.

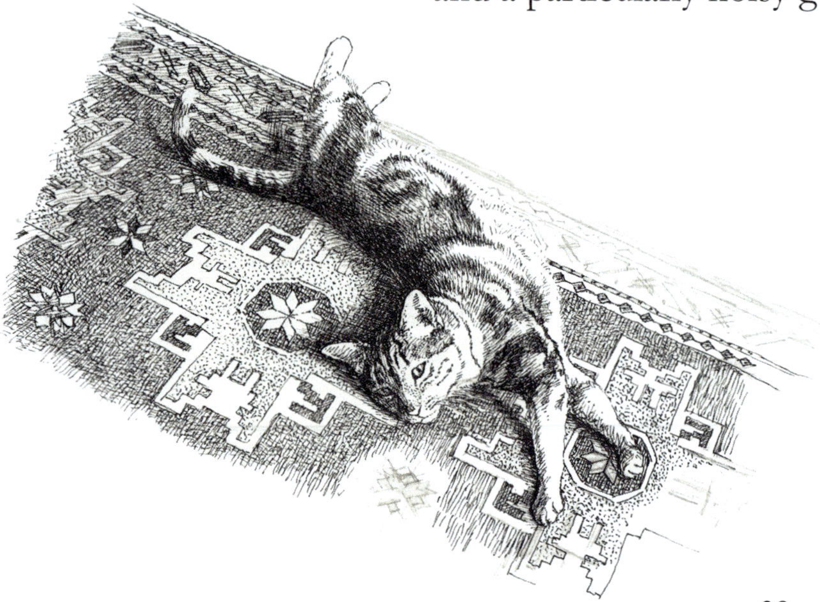

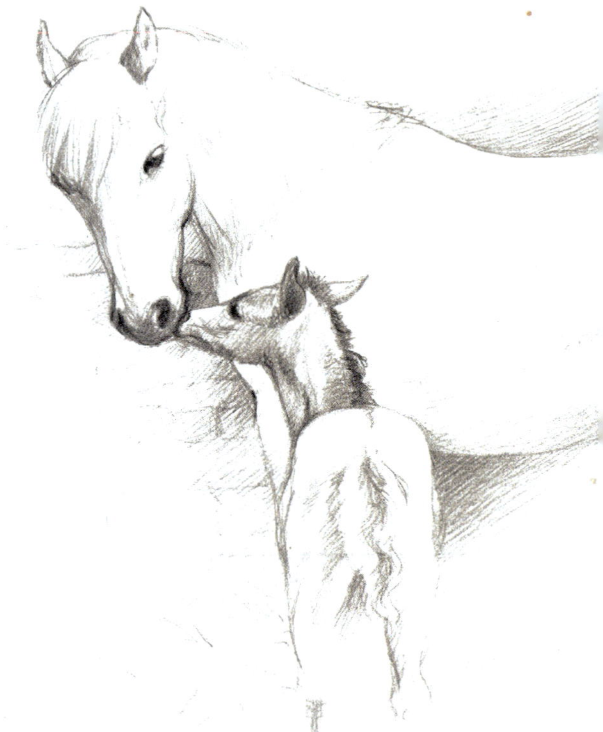

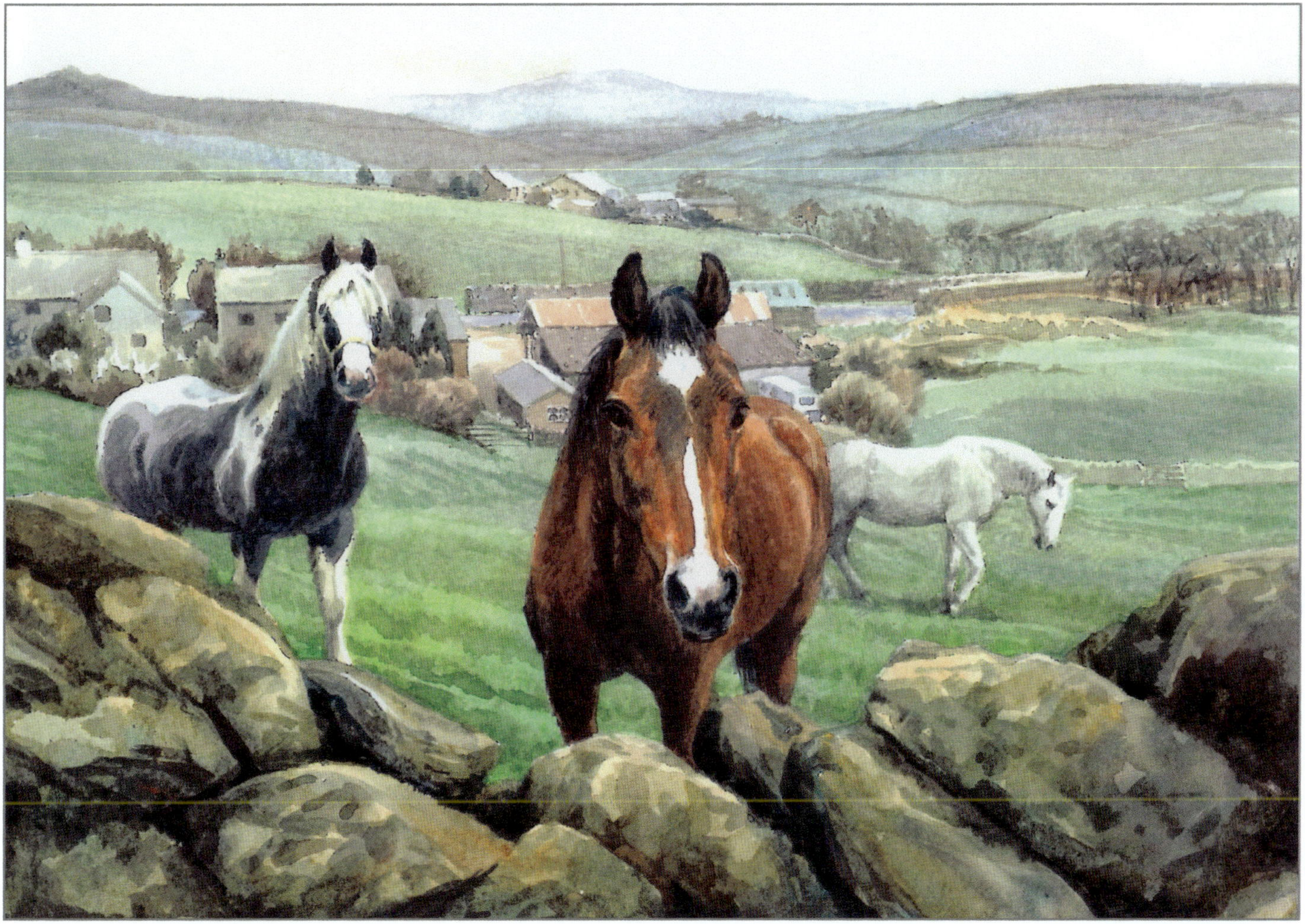

The fields in this area are separated by a mix of classic dry stone walls and hedgerows. The stone walls are an effective way of clearing the fields so that they can be grazed by cattle and sheep, and the occasional horse. A well built dry stone wall is a testament to the waller's art that can last for many years.

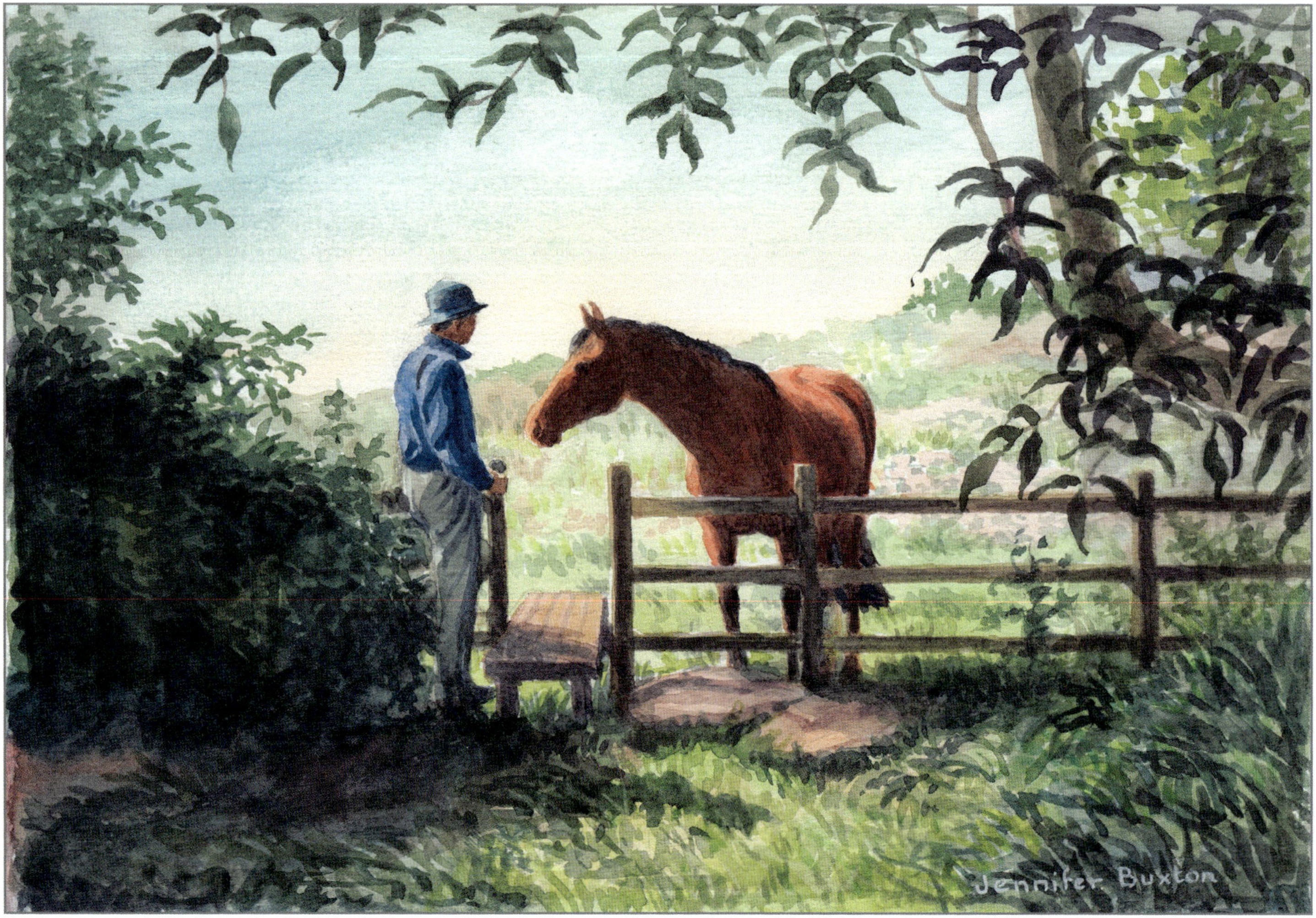

A Chance Encounter

Vic didn't often make it into Jennifer's paintings, so this one deserves a special mention.

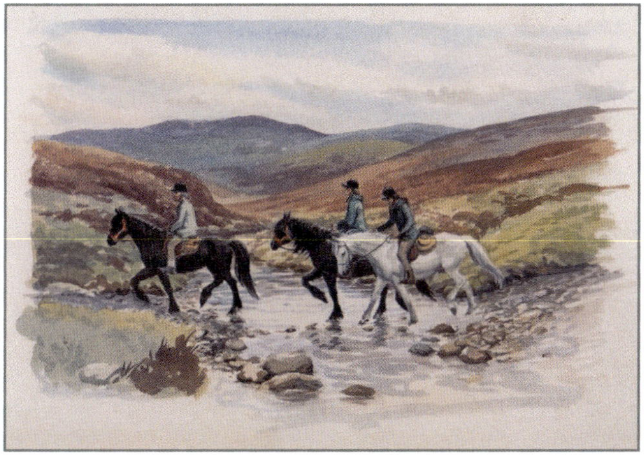

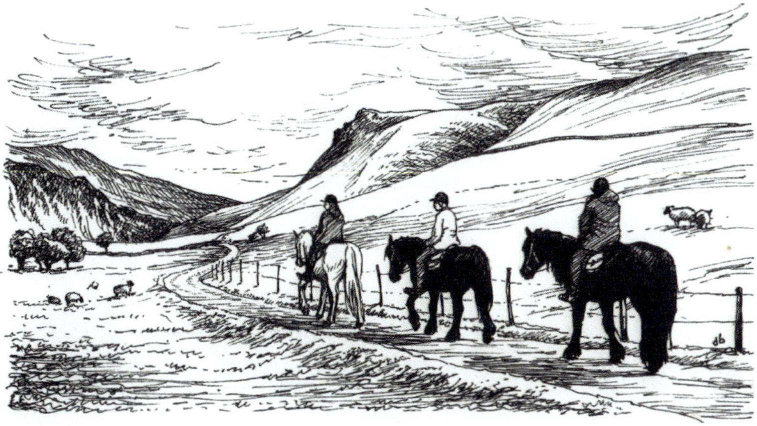

For many years Jennifer and Vic kept ponies at Windy Ash. Jennifer made a number of overnight treks with friends, and contributed sketches to the Fell Pony Society and the Connemara Society in association with their ponies Rosie and Jenny.

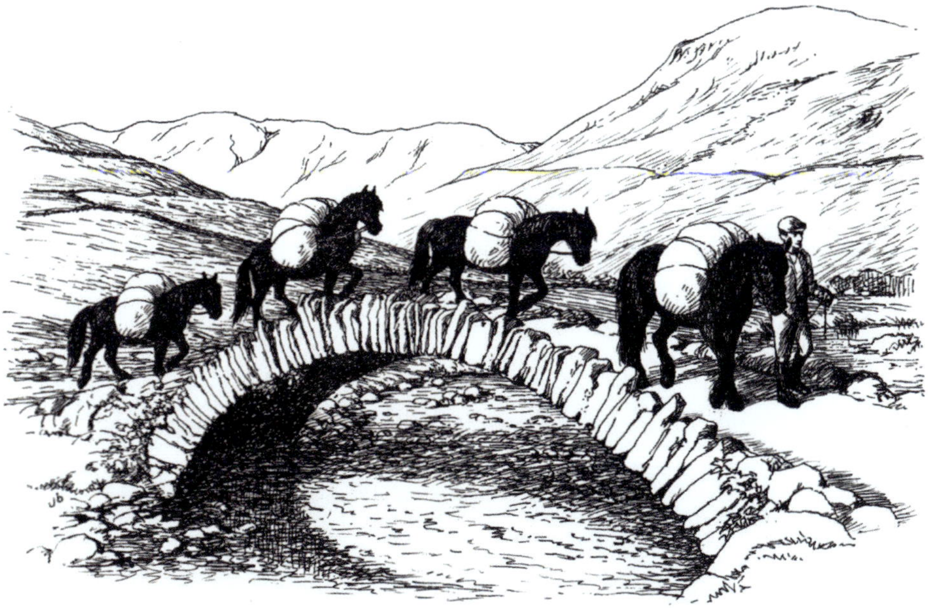

There's a long tradition of moving goods and produce by packhorse in the Lake District

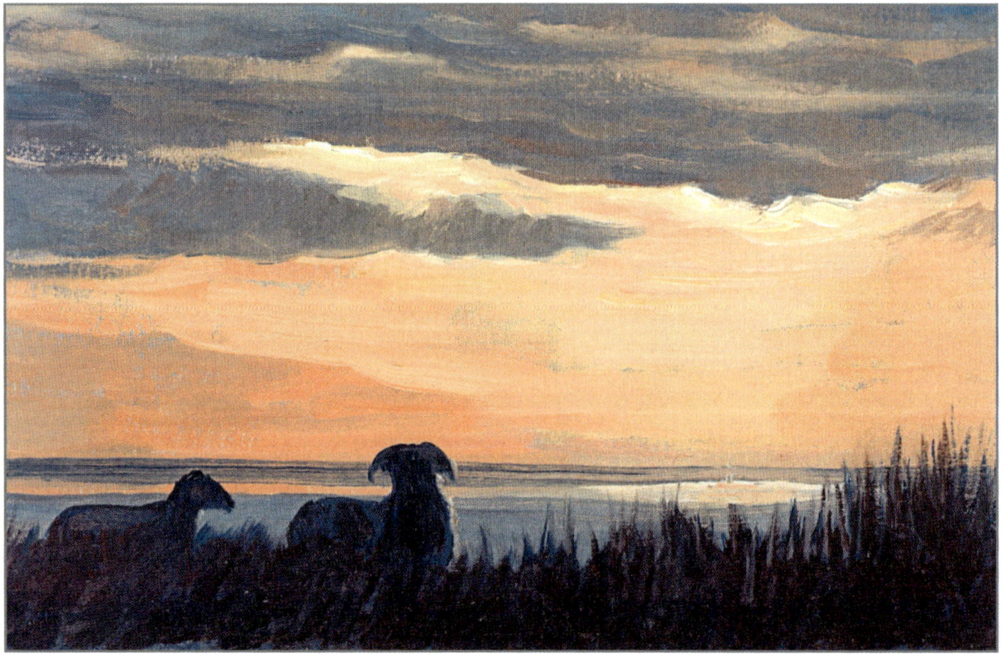

Towards the sunset

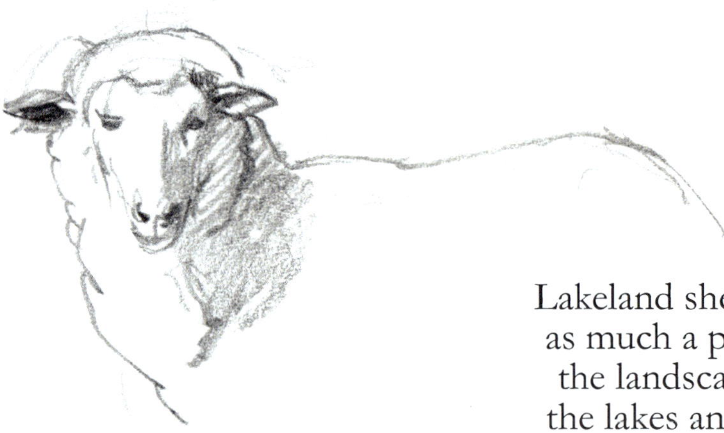

Lakeland sheep are
as much a part of
the landscape as
the lakes and fells

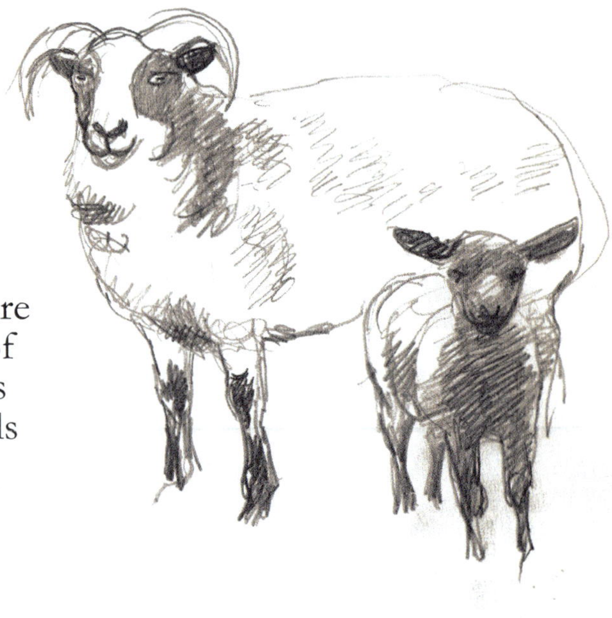

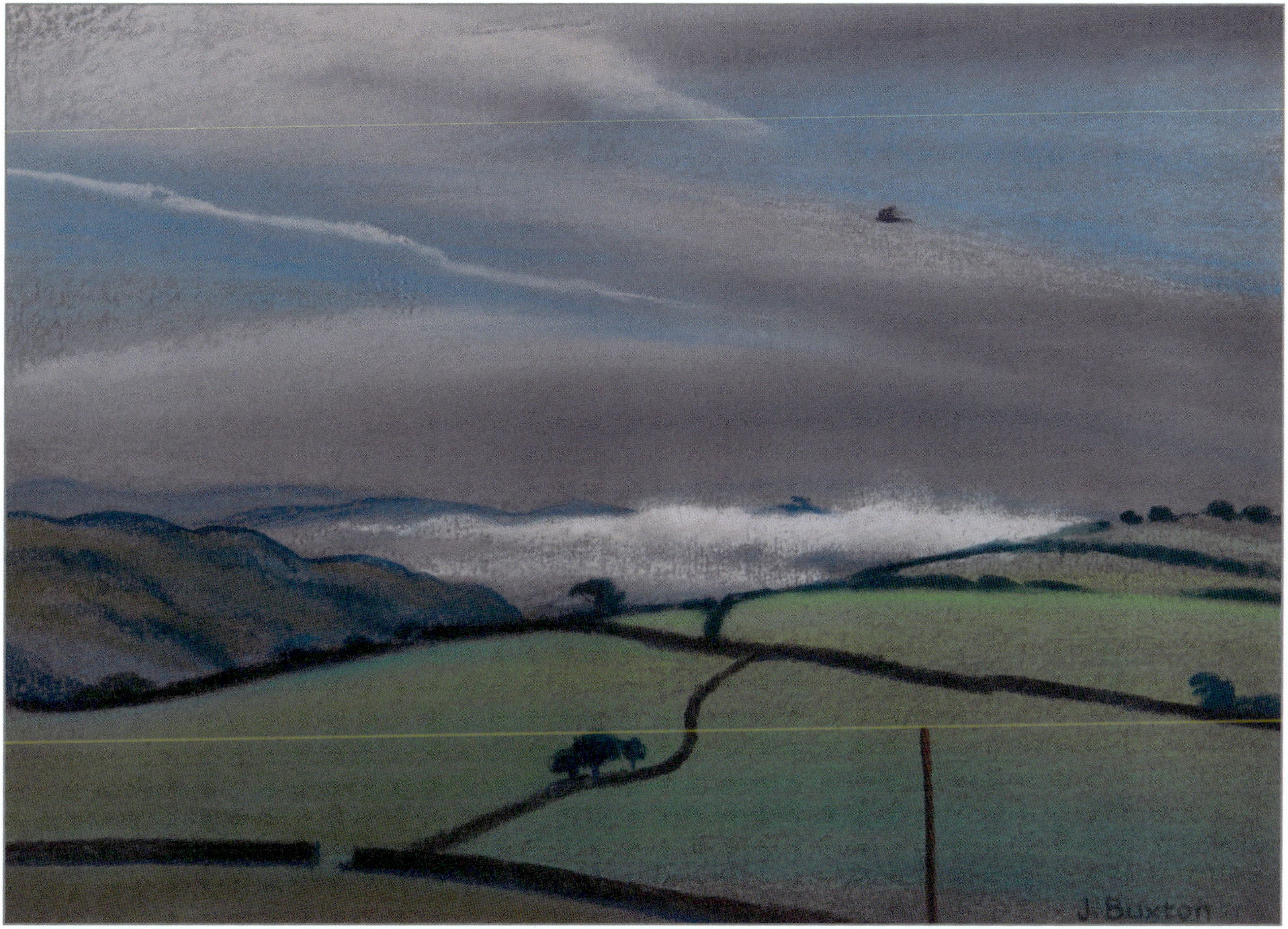

Morning Mist - across the fields towards Morecambe Bay

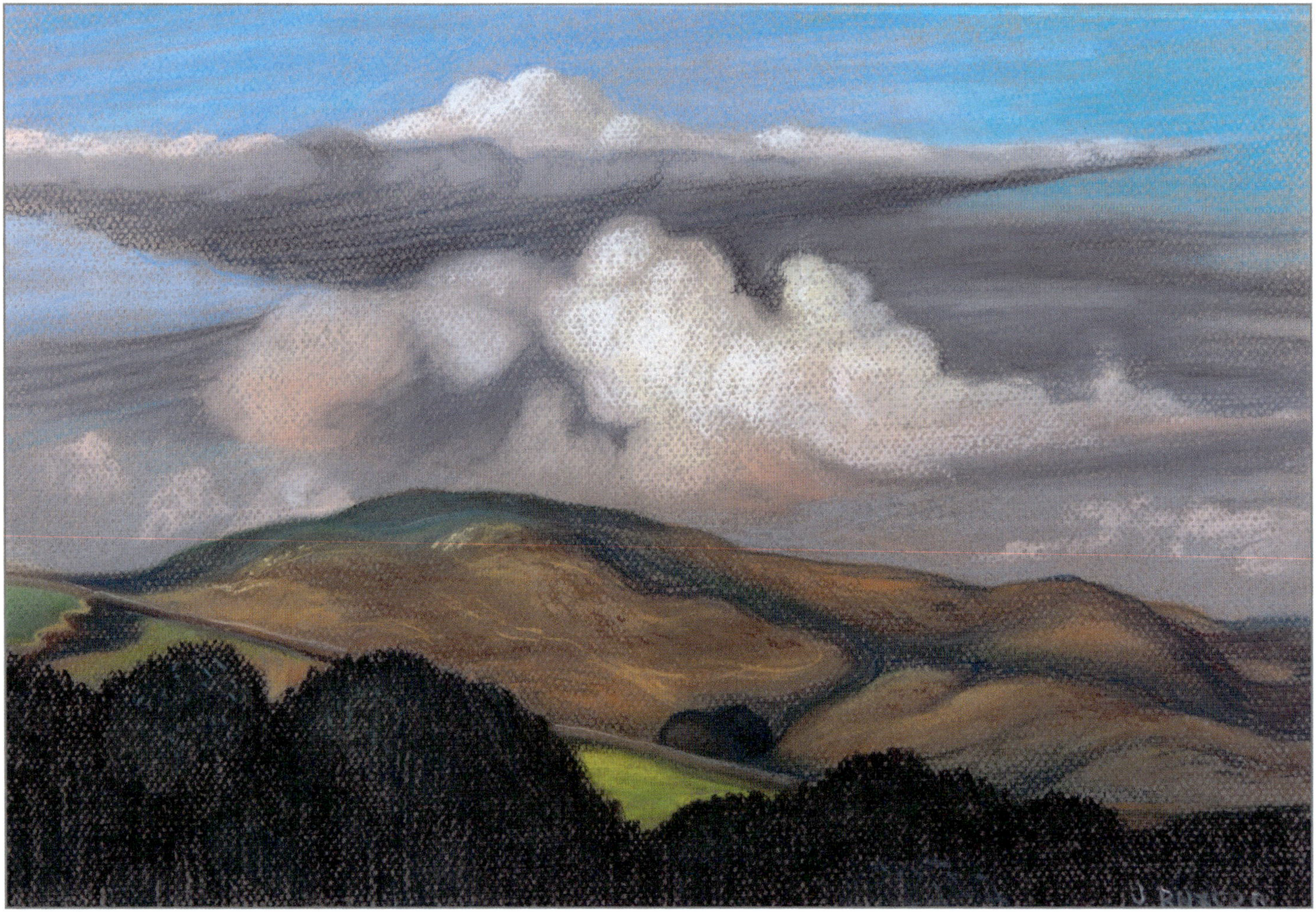

Clouds over Mansriggs. Lying to the north of Ulverston on the way to Osmotherley, these low-lying crags overlook Hoad Monument and Morecambe Bay.

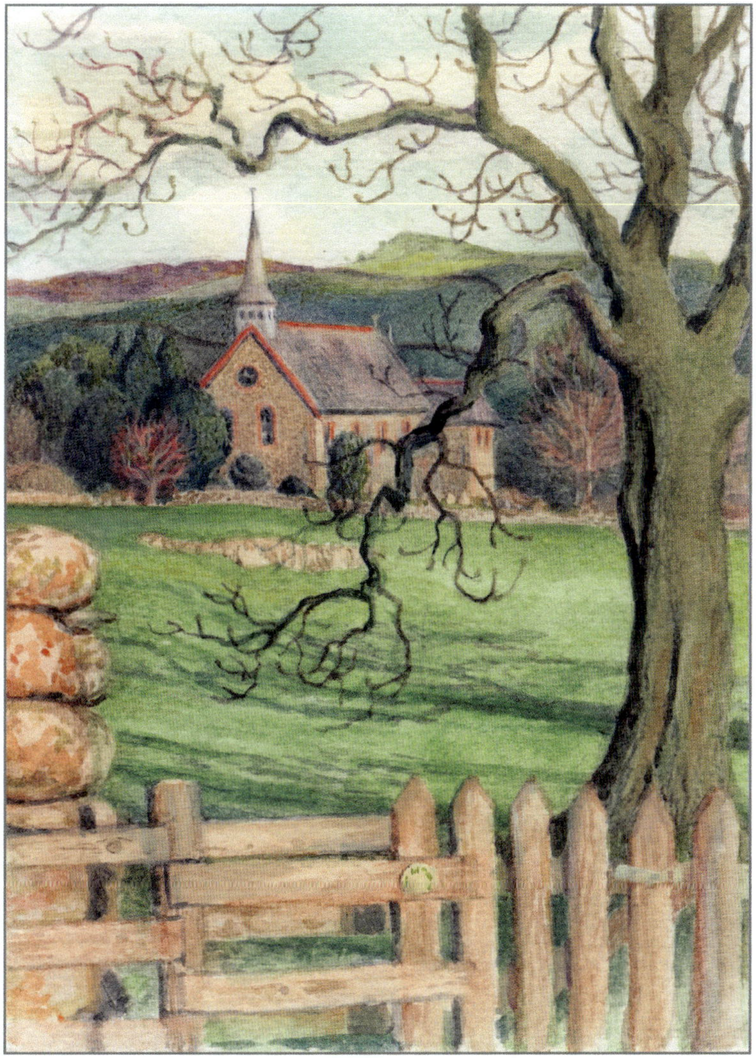

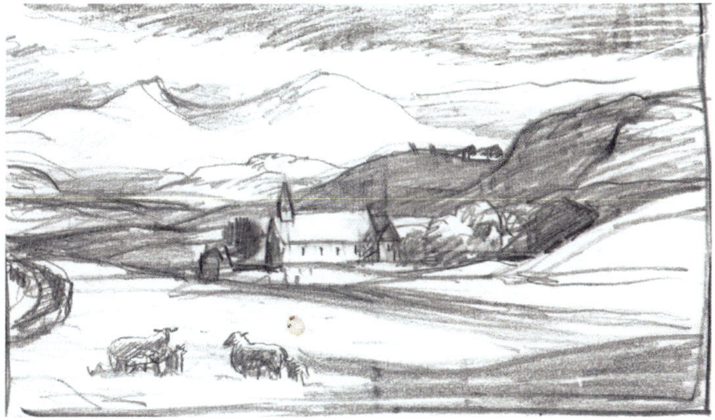

St. John's is the parish church of Osmotherley

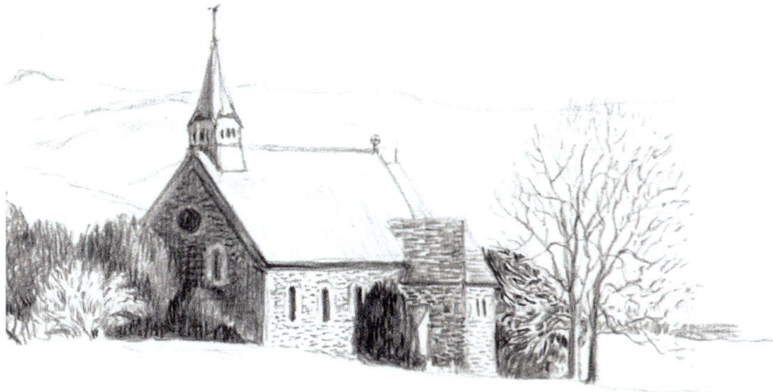

Jennifer was commissioned by Bridget from Bortree Stile to design the new stained glass window in the gable end in memory of her late husband Douglas.

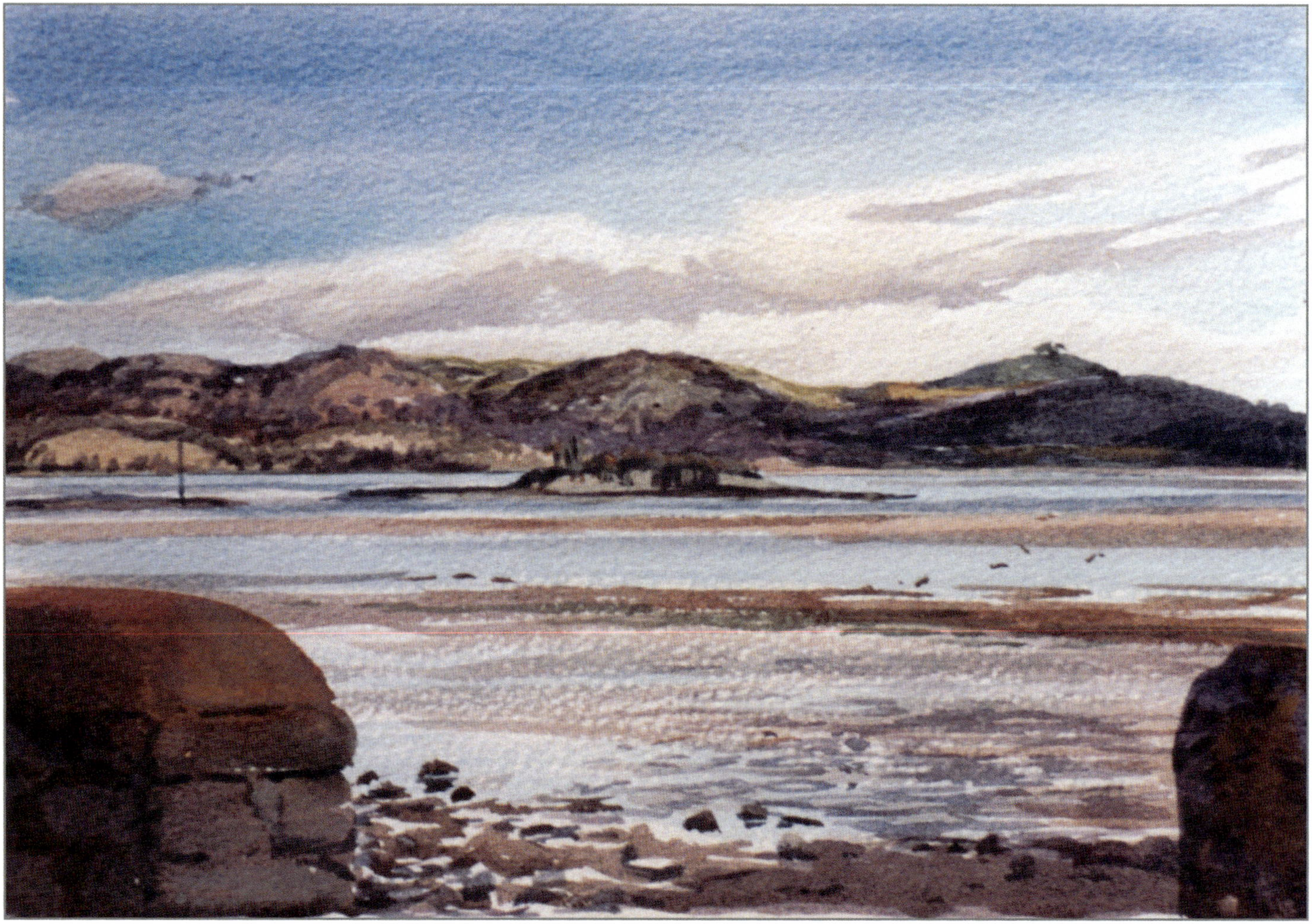

Seafront at Bardsea, with Chapel Island mid-channel

While predominantly mud and sand, the flats are broken up by areas of seagrass and by channels from where the sea spreads as the tide rises. Saturated areas of sand, or quicksands as they are known, can be hazardous if you should walk into them.

Morecambe Bay

From Ulverston it's just a short drive to the shoreline and the wide vistas looking south across Morecambe Bay towards the Yorkshire Dales, Lancaster and Blackpool.

Taking the dogs out over the mud flats was a favourite walk on our visits to the area; having a care to avoid the channels and quicksands of course.

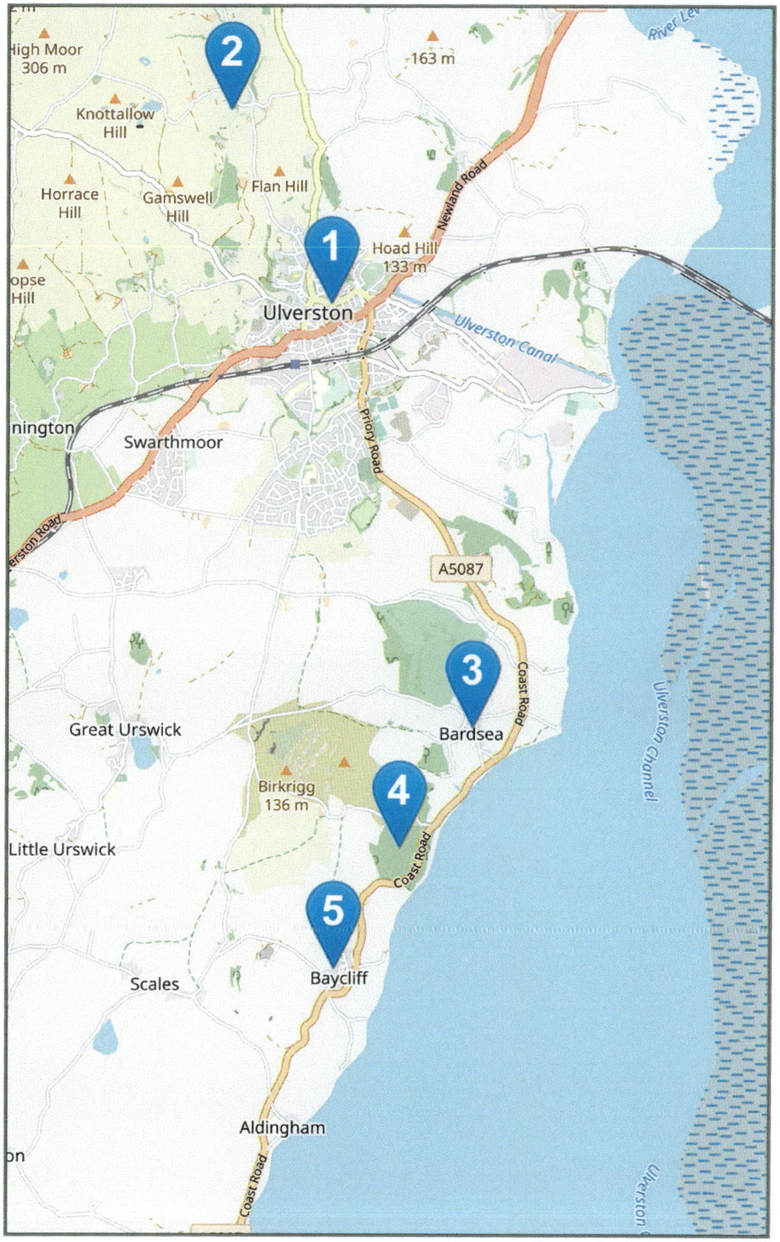

Map Locations

1. Ulverston
2. Windy Ash
3. Bardsea
4. Sea Wood
5. Baycliff

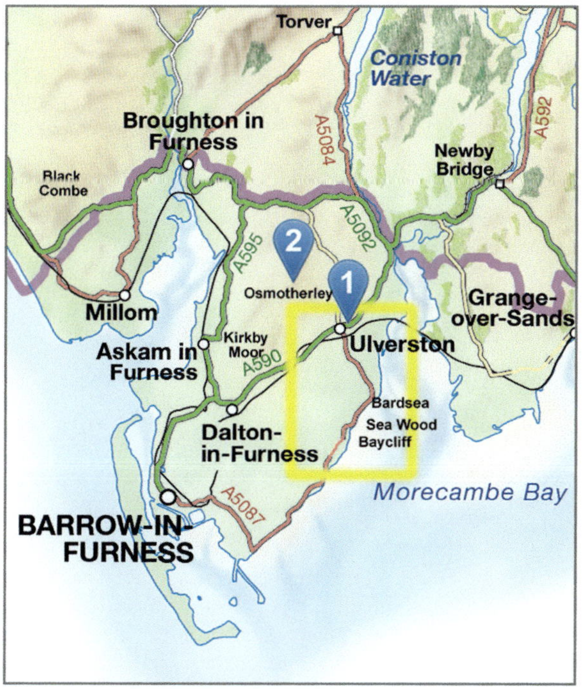

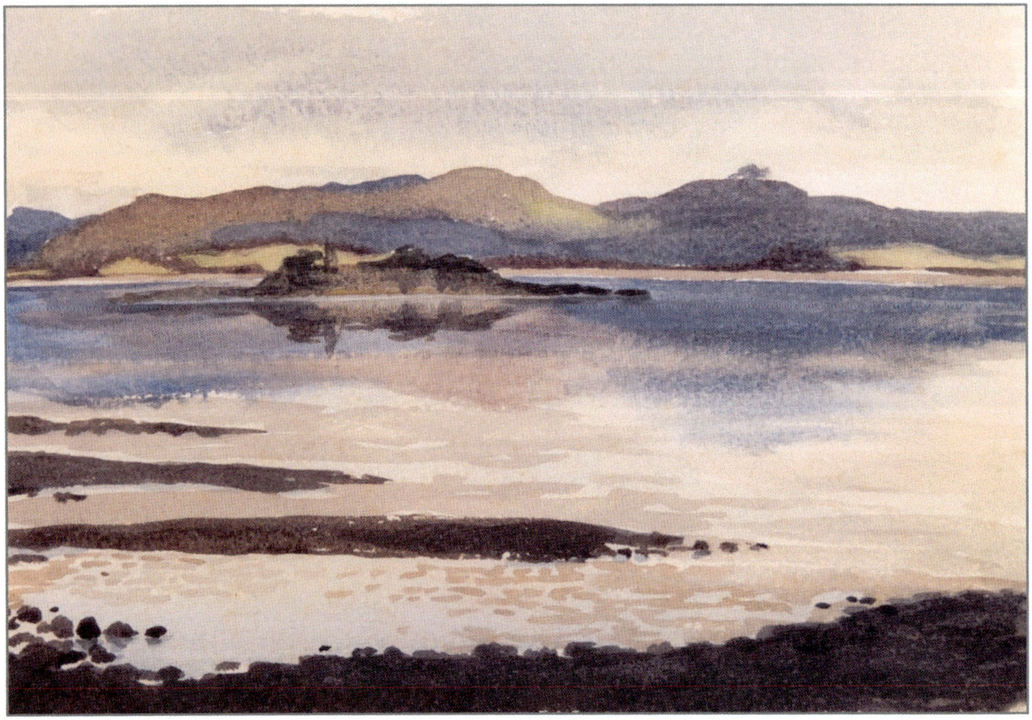

Chapel Island seems deceptively close but the mud flats between the island and the shore can be treacherous with quicksands

The seafront
by Bardsea

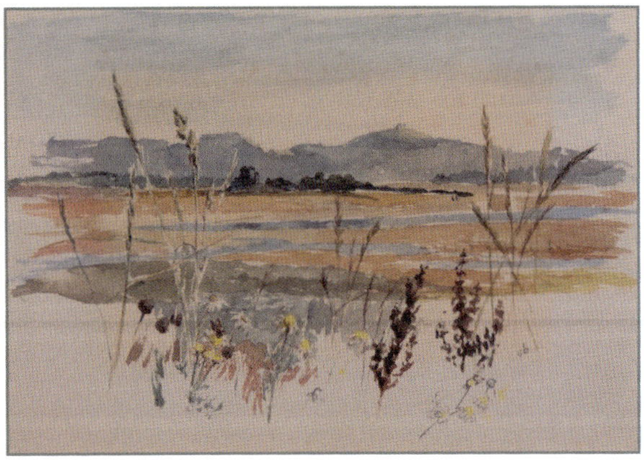

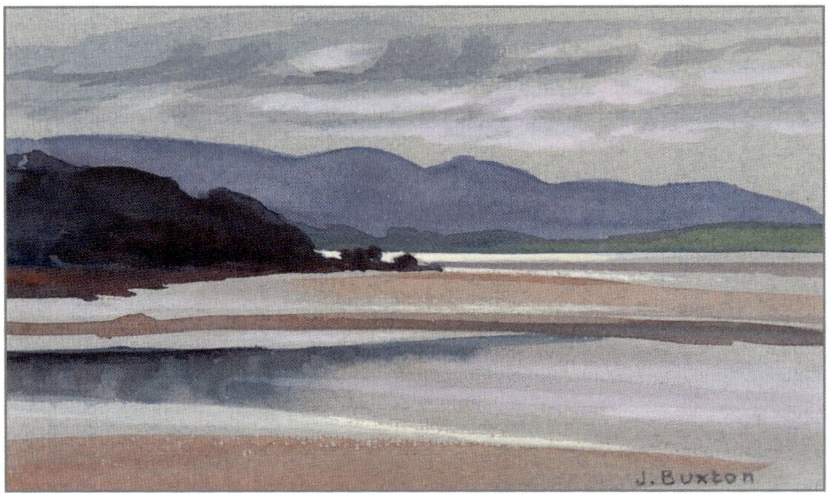

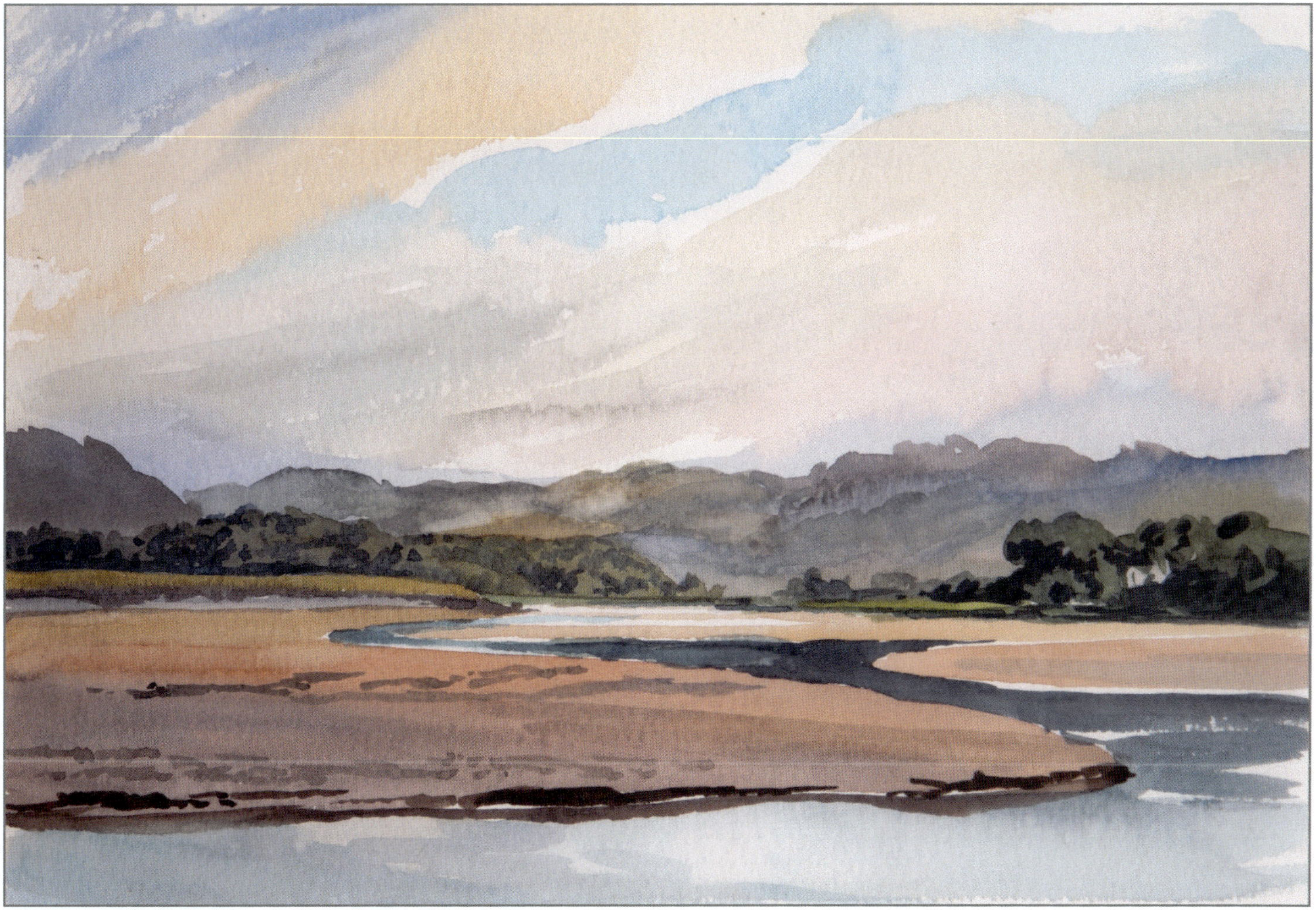

The River Leven Estuary, Morecambe Bay, from near Greenodd. Sometimes in winter the snow will settle on the flats, turning them white.

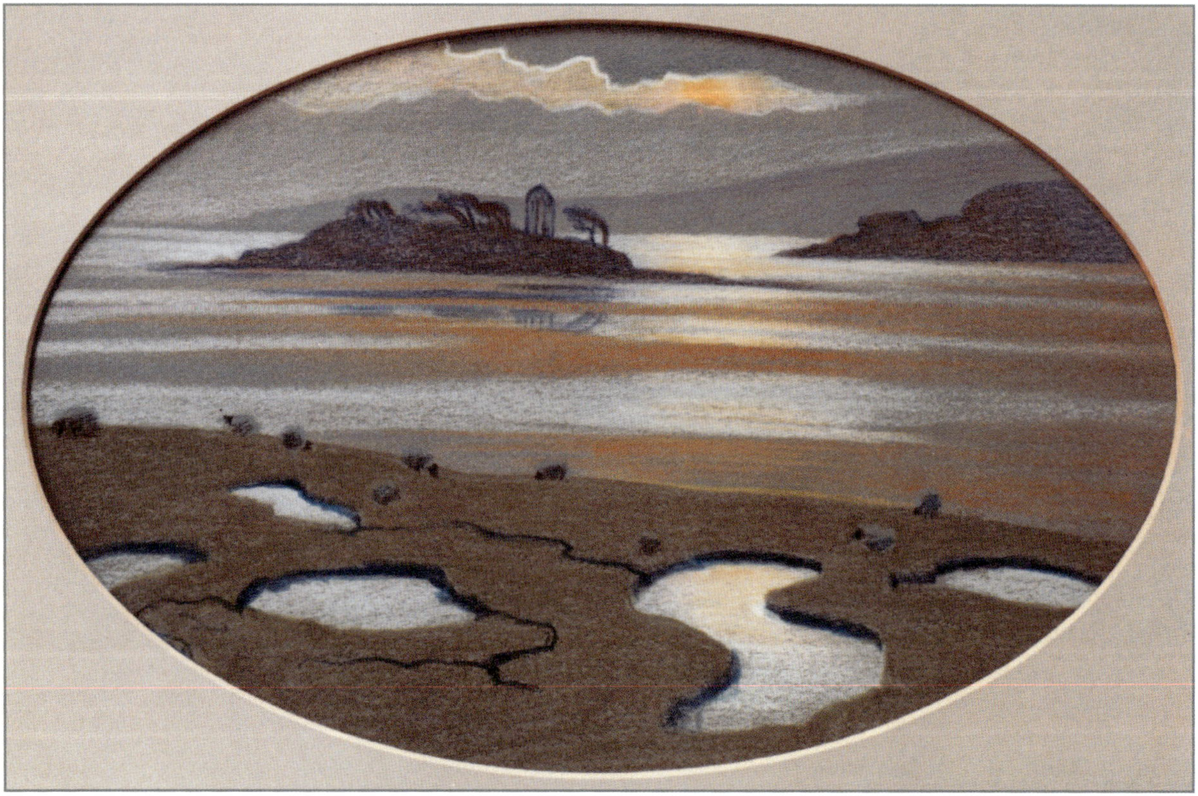

These are older works of Jennifer's that we only have access to from photographs. They were two of her favourites though as they made it into one of her photo albums - so many of her landscapes of the area were unfortunately sold without record.

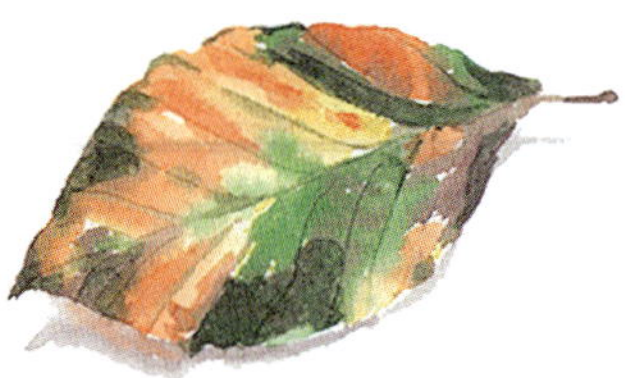

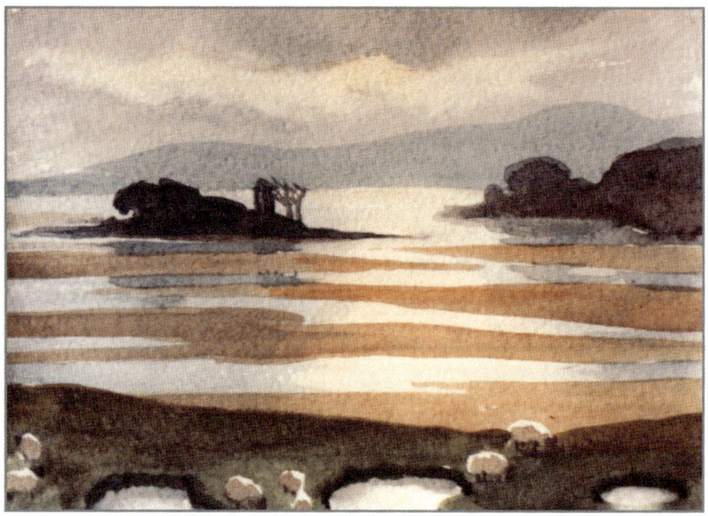

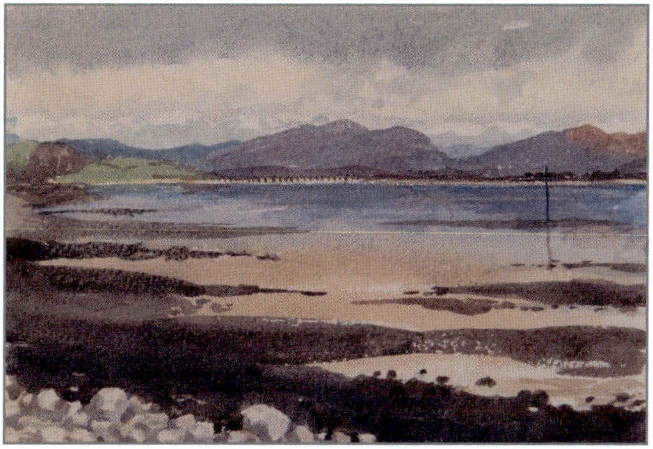

Plumpton viaduct from Canal Foot Ulverston. This is actually the railway route from Lancaster to Ulverston, which offers panoramic views of the bay.

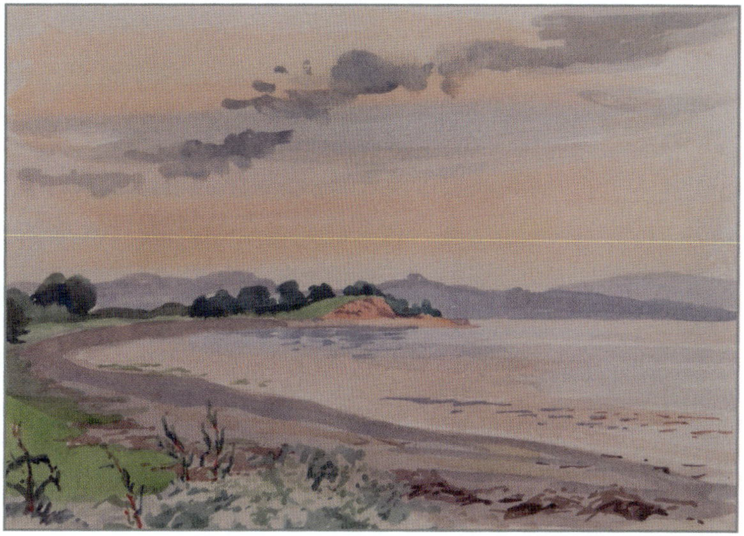

The shoreline at Bardsea

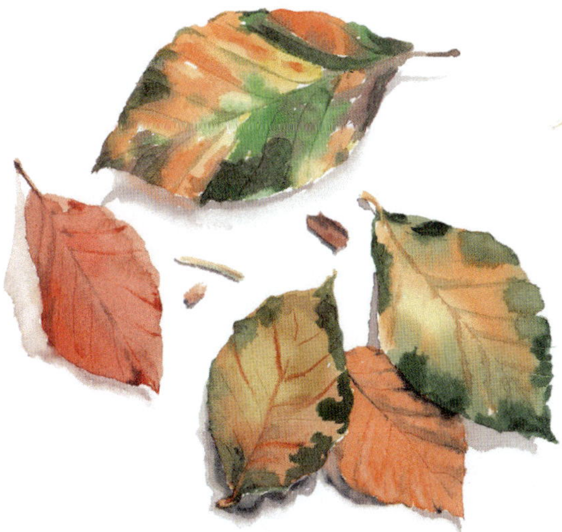

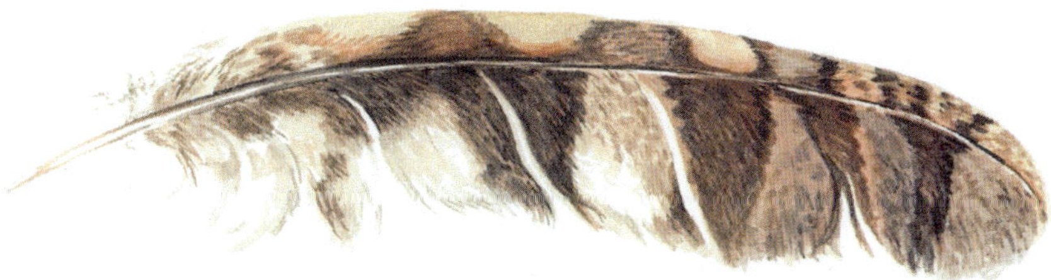

Jennifer would collect anything that caught her eye. Feathers, leaves, shells, rocks; sometimes they would become paintings, but more often they simply accumulated, sometimes to Vic's despair.

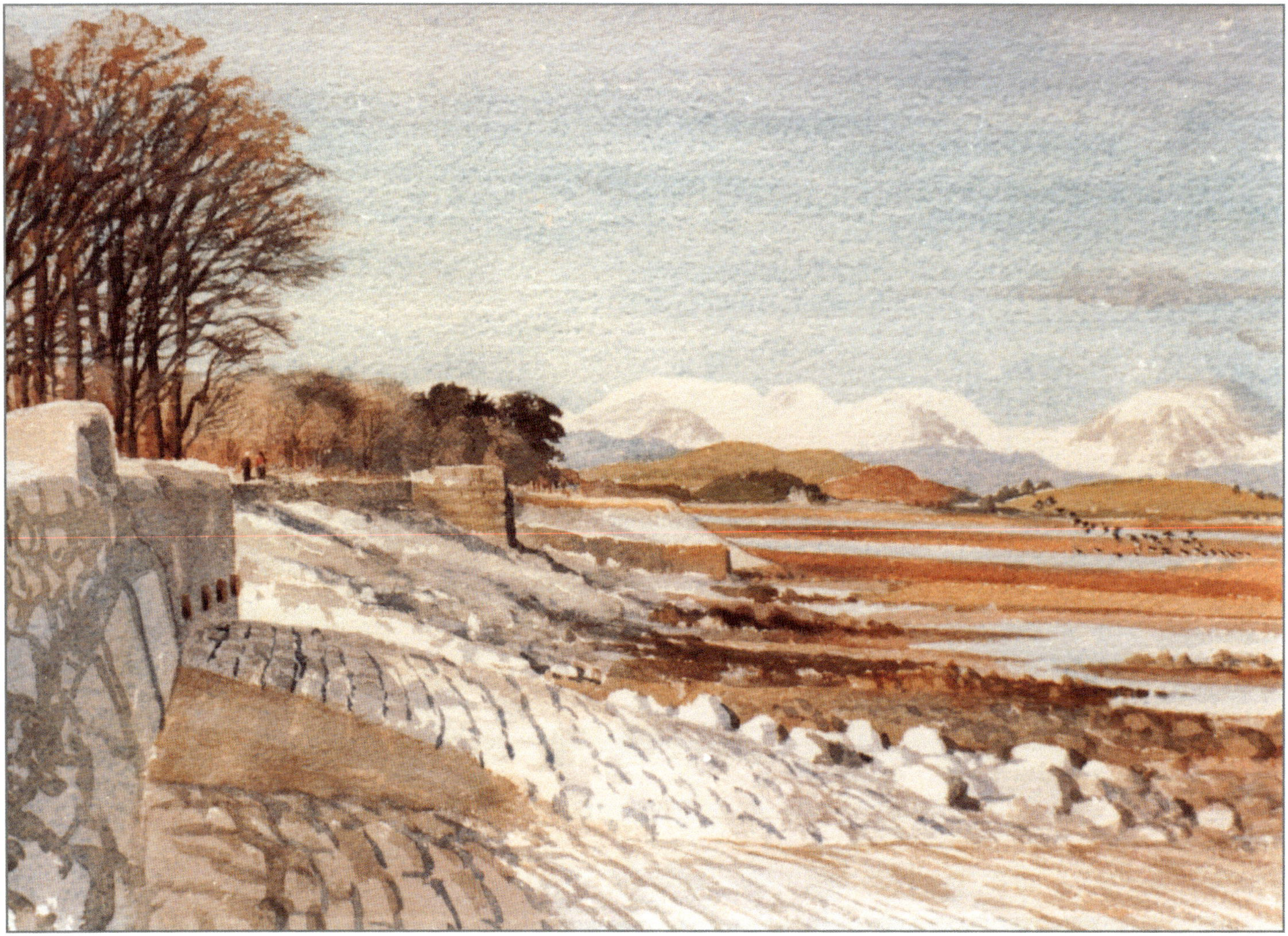

Bardsea shorefront, looking north towards the central fells

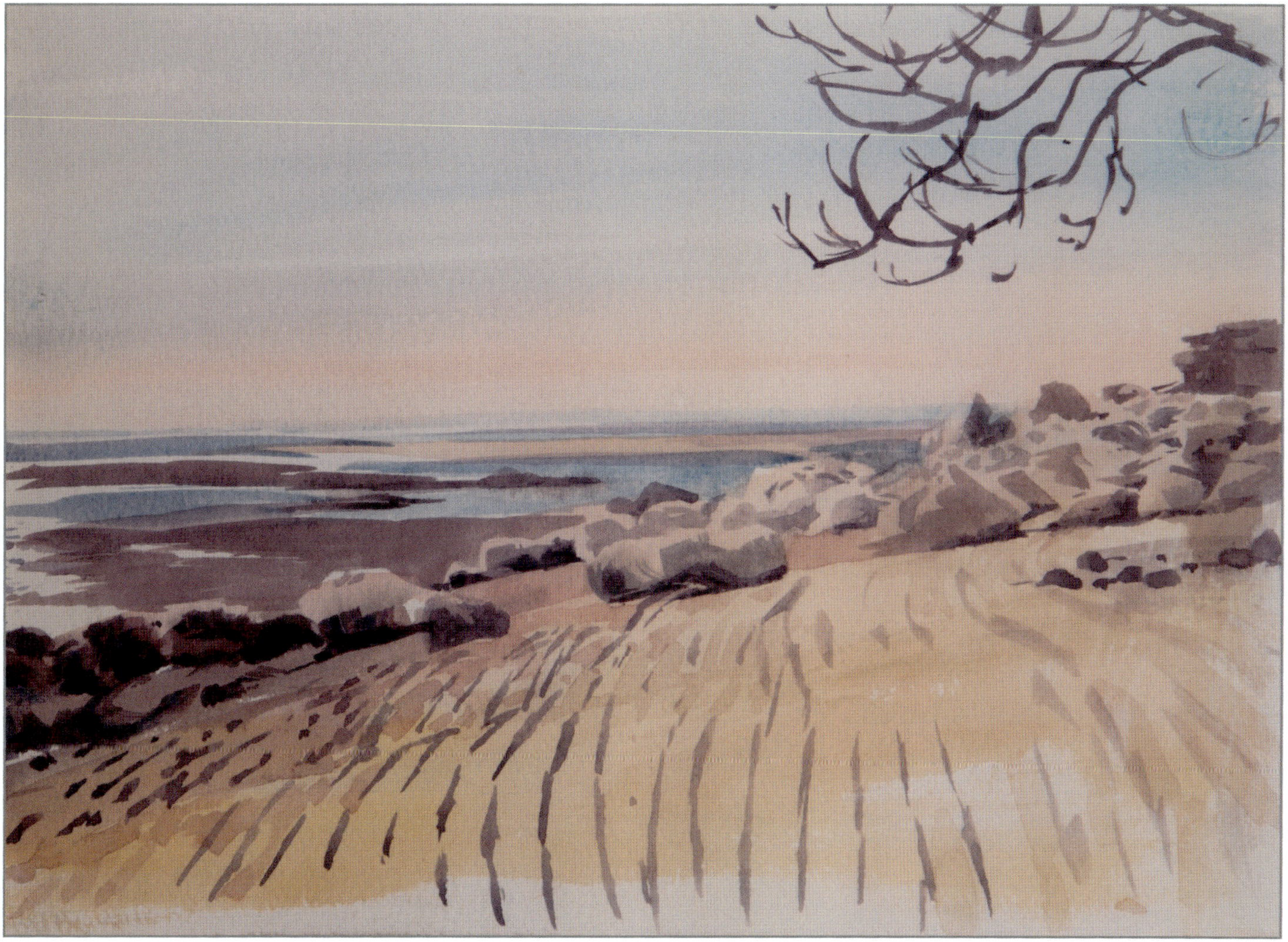

The Bardsea shoreline at low tide. Jennifer and I passed many an afternoon here, with Jennifer painting while I explored, or baited a long line for elusive flounder and dabs. In the winter it can be bitterly cold, but in the summer it's warm and sheltered in the lee of the bluffs.

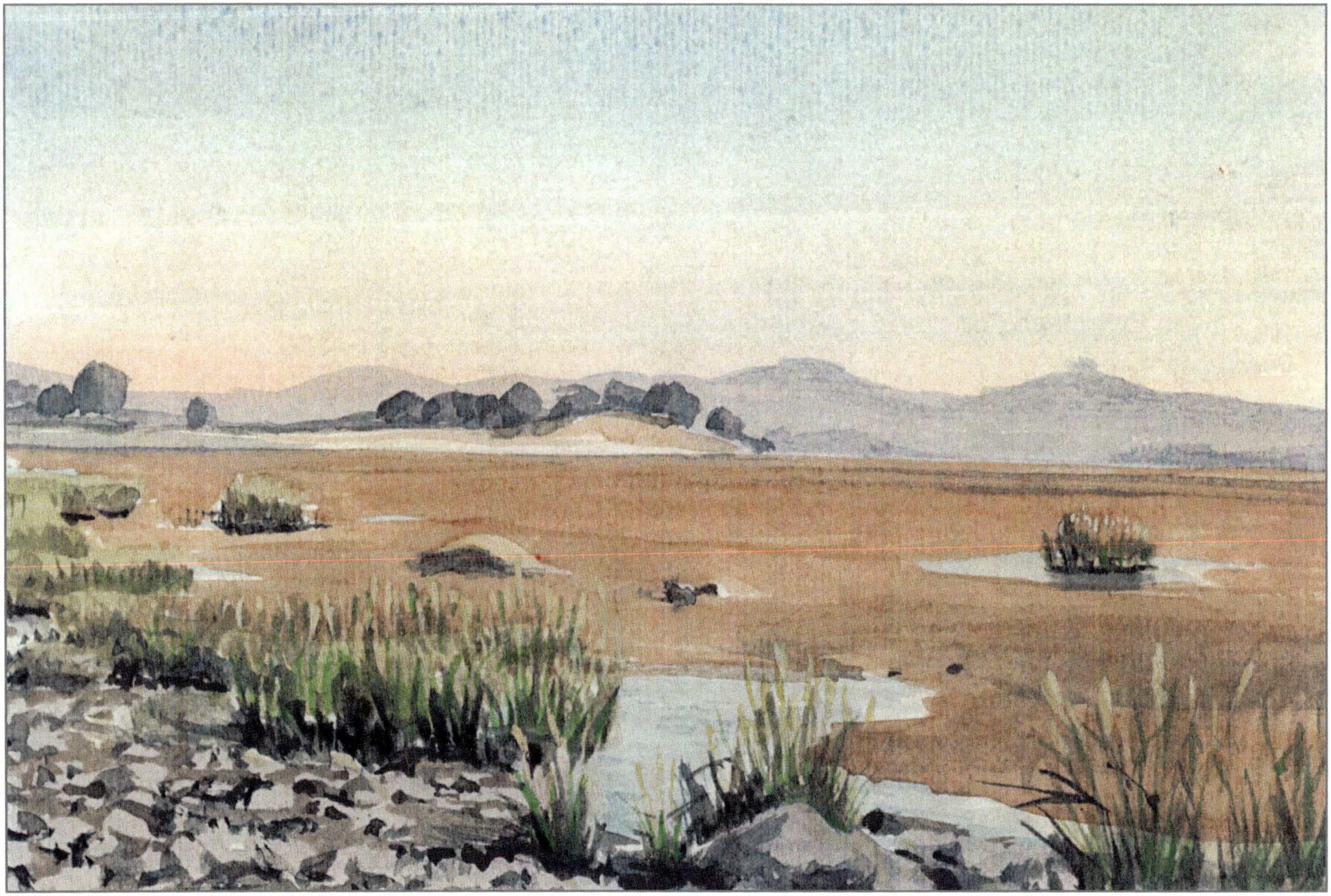

Looking south across the bay from close to Bardsea. The water recedes for miles at low tide, but returns at a fast clip that can overtake you if you're caught unawares. An occasional bore can flood the mudflats faster than you can run.

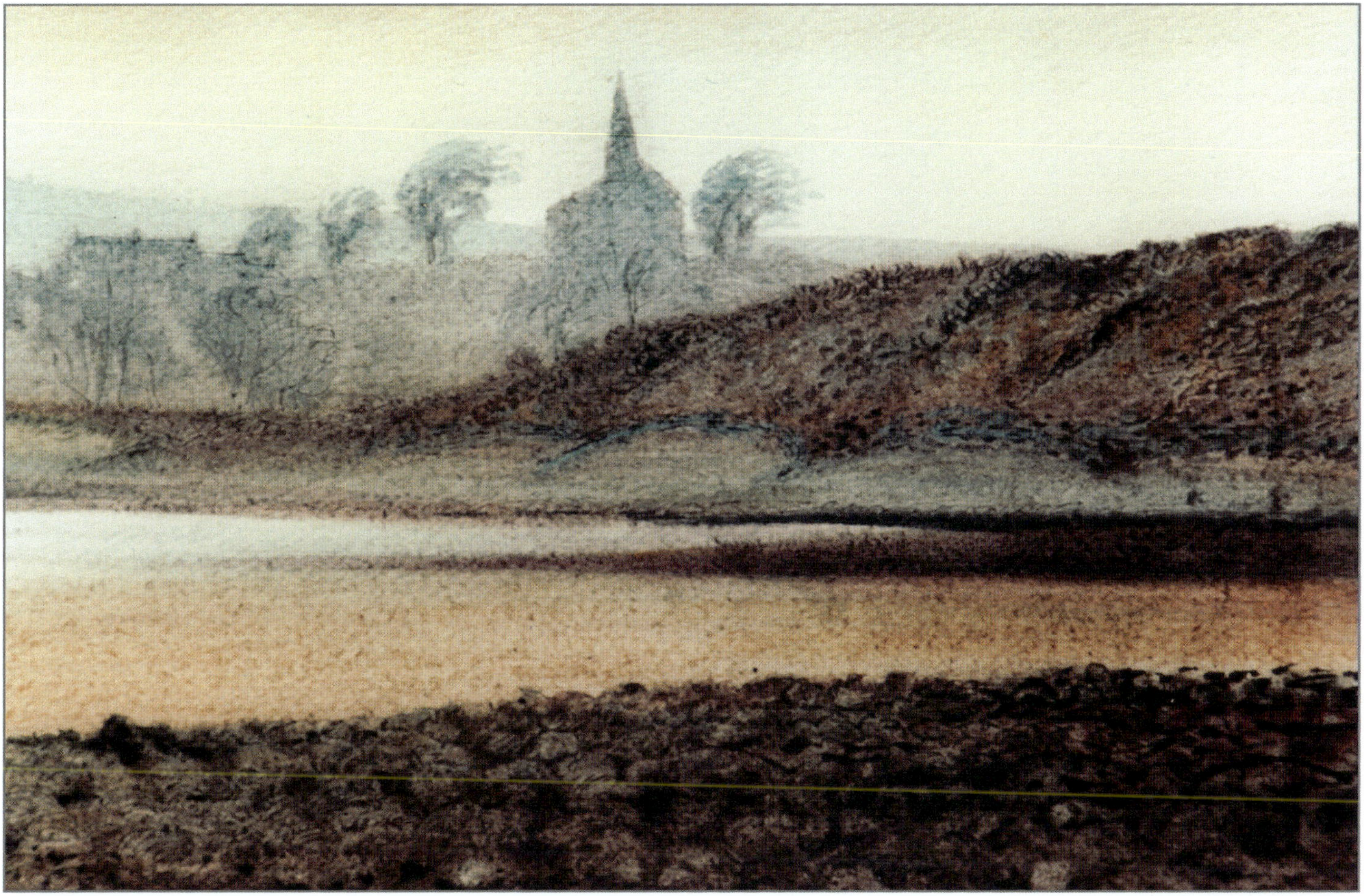

An early watercolour. Bardsea church, with Bayview to the left where Jennifer and Vic lived when my brother Henry was born. Harry and Gladys, the owners of Bayview, became my godparents three years later when I was born, and through them we have maintained a connection with Bardsea throughout our lives.

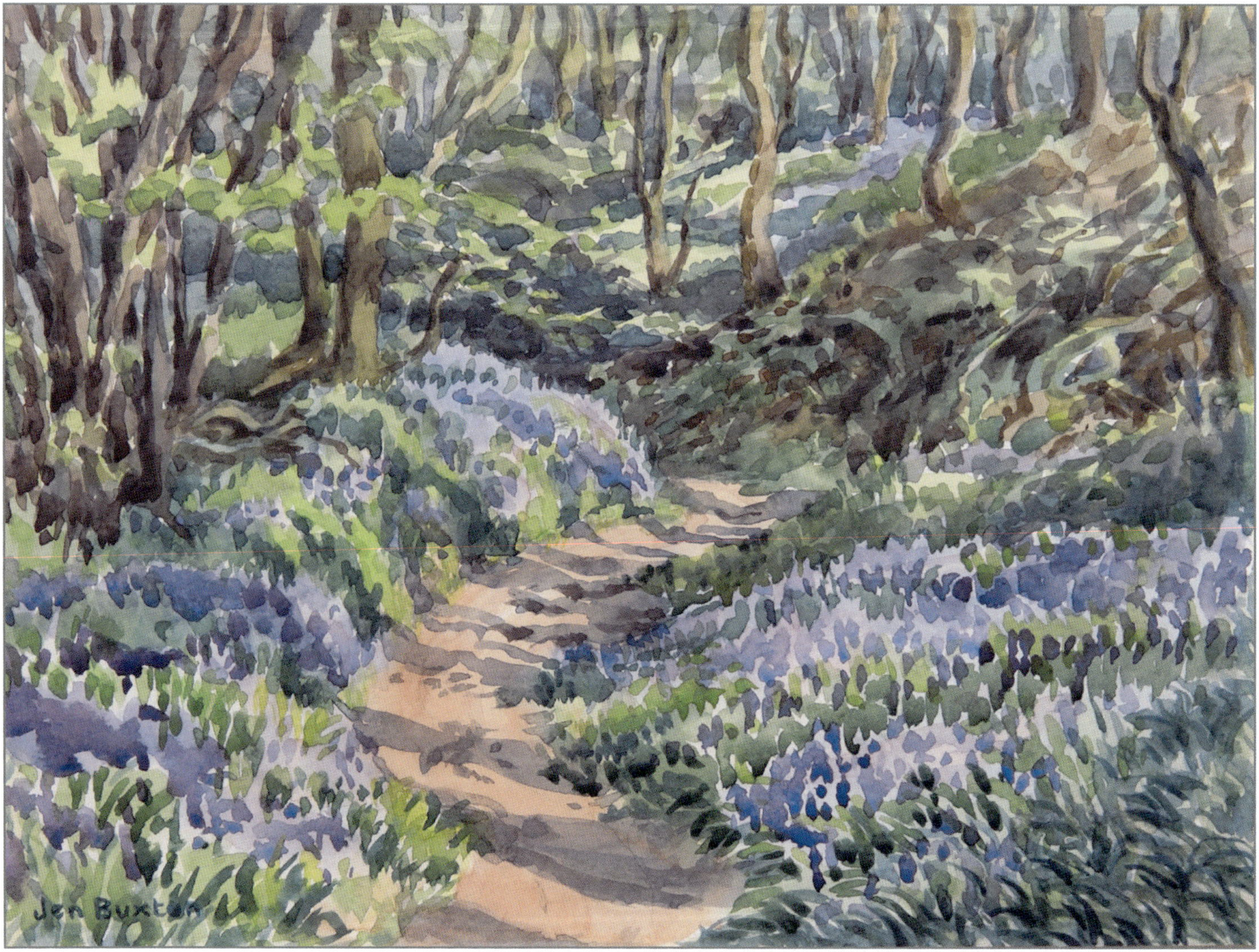

Sea Wood lies between Bardsea and Baycliff, which has the shore to its front and Birkrigg Common behind.

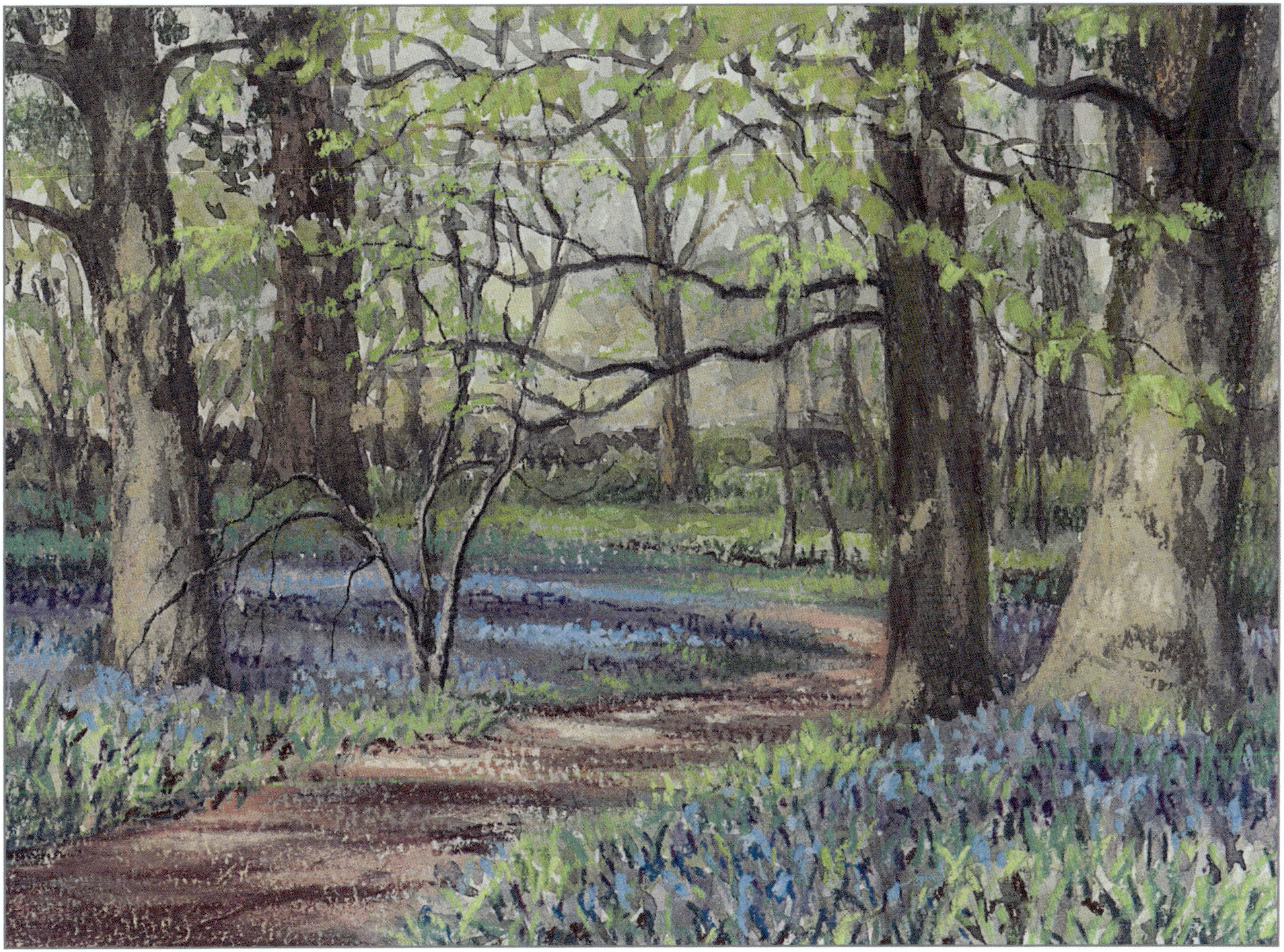

Jennifer loved to walk the dogs in Sea Wood with our friend Ruth, especially in April and May when the bluebells transform the leafy glades into a sea of blue.

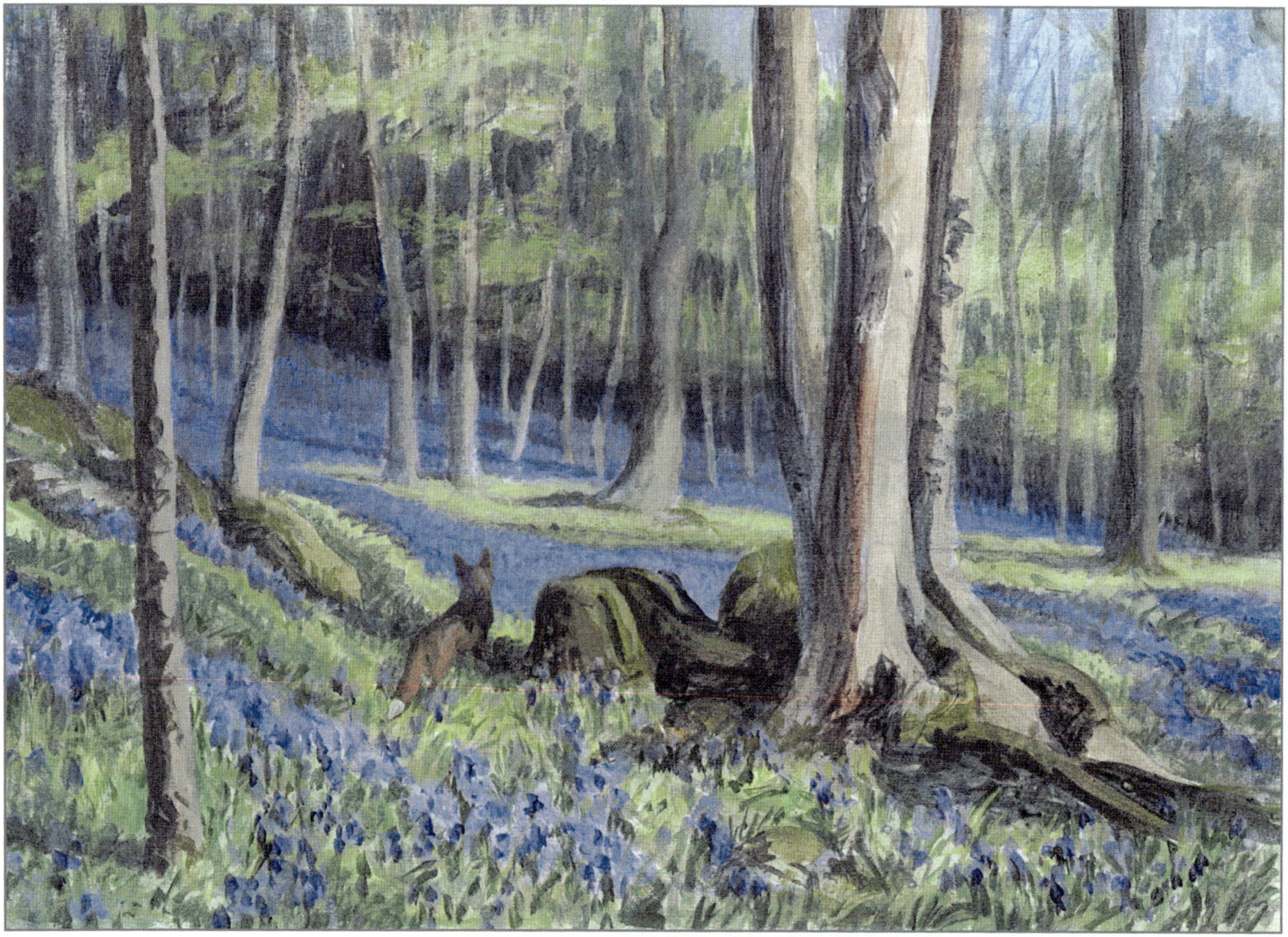

Sea Wood in May

We used to take the dogs for walks in sea wood when we stayed at our cottage in Baycliff during school holidays. Our friends Martin and Helen, who we got to know during those years, own the Olde Mill along the shore from Sea Wood, where we gathered with friends after our parents died.

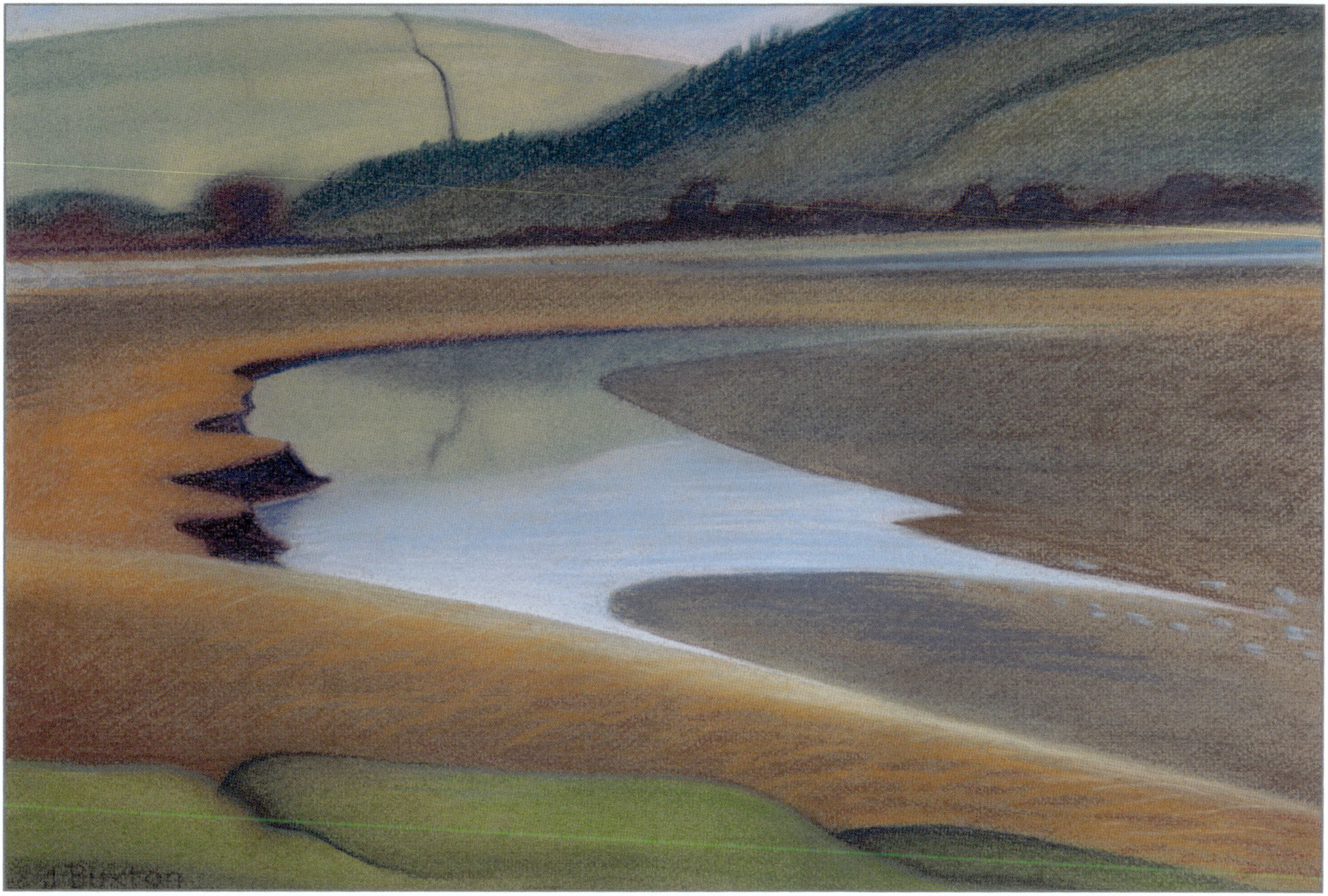

Wings Across the Bay

Jennifer would see patterns and shapes in everything. She would point to dragons that were trees, sometimes in a rather alarming fashion as we drove by. She'd see mountains in the sky, and birds in the water, as was the case here where she named this painting for the shape of the wings of a swallow that she could see in the channels at low tide.

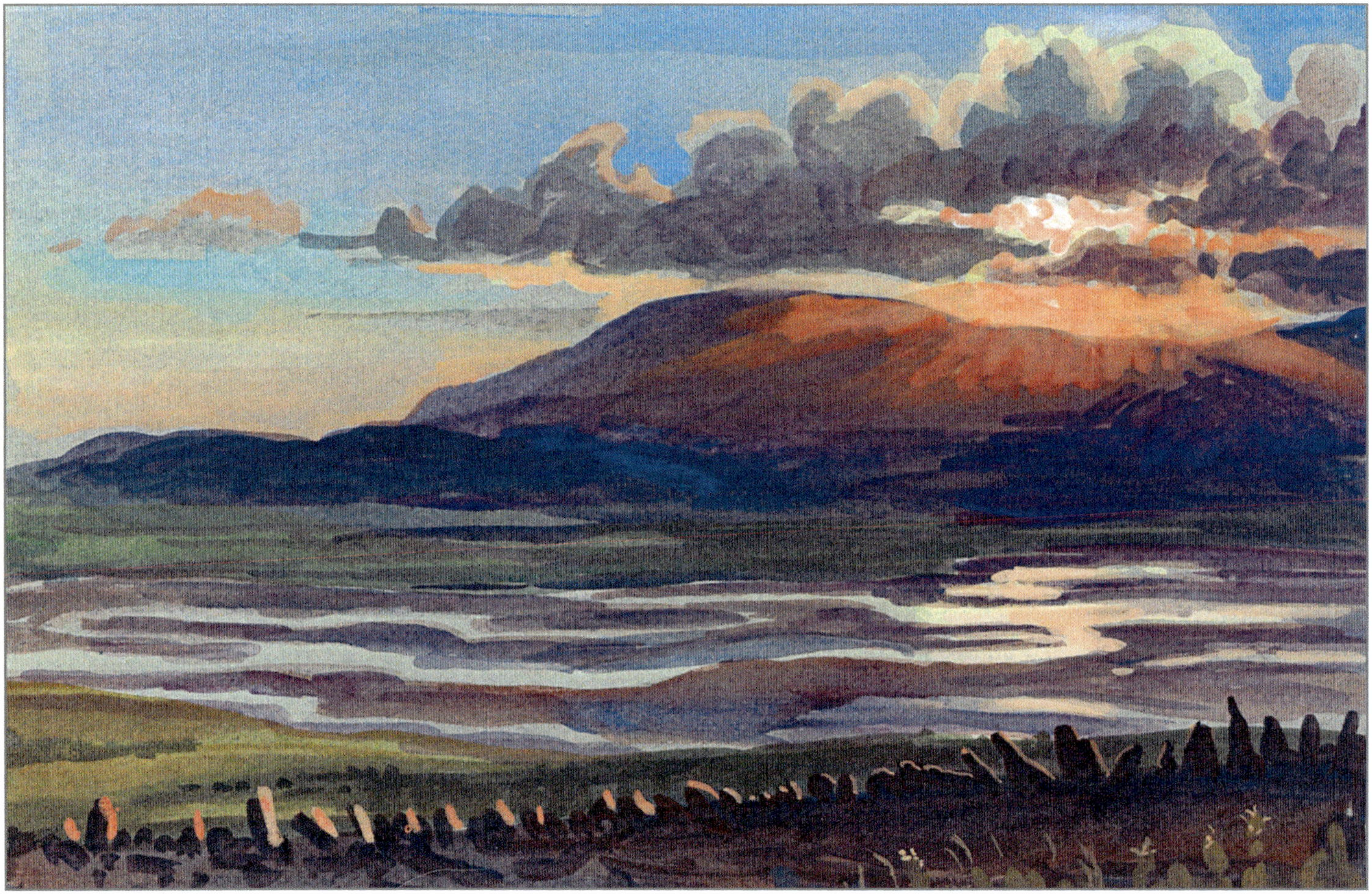

Sunset over Black Combe

Unfortunately the quality of this painting has suffered as it was a relatively quick sketch of Jennifer's and we don't have the original. I love the light on the capstones on the wall.

Kirkby Moor

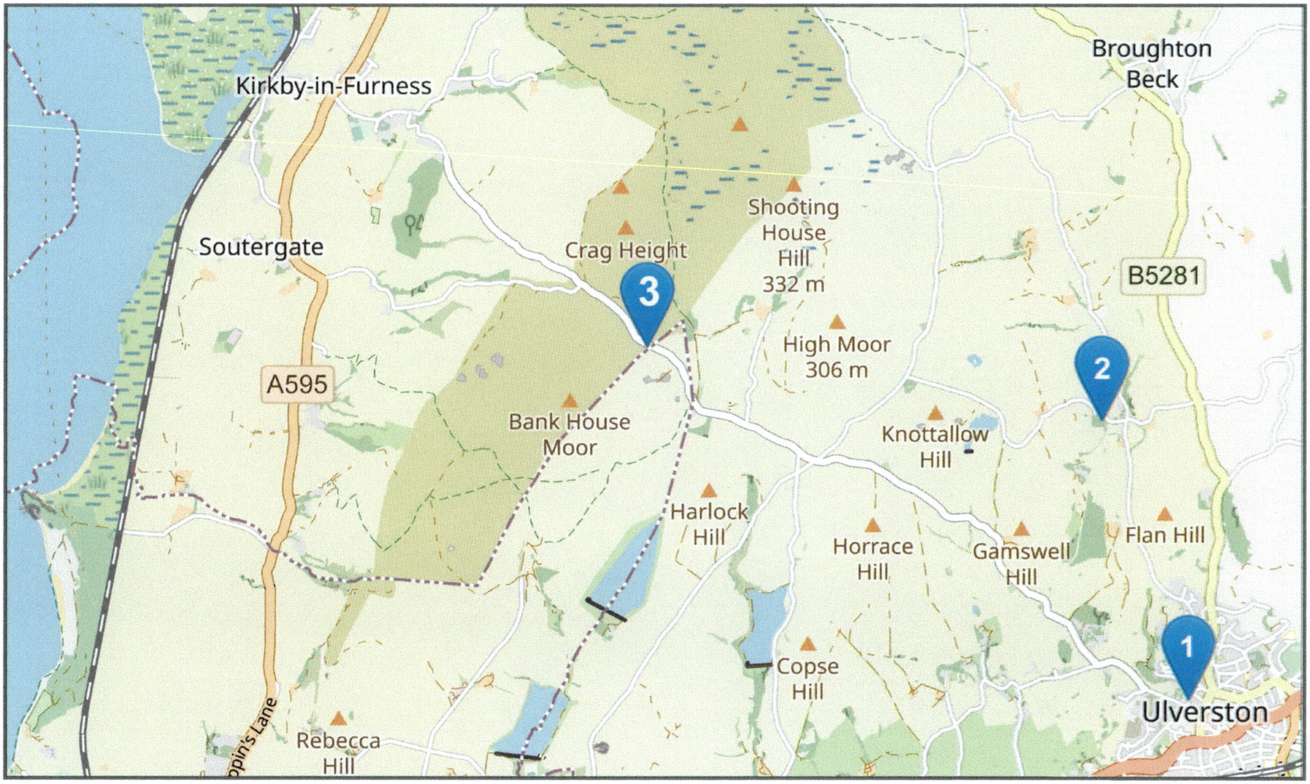

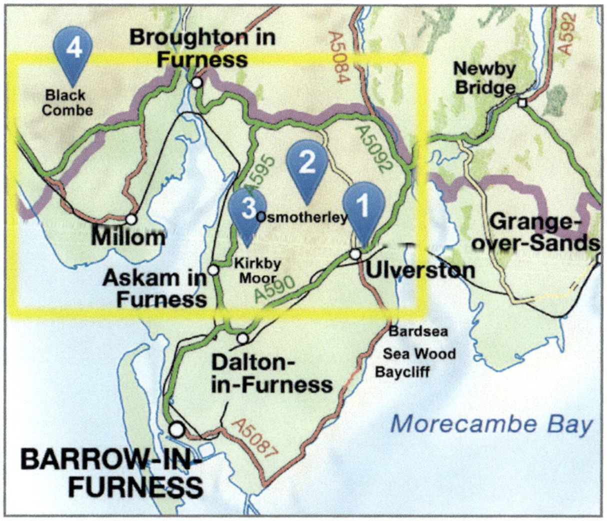

Map Locations

1. Ulverston
2. Windy Ash
3. Kirkby Moor
4. Black Combe

Kirkby Moor lies to the north west of Ulverston. Exposed on all sides, the wind sweeps uninterrupted across the marshy moorland, home to sheep and intrepid hikers walking their dogs.

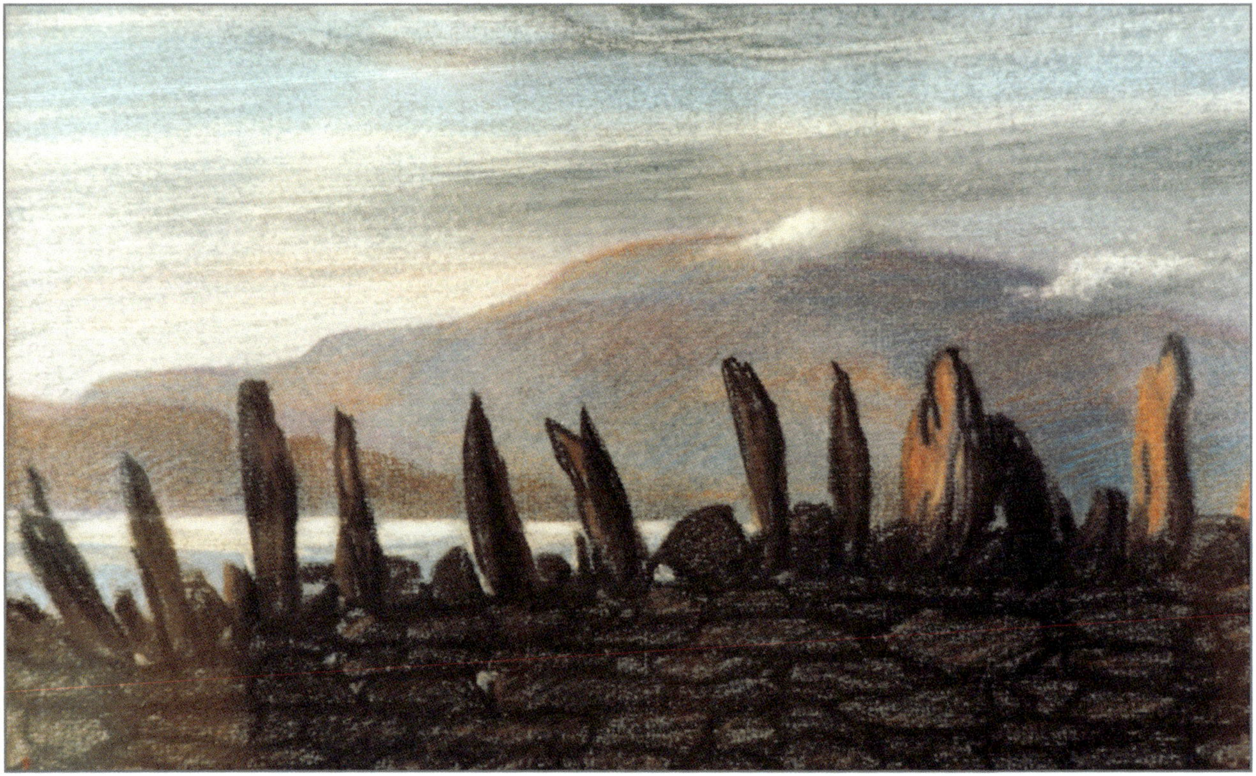

Vic was particularly fond of this dry stone wall with its distinctive capstones, and Jennifer painted it often. The moor behind can be particularly damp in the winter making sitting and painting for too long rather uncomfortable!

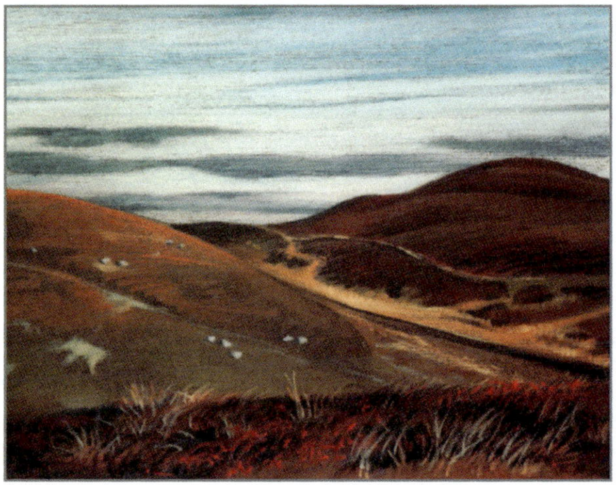

Kirkby Moor looking north

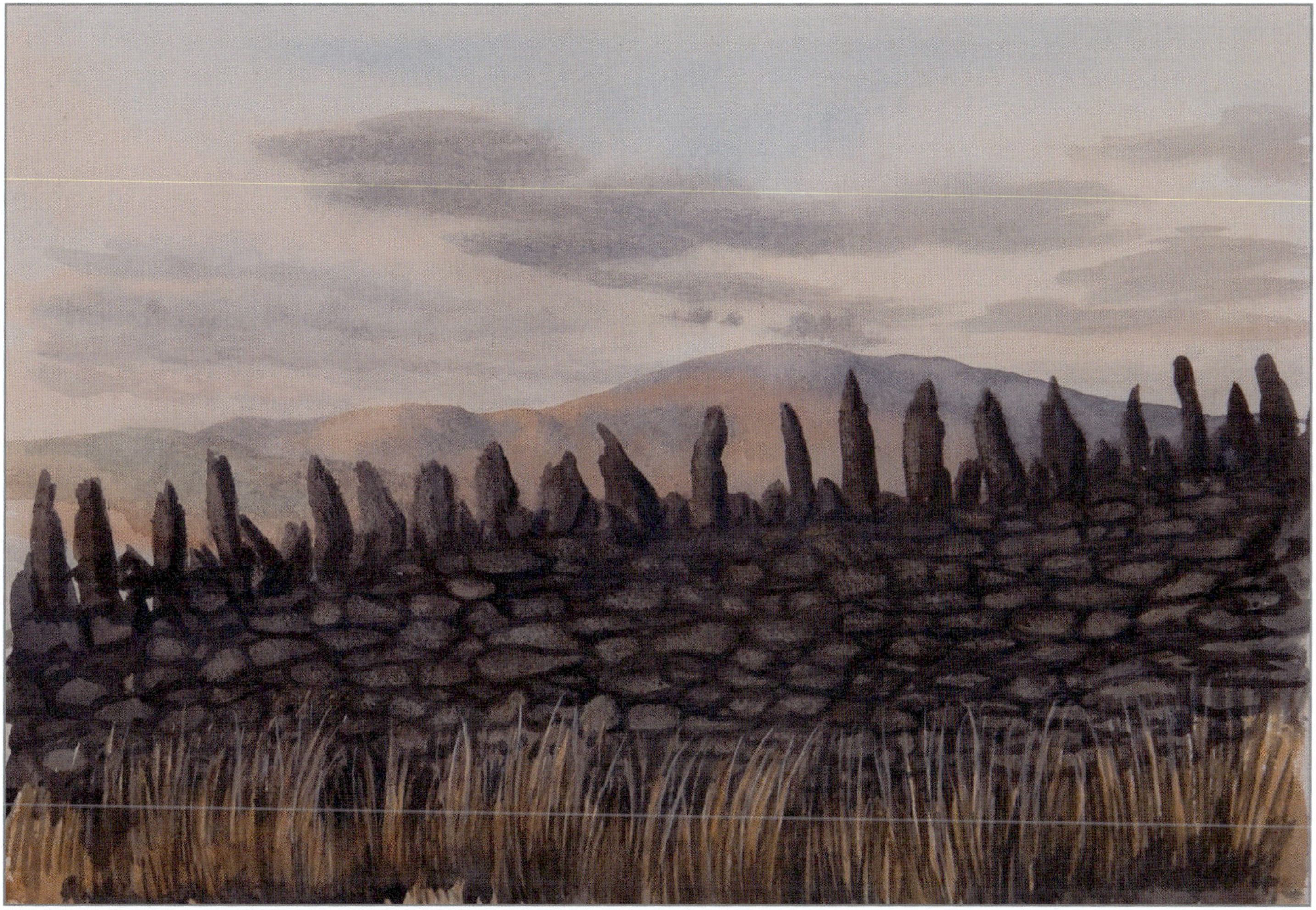

Black Combe from Kirkby Moor

The wall again! On a dry autumn day like this you can sit in the lee of the wall and enjoy the views without risking a damp behind!

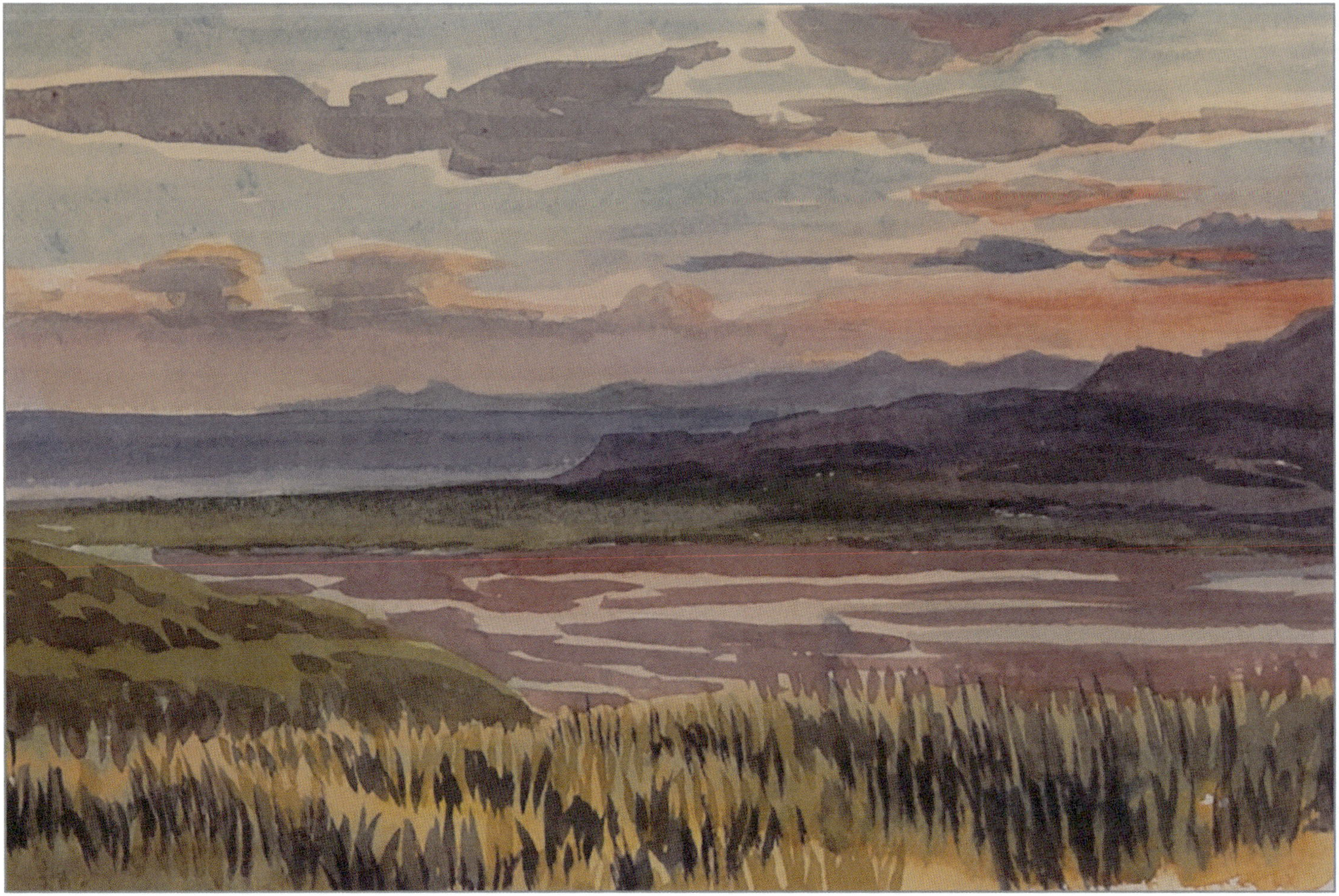

Looking north west over the Duddon Estuary
towards Millom and the western coast

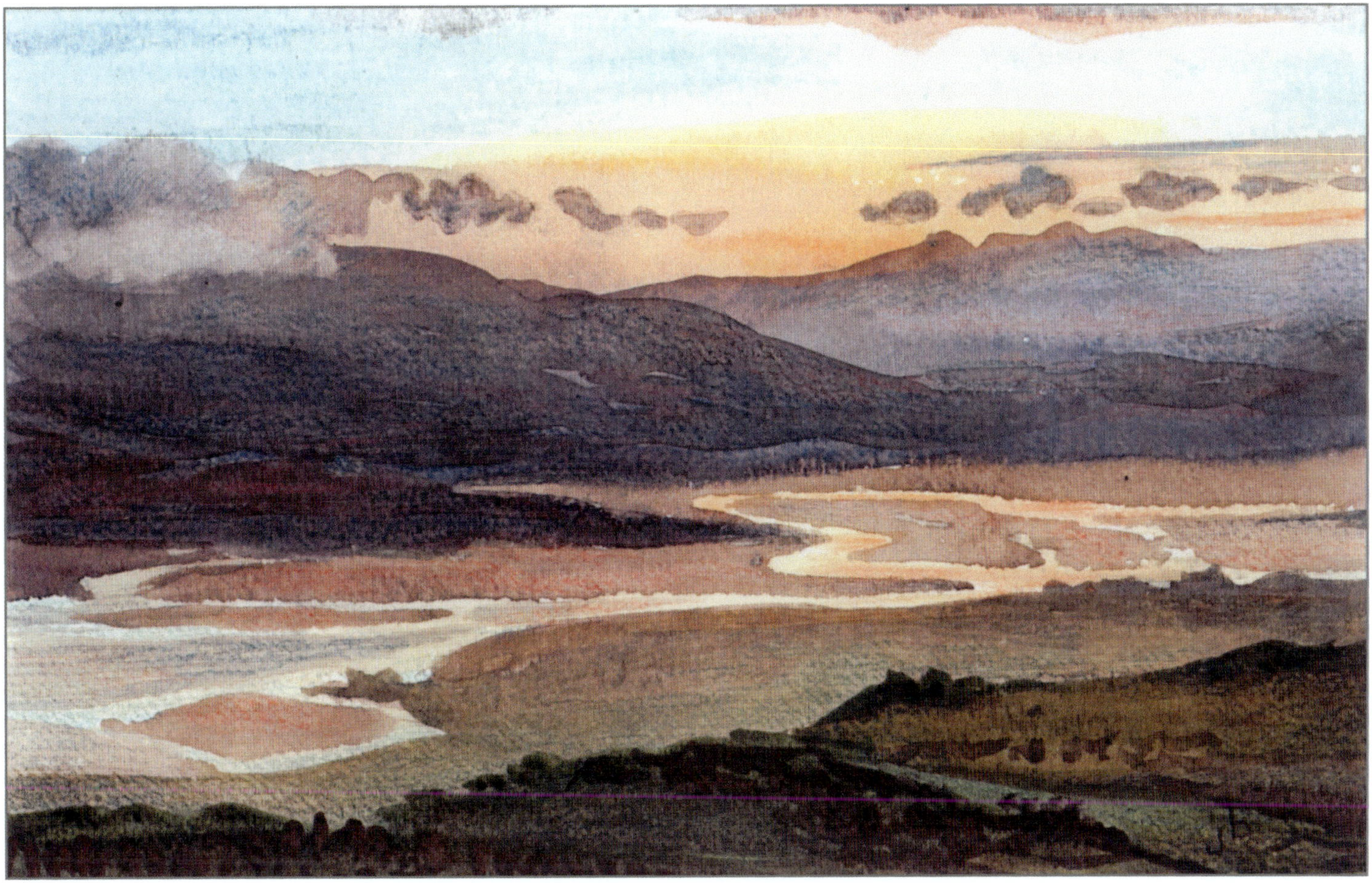

Looking north east over the Duddon Estuary
towards Broughton-in-Furness and Ulpha

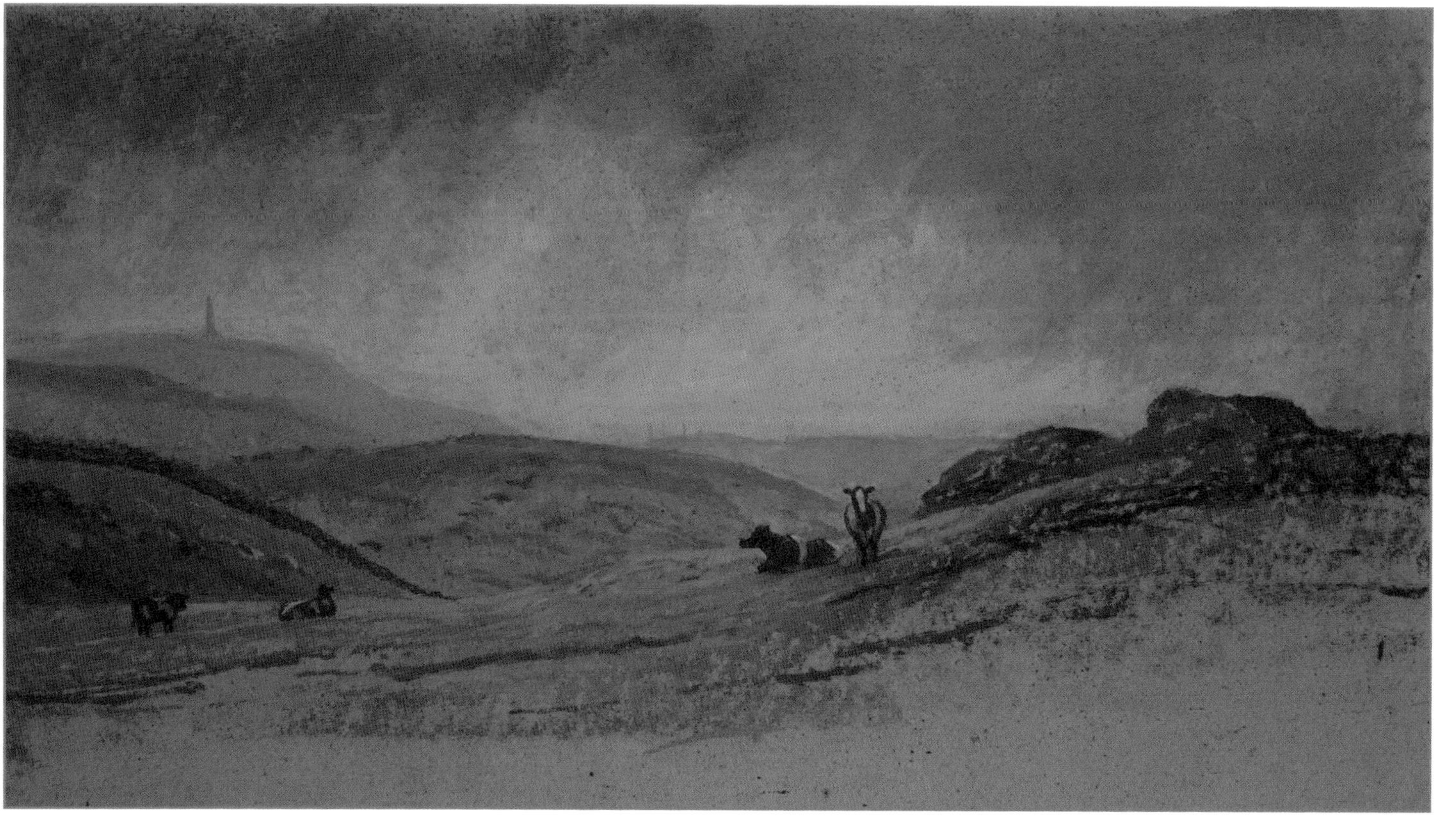

Cows hunker down as a storm moves in over the bay

Jennifer painted this picture from the road up to Knottallow Tarn above Windy Ash in Osmotherley. Hoad Monument is visible on the skyline to the north east. The road on from Knottallow Tarn takes you across the moor to Kirkby-in-Furness.

South Lakes

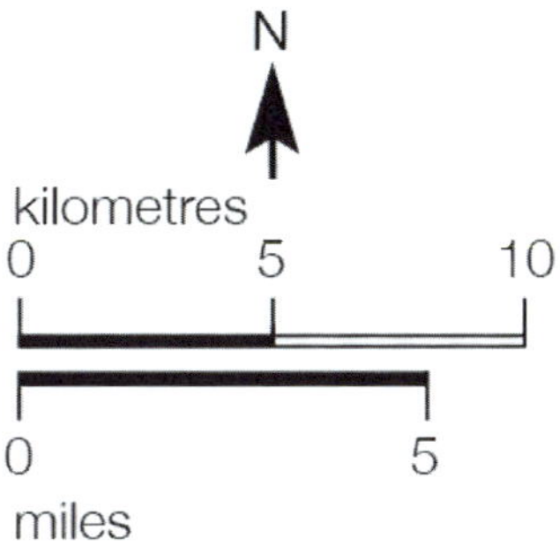

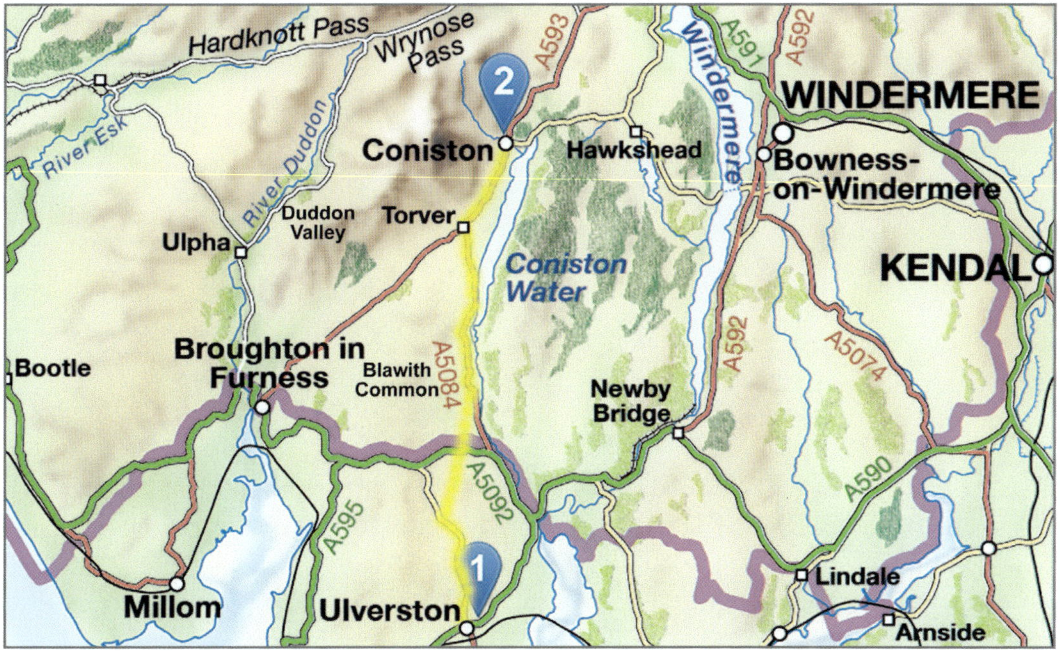

Map Locations
1. Ulverston
2. Coniston

It's a beautiful drive north from Ulverston. This route takes us past Osmotherley and St. John's church along the Broughton Beck road and then on past WoodGate where Jennifer and Vic lived when I was born. The road along the west side of Coniston Water towards the town of Coniston at the head of the lake offers beautiful views up towards Coniston Old Man and Dow Crag, two of the most recognizable of the southern fells. Between Coniston and Windermere, just south of Hawkshead, lies Esthwaite Water which is a hidden gem well worth the less travelled route.

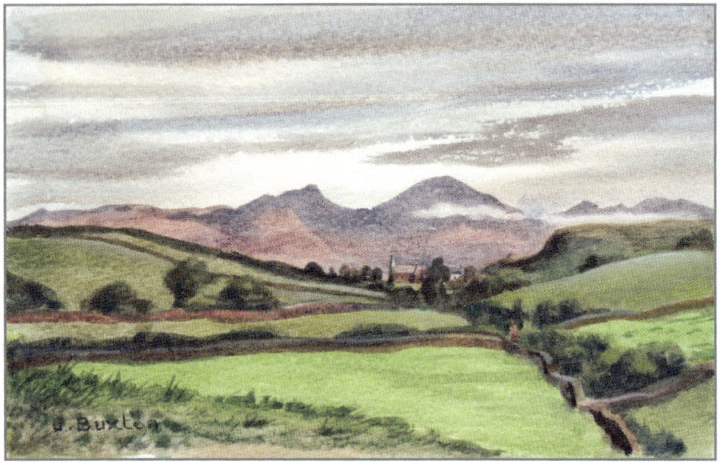

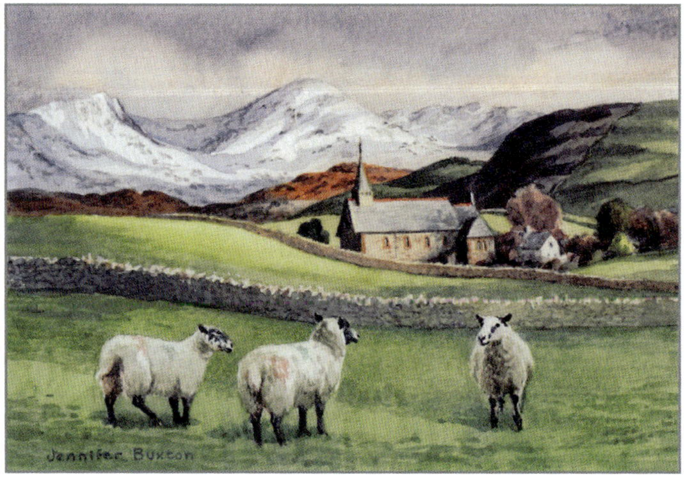

St. John's Church in Osmotherley lies just off
the Broughton Beck road north of Ulverston

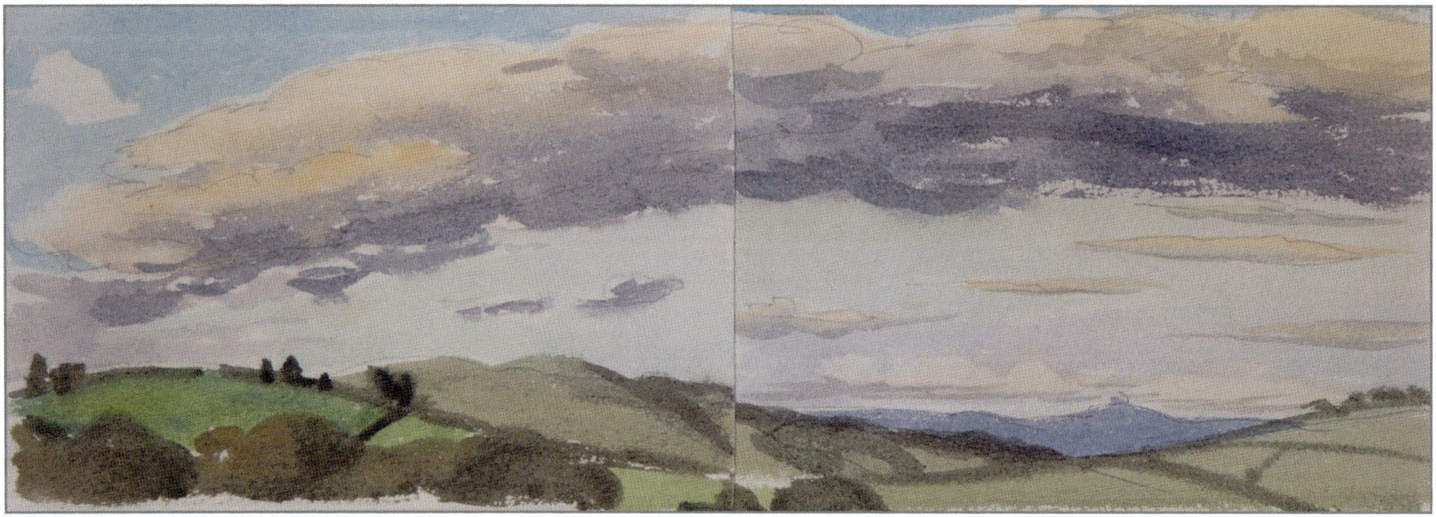

Jennifer painted across the centre of her spiral bound
pad so the two sides don't quite line up!

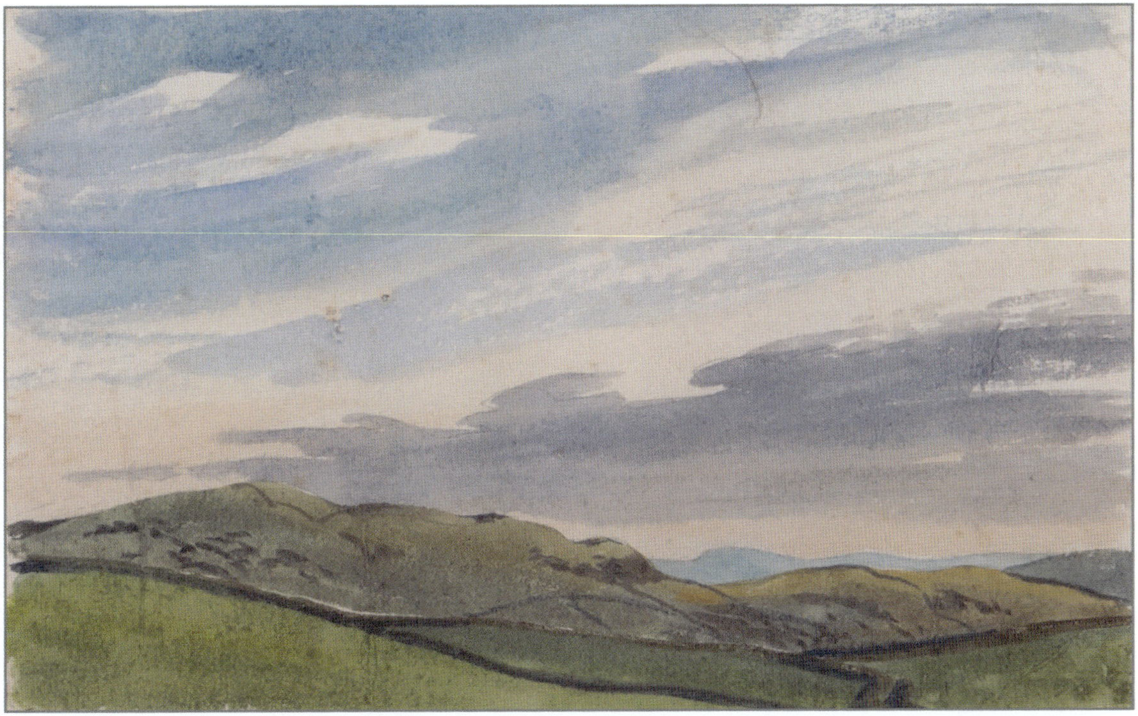

North from
Osmotherley

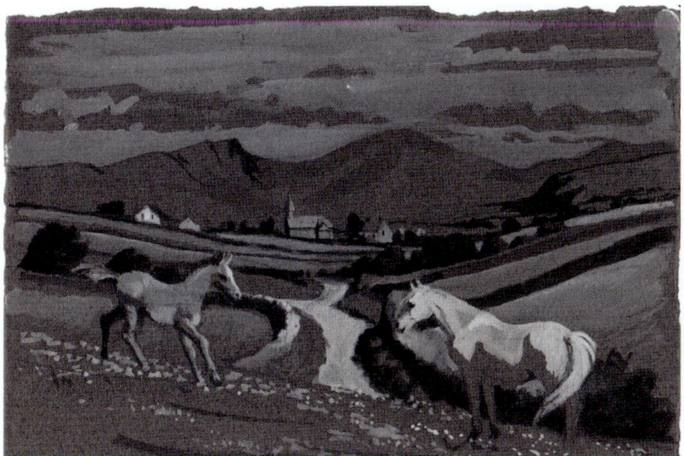

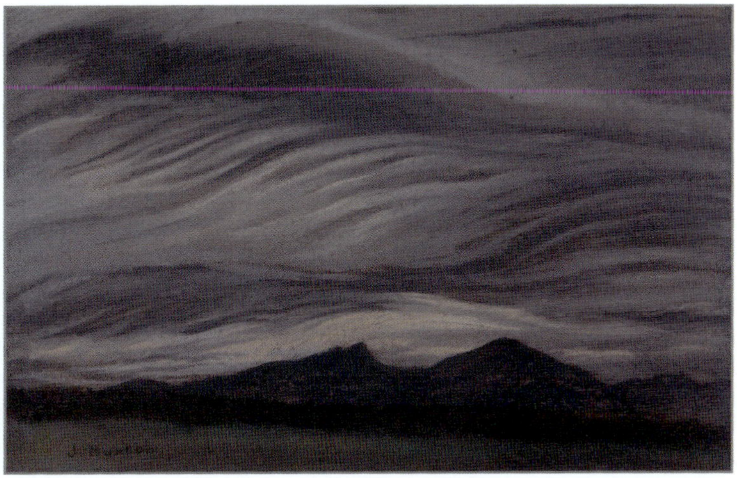

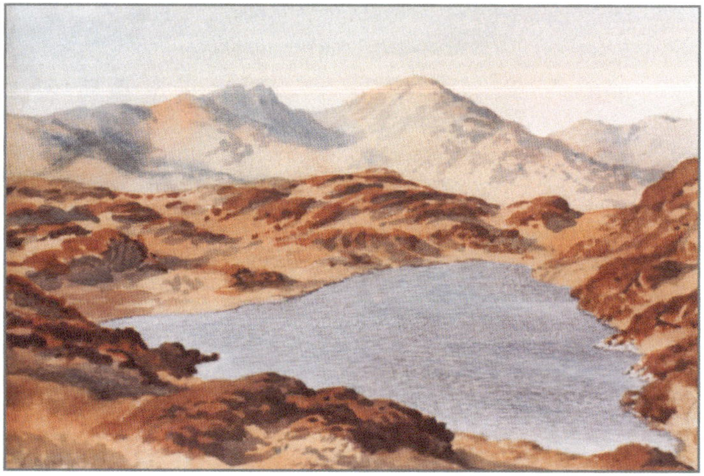

Beacon
Tarn

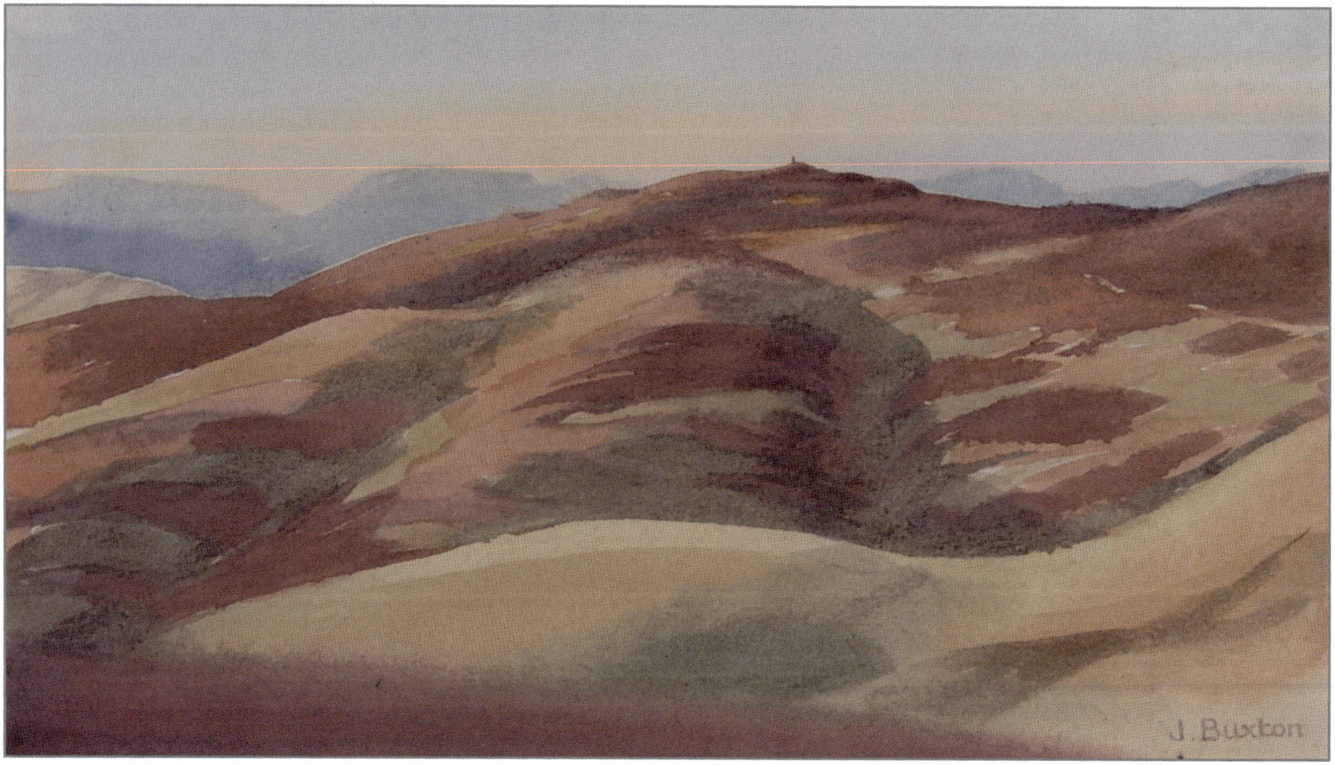

Blawith Common

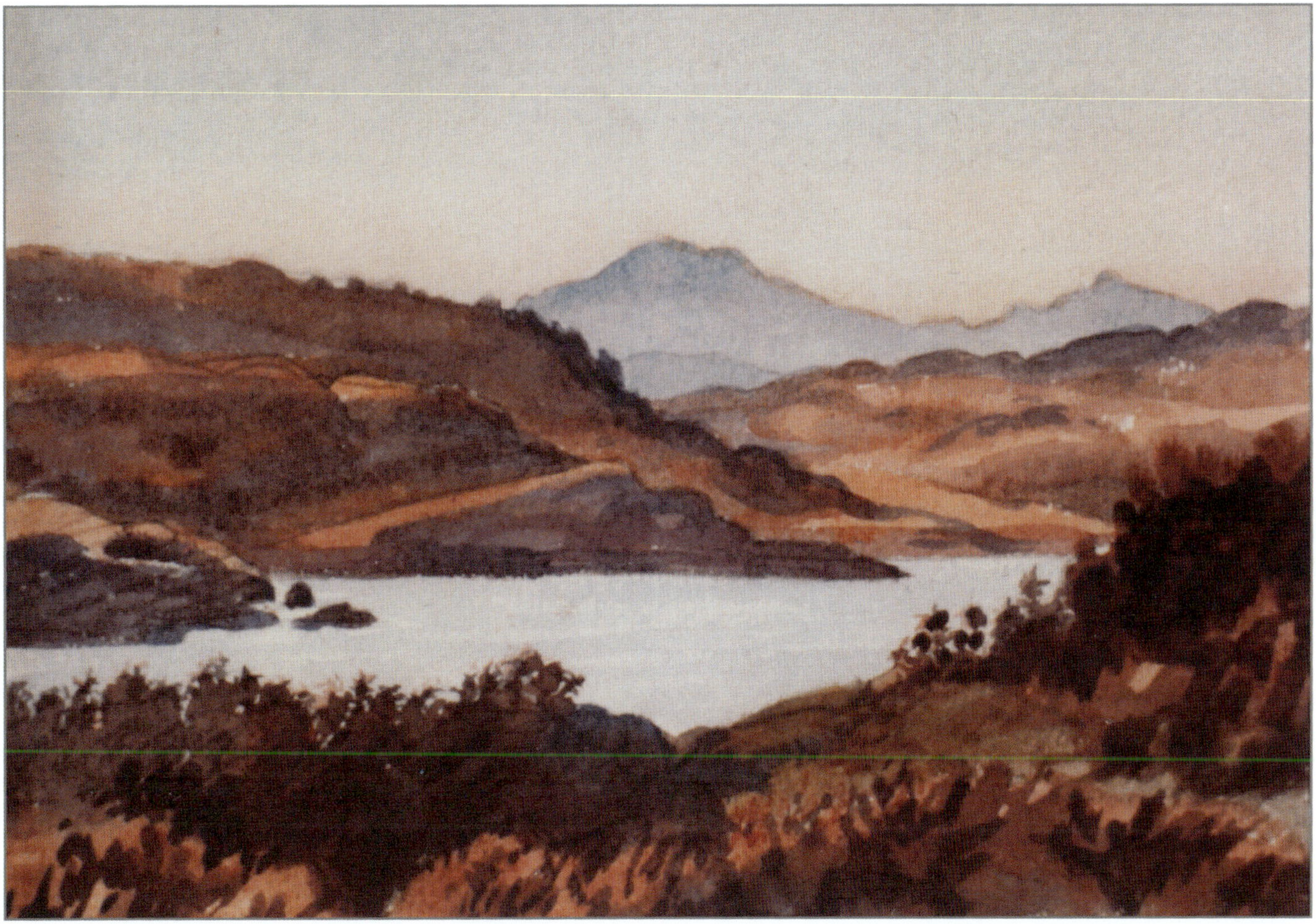

Beacon Tarn above Blawith at the southern end of Coniston Water

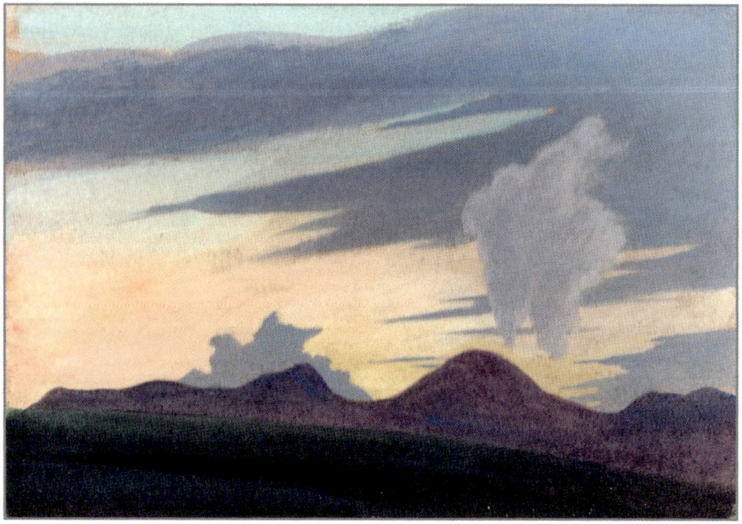

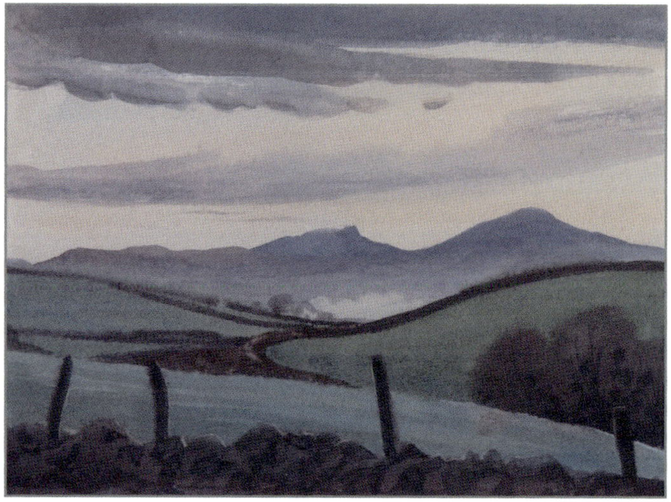

Dow Crag and Coniston Old Man

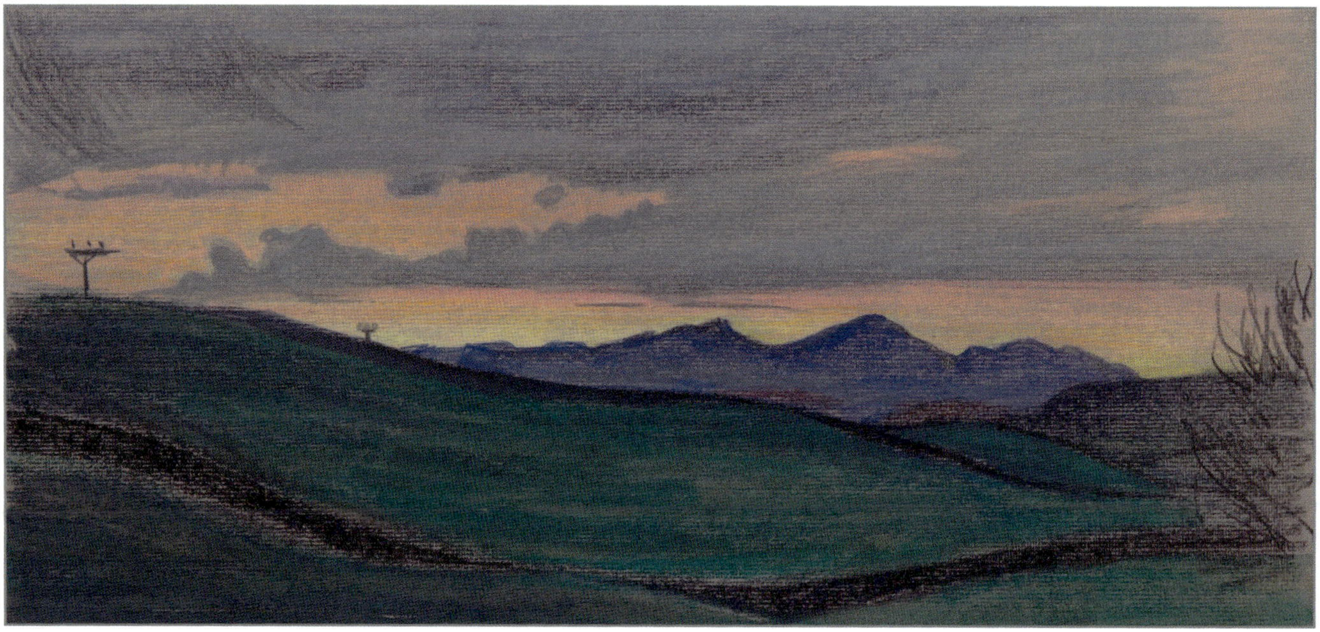

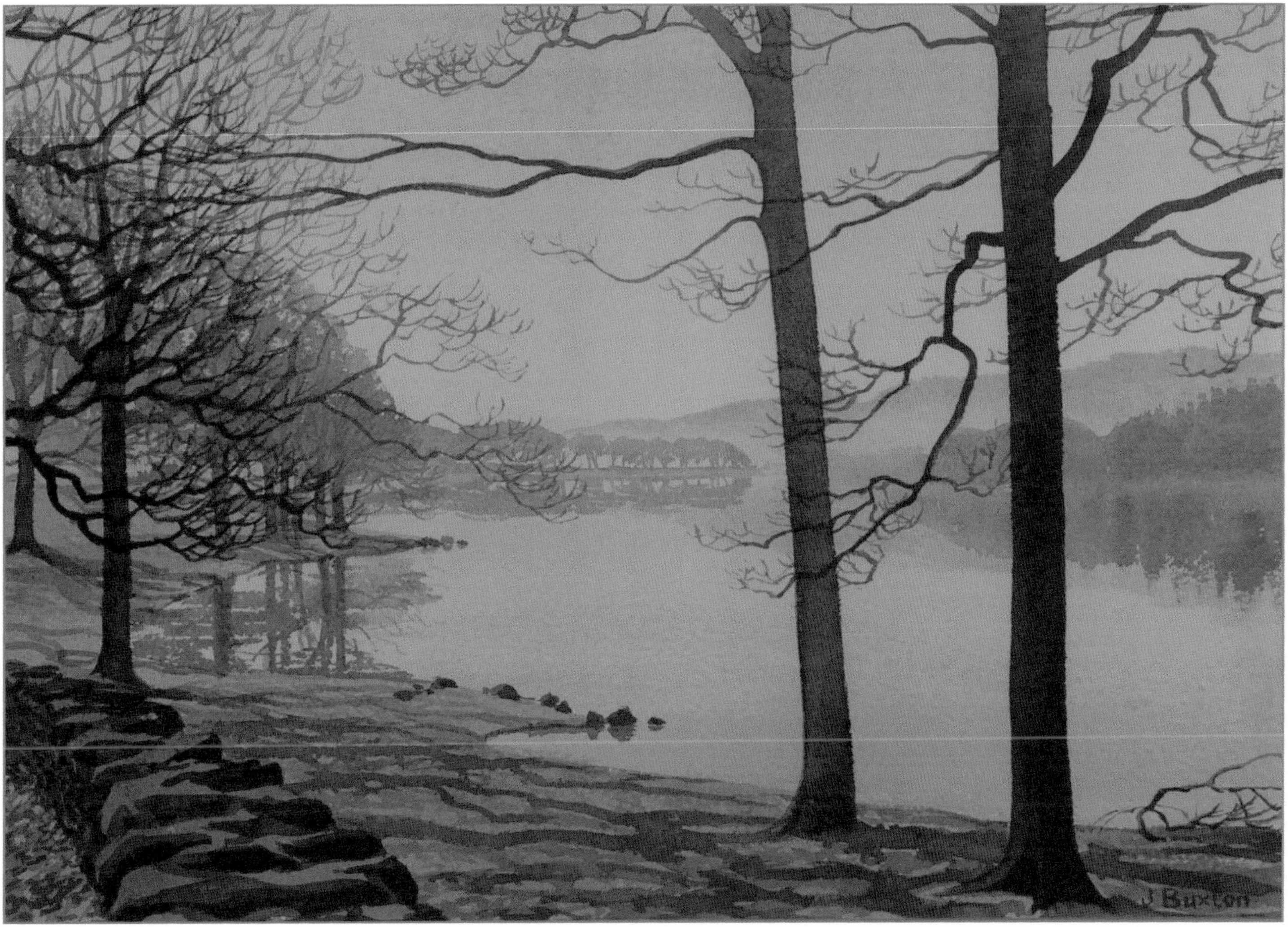

Coniston Water looking north east. Sometimes the winter brings sharp frosty days like this, and an uncustomary calm on the surface of the lake.

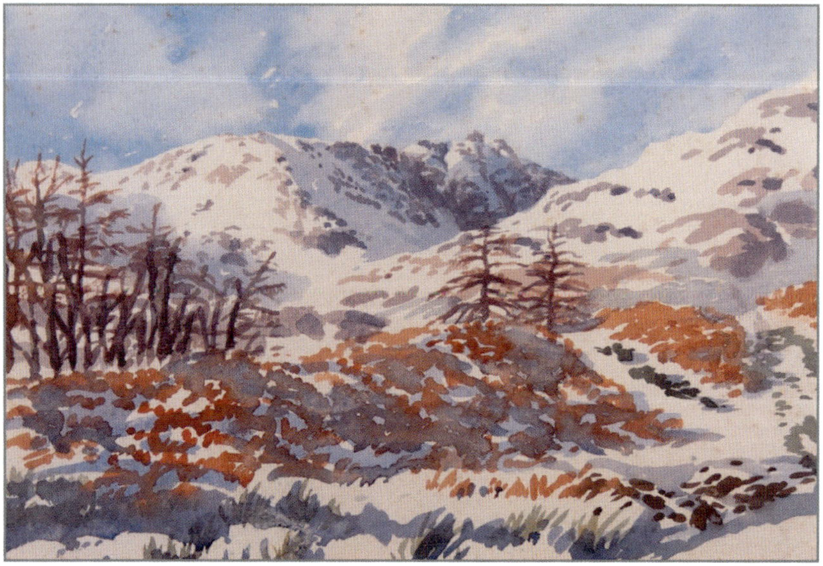

Dow Crag

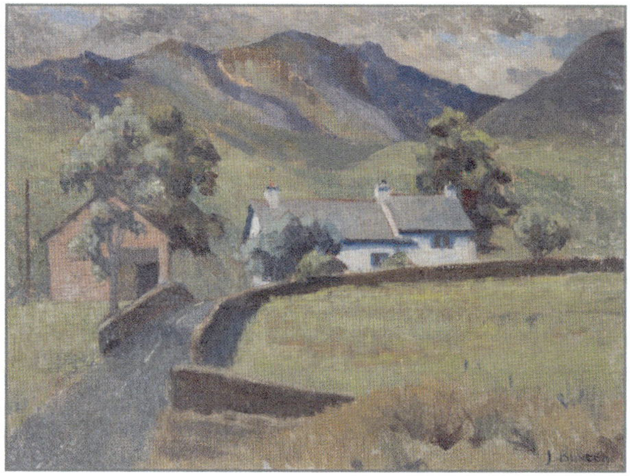

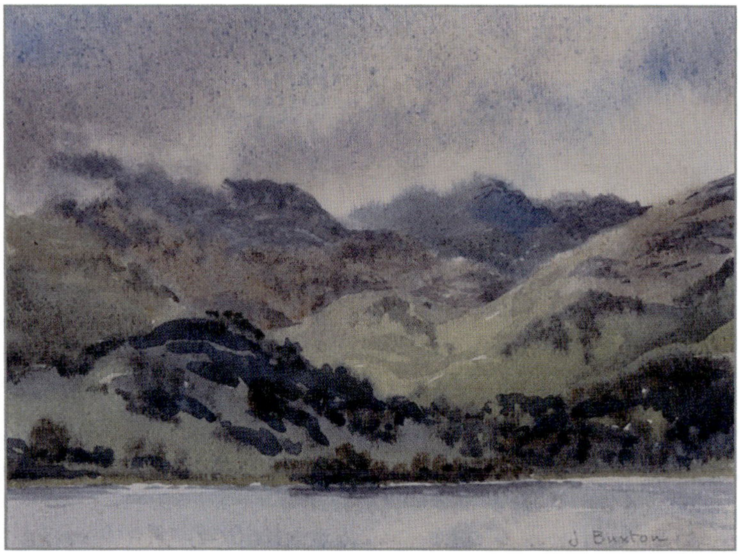

One of the classic walks up to Dow Crag and the Old Man of Coniston is from Torver. This is an early painting of Jennifer's in oils: she had to switch to watercolor as Henry and I would make a terrible mess with the slow-to-dry oil paints!

Often Jennifer would paint from around here while Vic and Henry would walk up into the fells and I would play happily around one of the many streams.

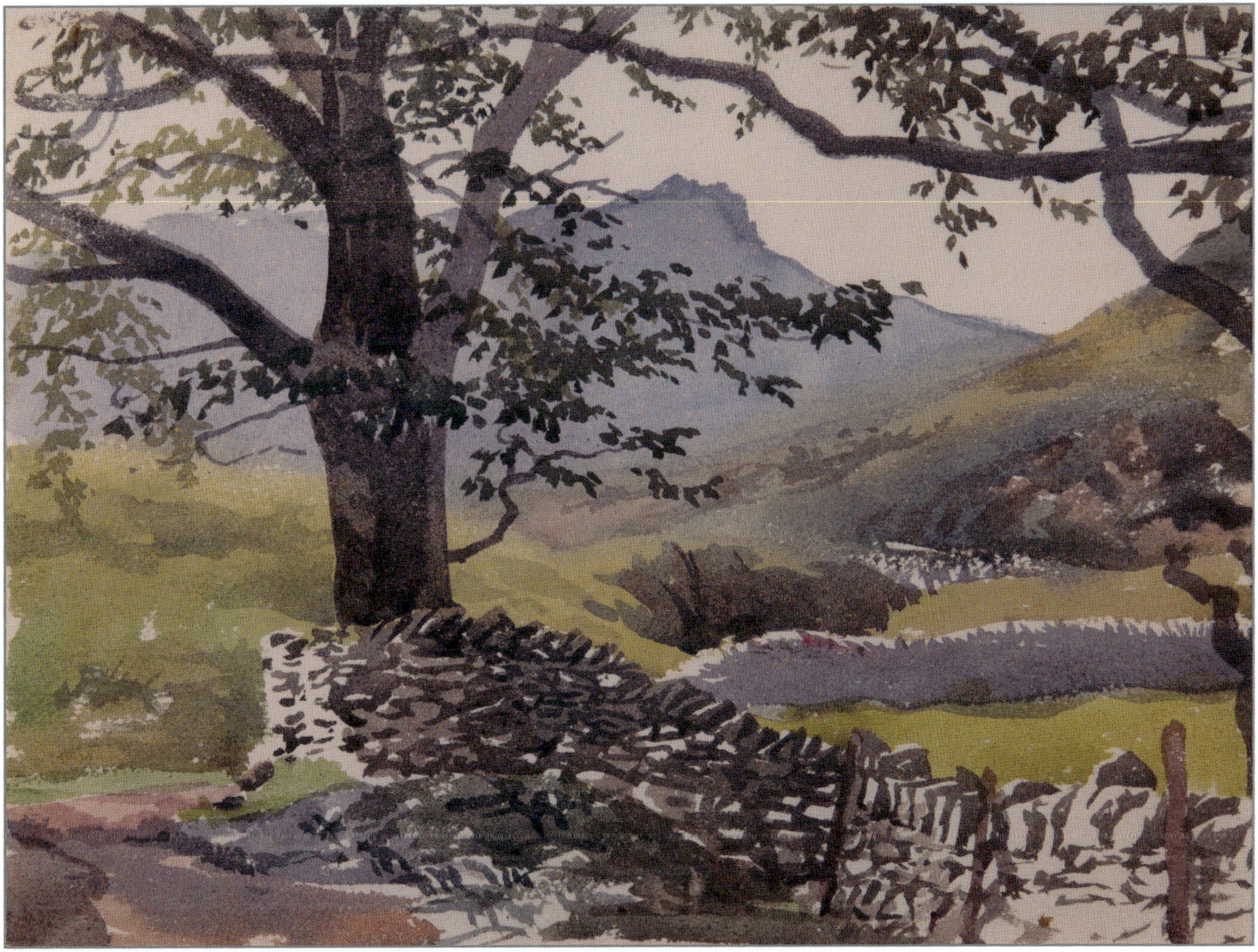

Dow Crag

The path up to Dow Crag from Torver approaches via the slate quarries that made Coniston famous.

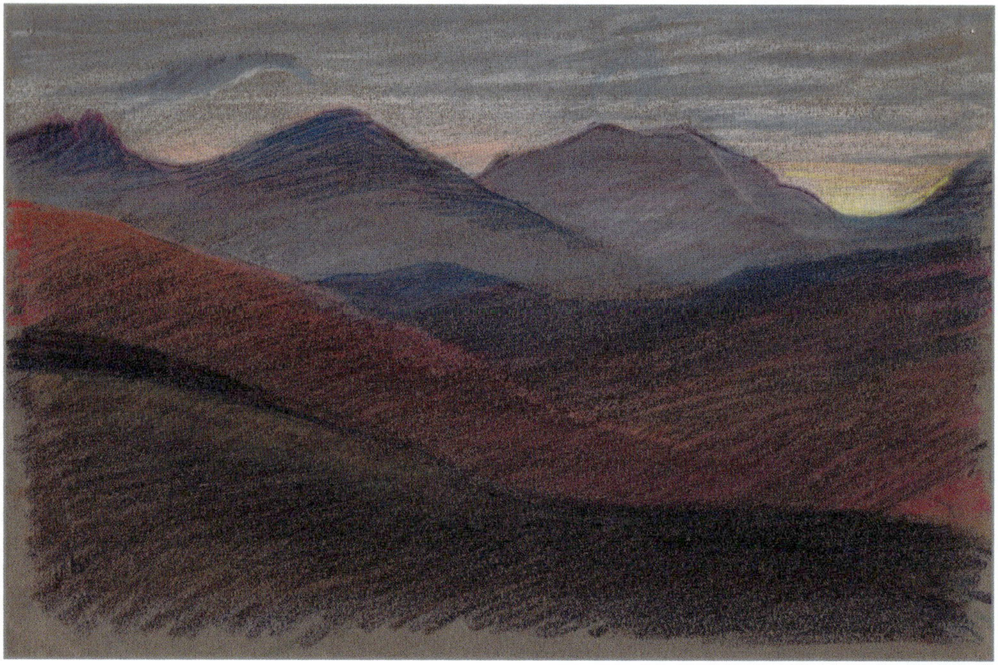

Sunset over Dow Crag,
Coniston Old Man
and Wetherlam

In autumn the bracken transforms the fellsides to this beautiful rusty red. Jennifer loved the change in hue as green was not her favourite colour!

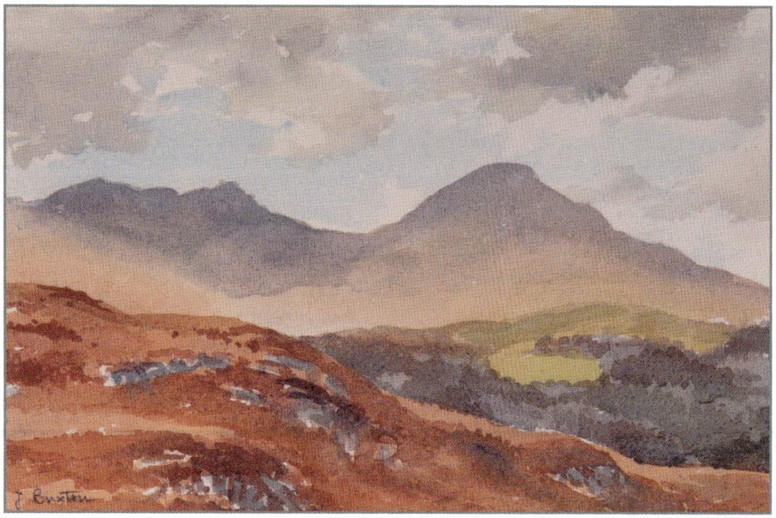

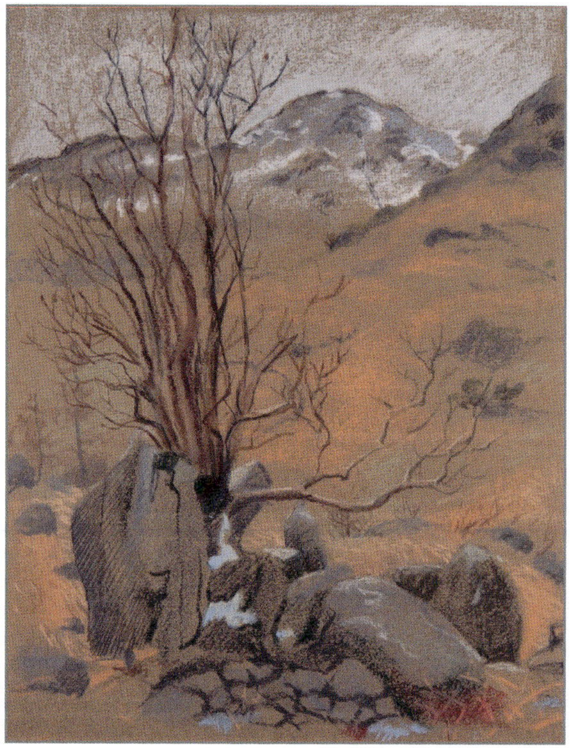

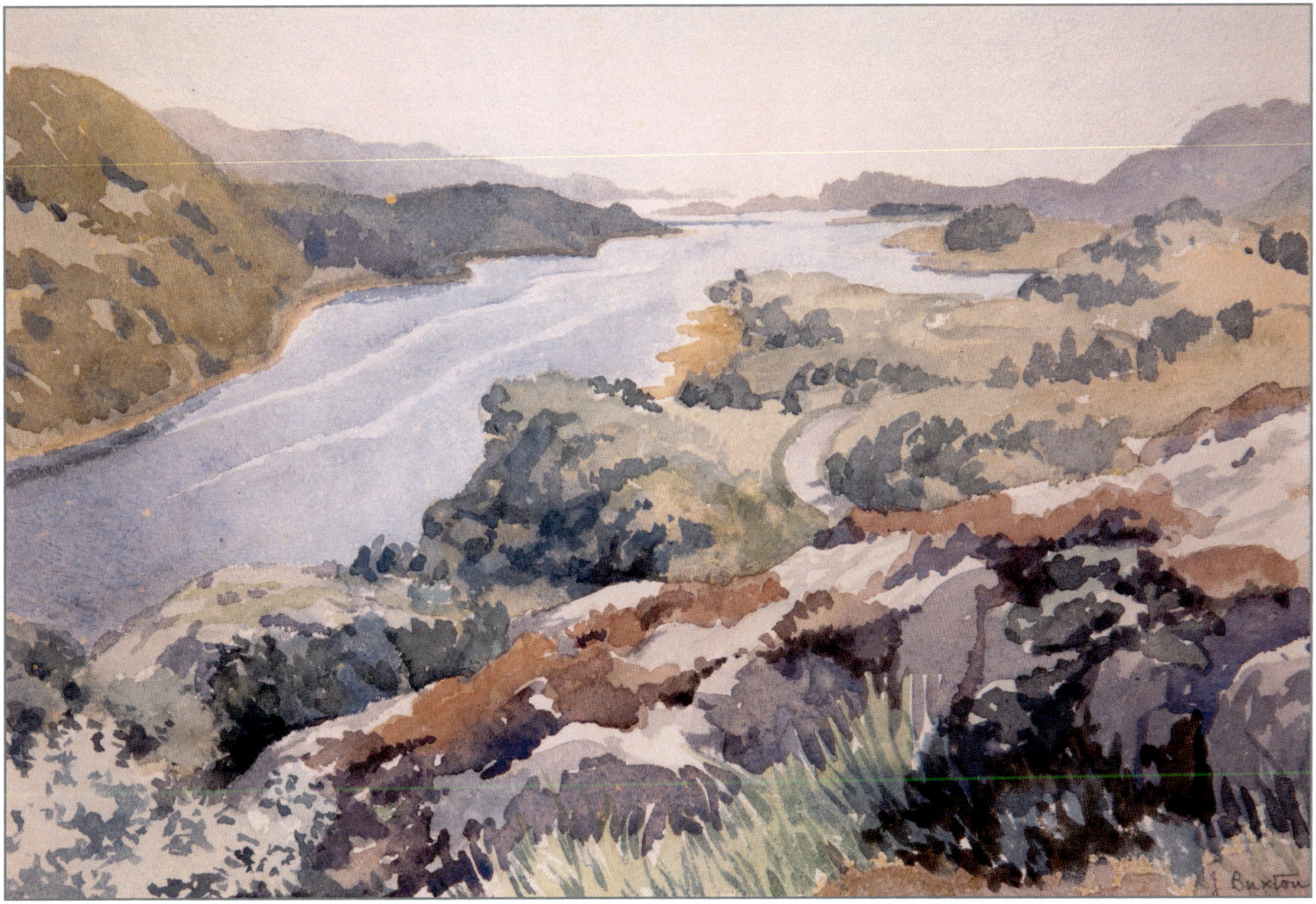

Coniston Water, looking south from the path up to Thrang Moss Reservoir above the road around Sunny Bank on the way to Torver.

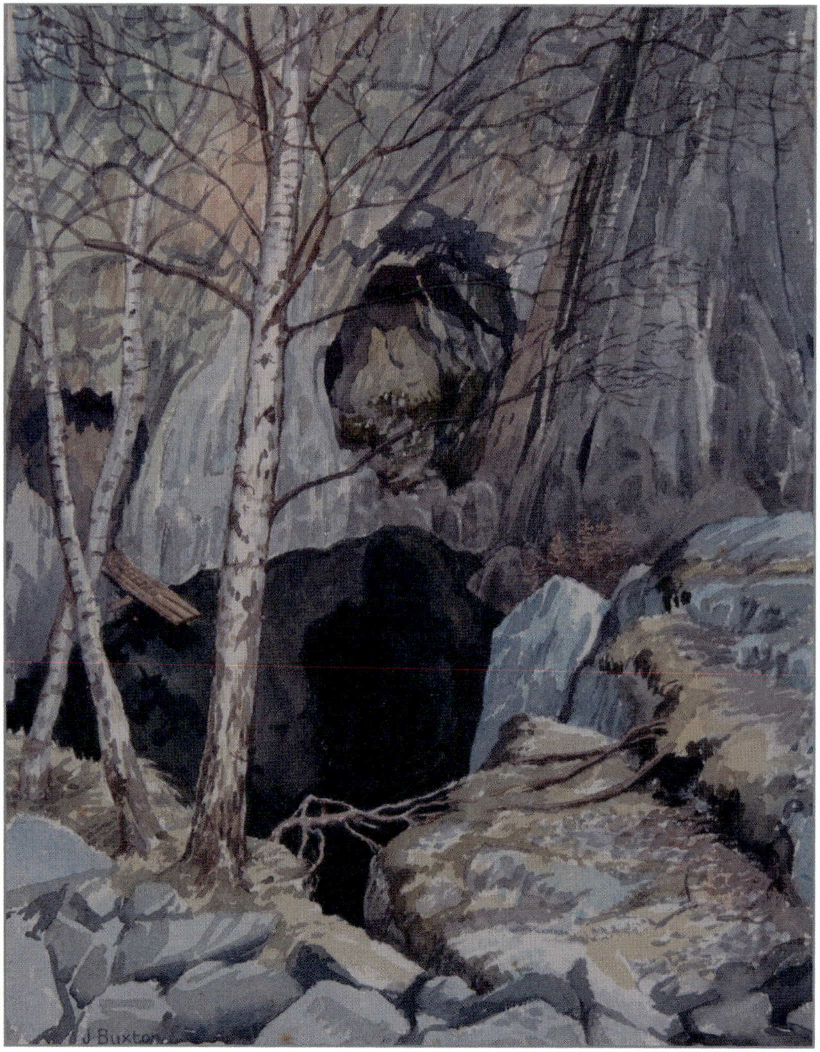

I remember Henry and I coming to Hodge Close one Christmas Day and climbing the inclined crack-line to the right of the jetty; I was probably 16 or 17 at the time. Henry was a keen rock climber and for a few years in our teens he seemed to spend a fair amount of his time coaxing me up climbs in the Lakes and around Bath where we were living at the time.

Hodge Close Quarry between Coniston and Little Langdale

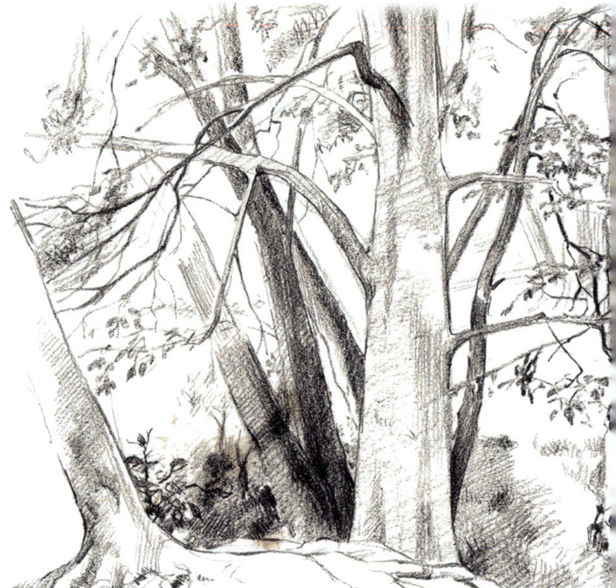

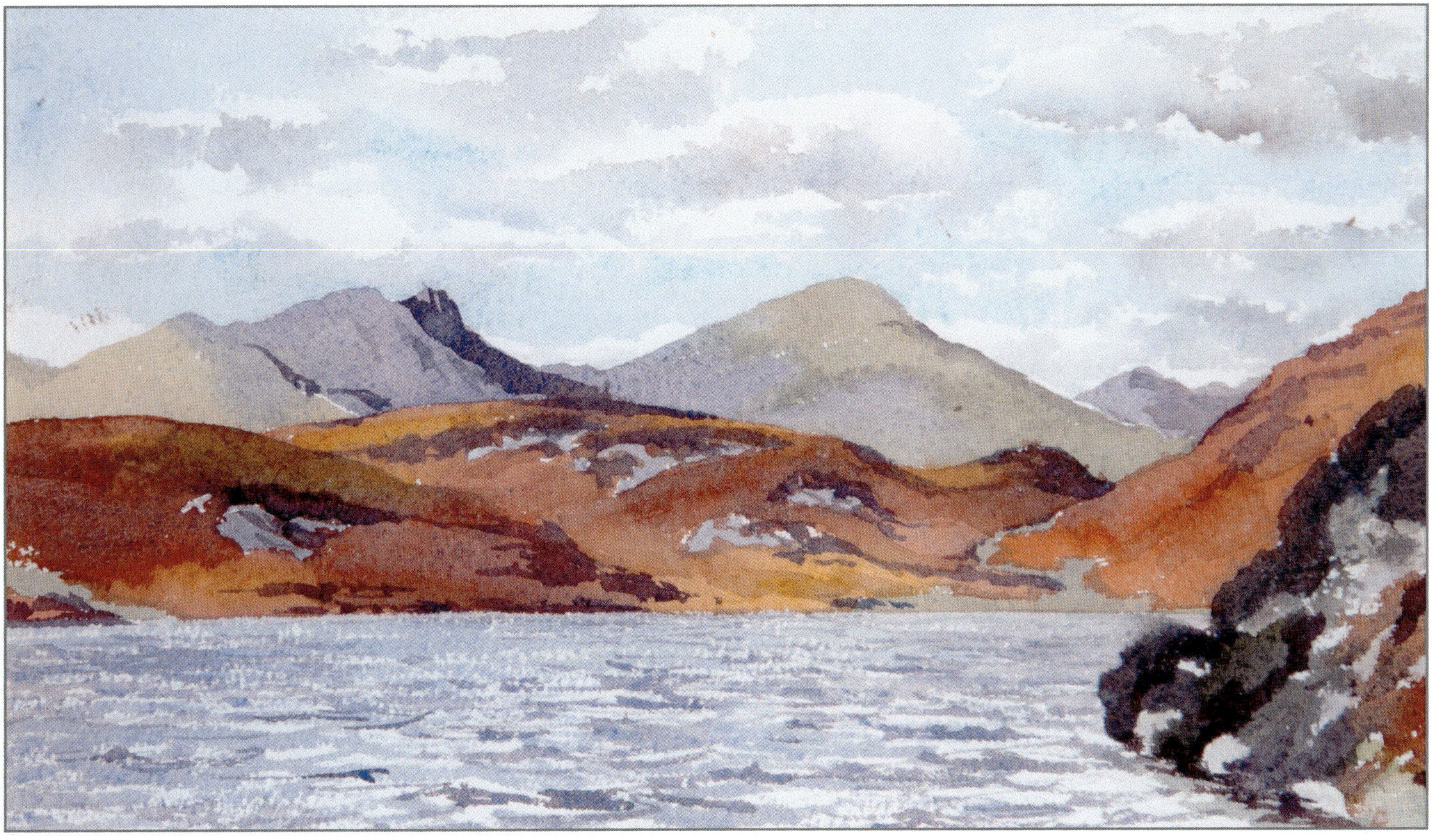

Thrang Moss Reservoir, west of the A5084 between Blawith and Torver. We used to walk the dogs up to the reservoir and even swim in the summer.

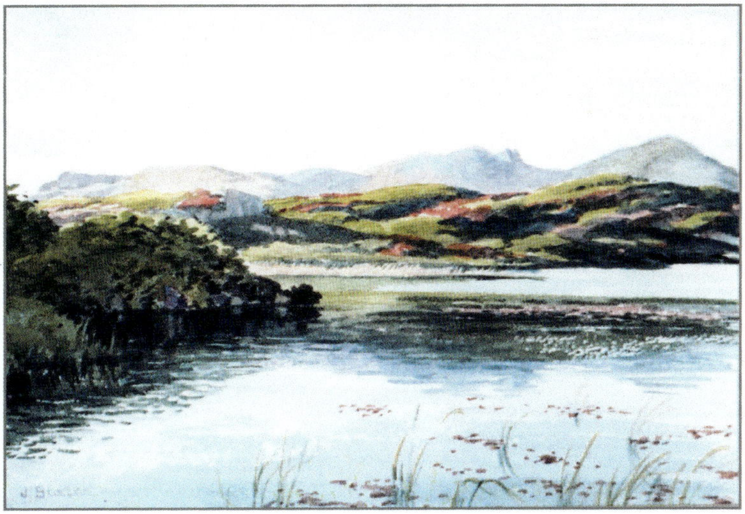

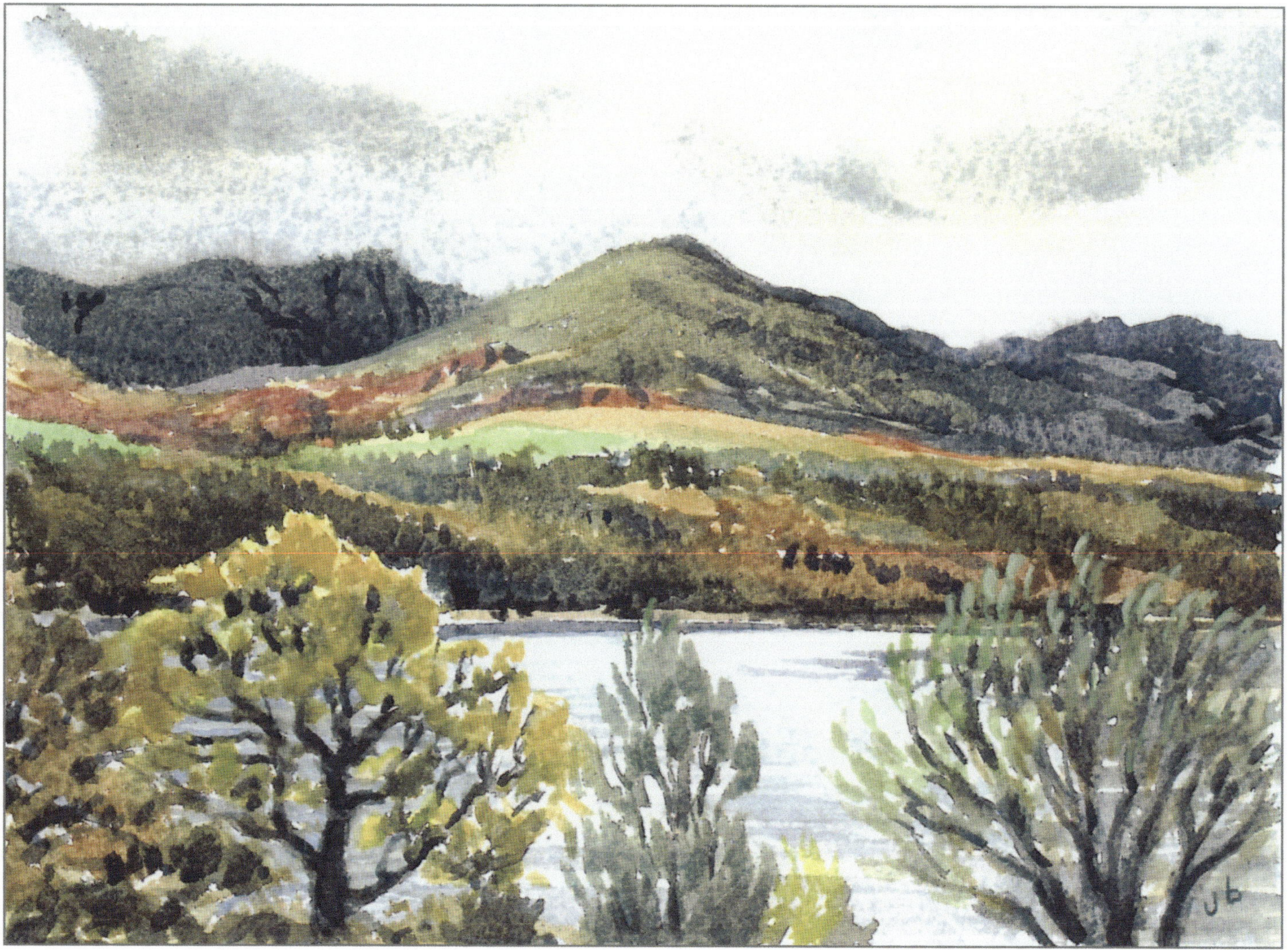

Coniston Old Man and Dow Crag looking across Coniston Water from Brantwood

Brantwood and East of Lake

Brantwood is a museum and art gallery dedicated to the Victorian painter and philanthropist John Ruskin. The area was famous for its views across the lake even before the time the main house was built in the late 1700's. Today there's a wonderful little restaurant and coffee shop in a converted stable on the site.

This was one of Jennifer's favourite places for a lunch stop, with home made soup and coffee, and also perhaps a cream cake; her propensity for chocolate deserts was well known among her friends.

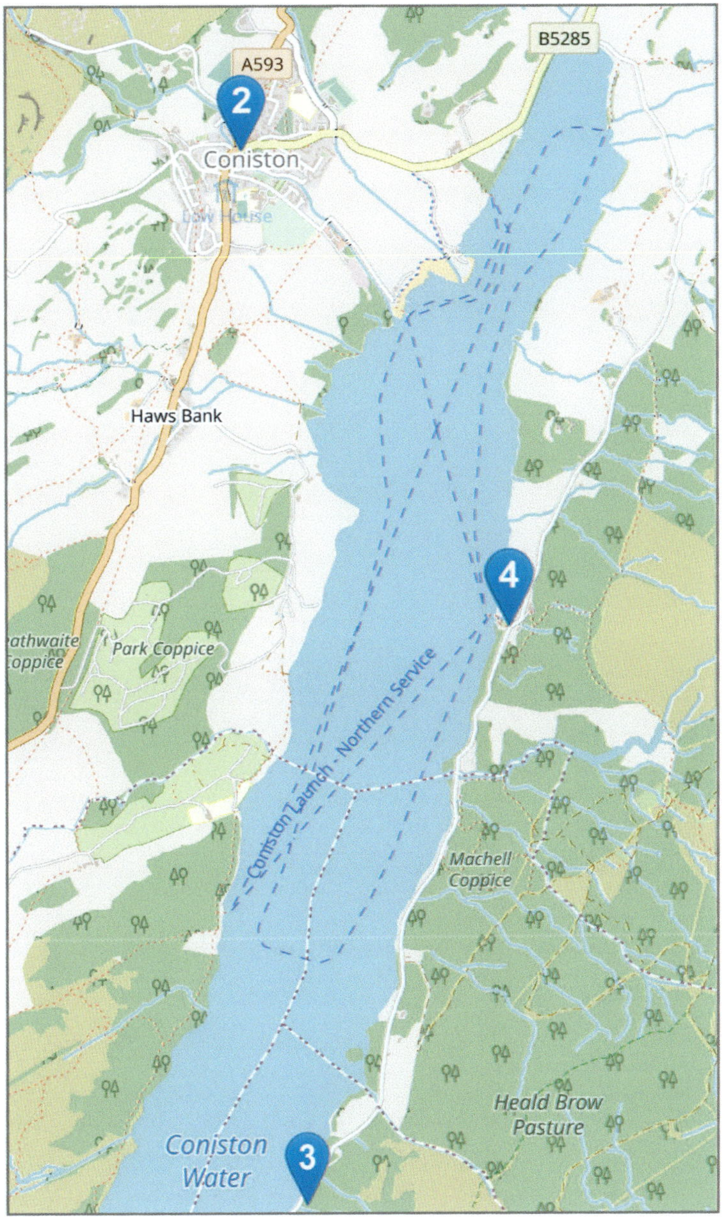

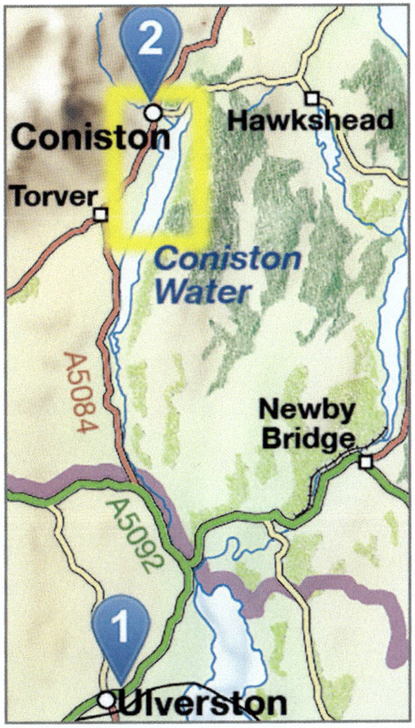

Map Locations

1. Ulverston
2. Coniston
3. East of Lake
4. Brantwood

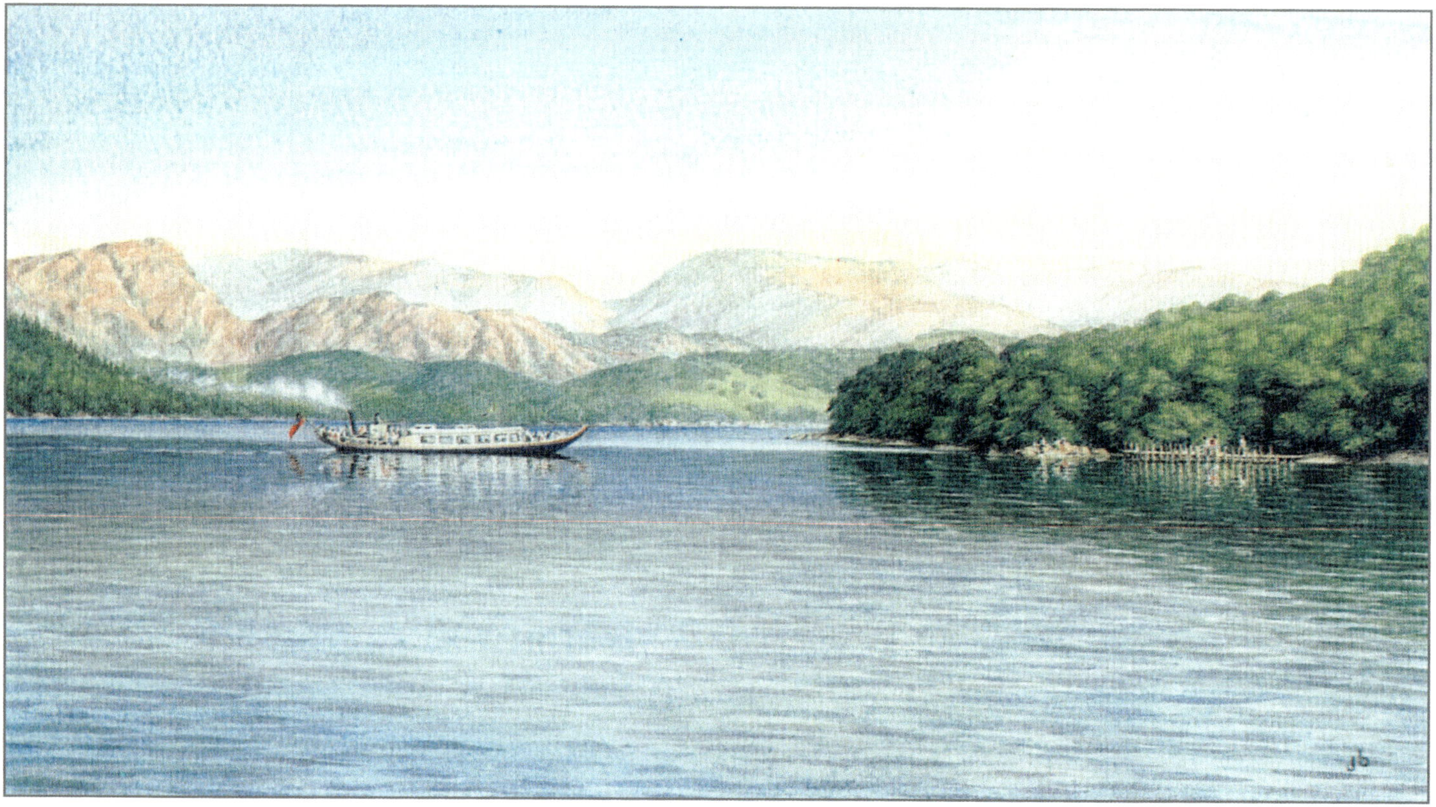

The Gondola heading towards Brantwood, Coniston Water

In 2008 Vic and Jennifer celebrated their 50th wedding anniversary with a group of close friends and an afternoon cruise on the Gondola. As a former naval engineer Vic appreciated the mechanics of the steam ship, and Jennifer was always enthralled by the different perspective the Gondola provides of the views north to the central Lakeland fells.

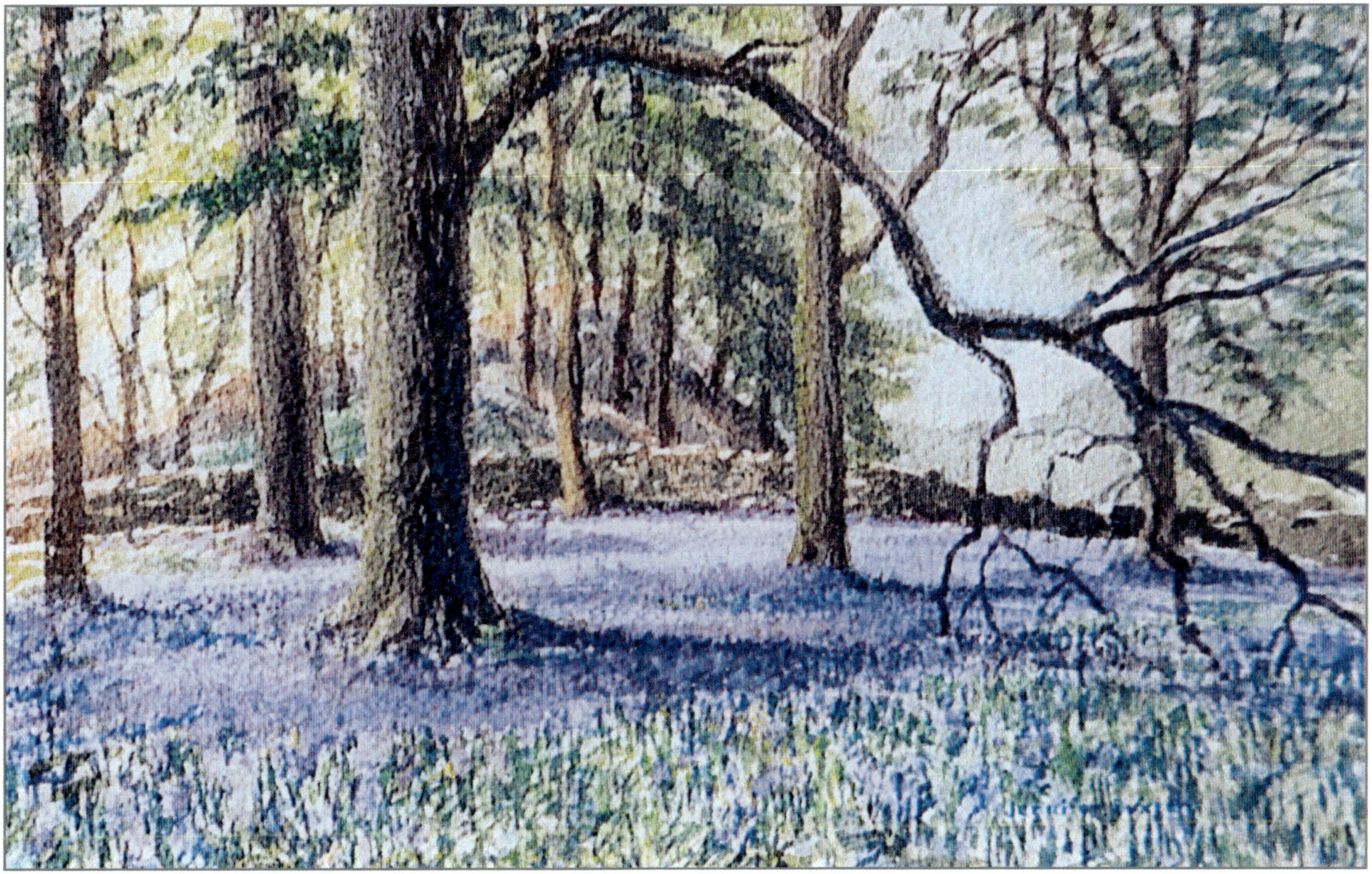

Anna's Wood is south of Brantwood on the east side of Coniston Water

Like Sea Wood near Bardsea, Anna's Wood is transformed by the bluebells in May. In the summer it was a favourite spot of ours for picnics by the lake. This is the only one of Jennifer's four bluebell paintings where we don't have access to the original, so this image was scanned from a greetings card which has affected the quality unfortunately.

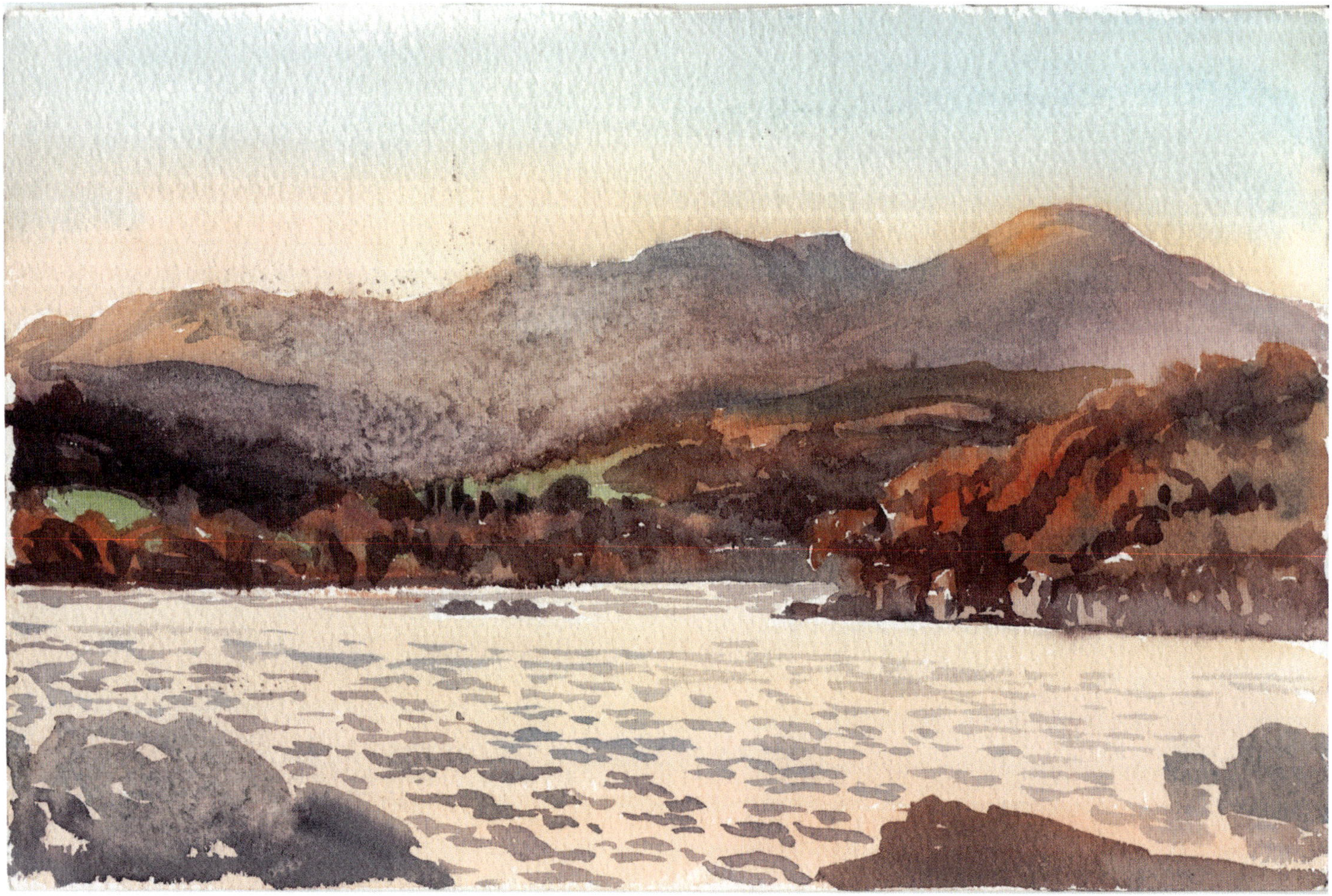

Dow Crag and Coniston Old Man, looking across Coniston Water with East of Lake on the right. It must have been a cold autumn day as the paint froze as Jennifer was painting Walna Scar!

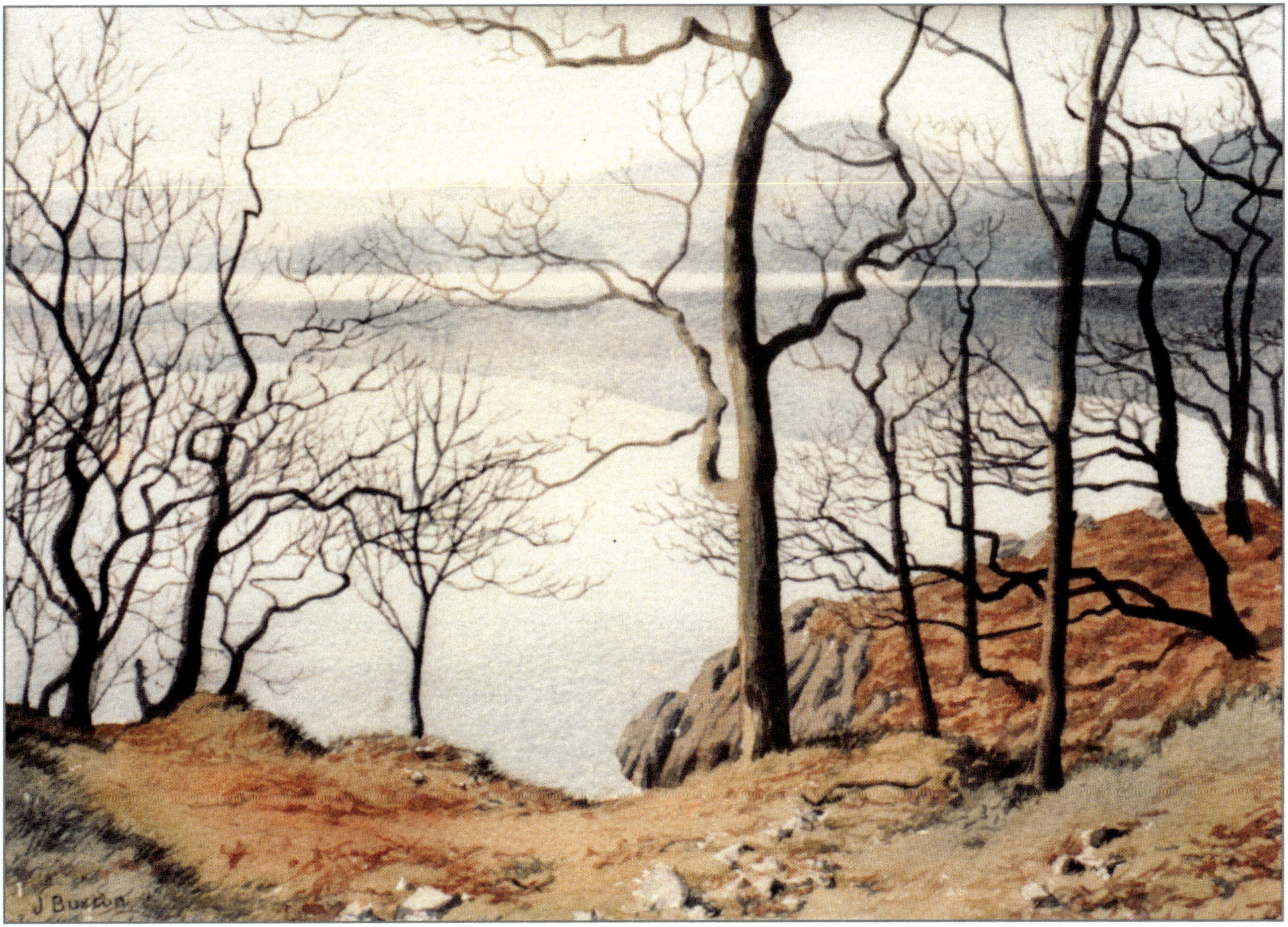

A crisp autumn day at East of Lake, Coniston Water. Anna's Wood crowds the shore but there is just room on the rocky beach to change for a dip, though on a warmer day than this one.

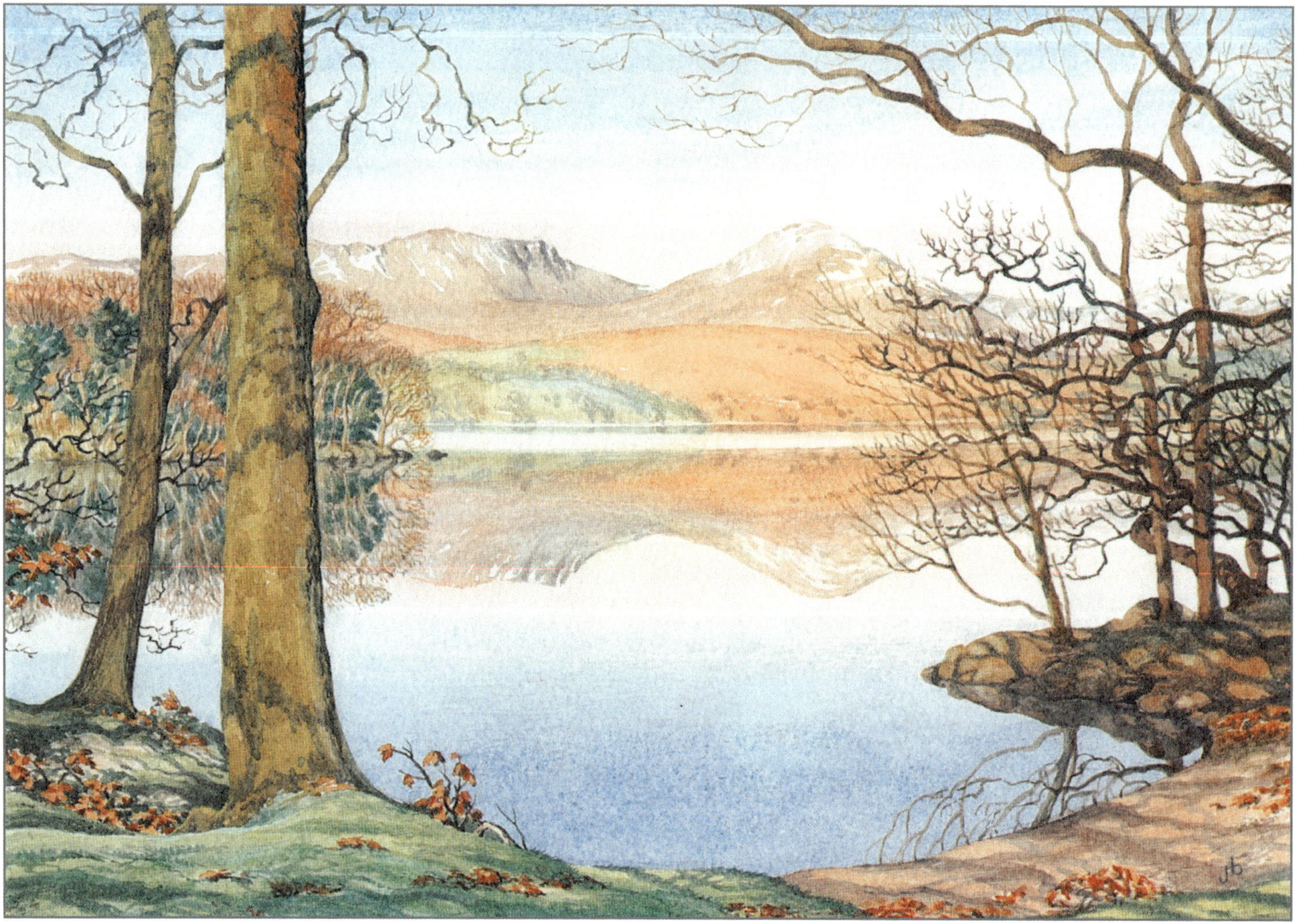

Coniston Old Man and Dow Crag from Anna's
Wood on the east side of Coniston Water

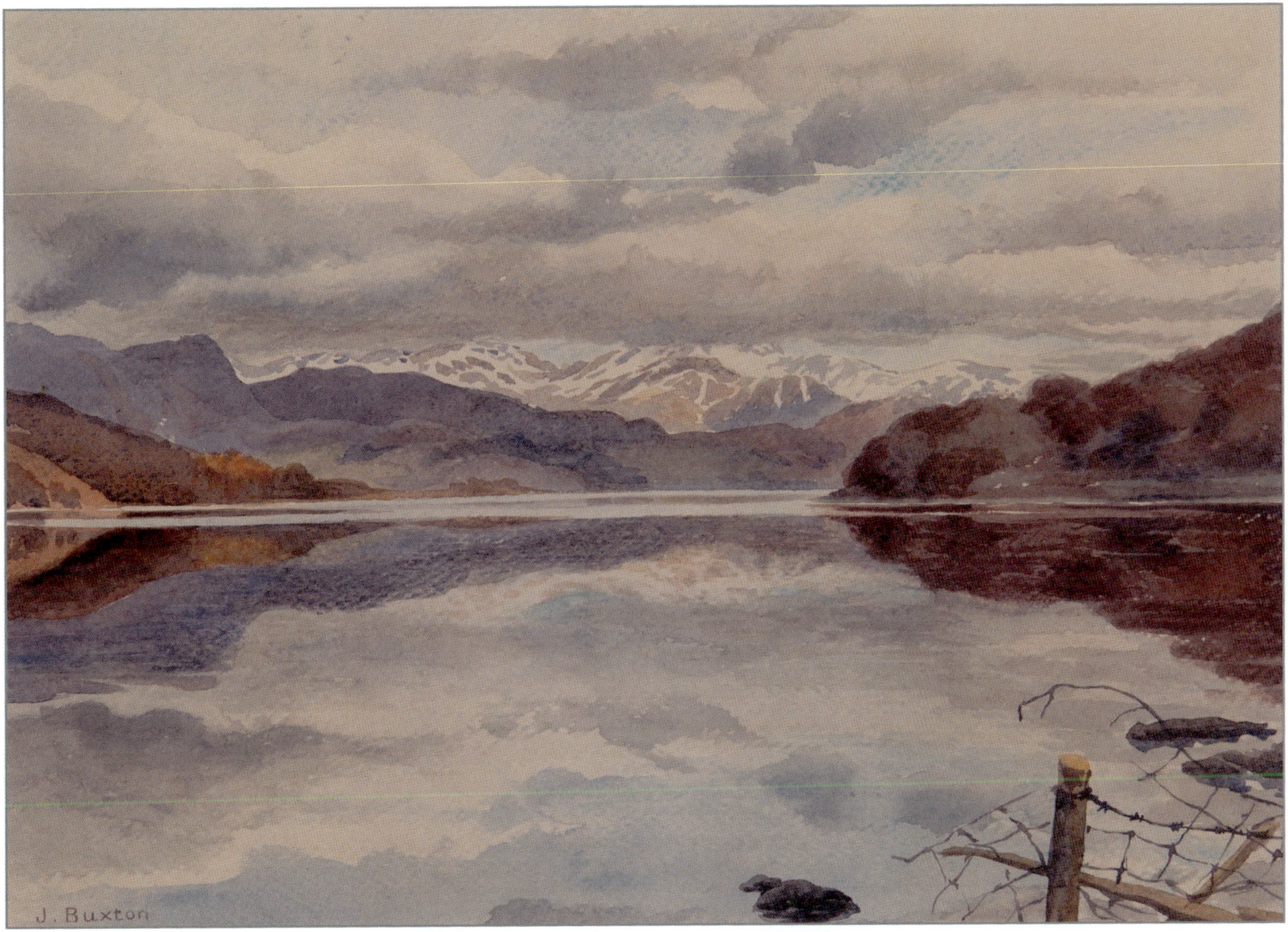

Looking north across Coniston Water to the central fells

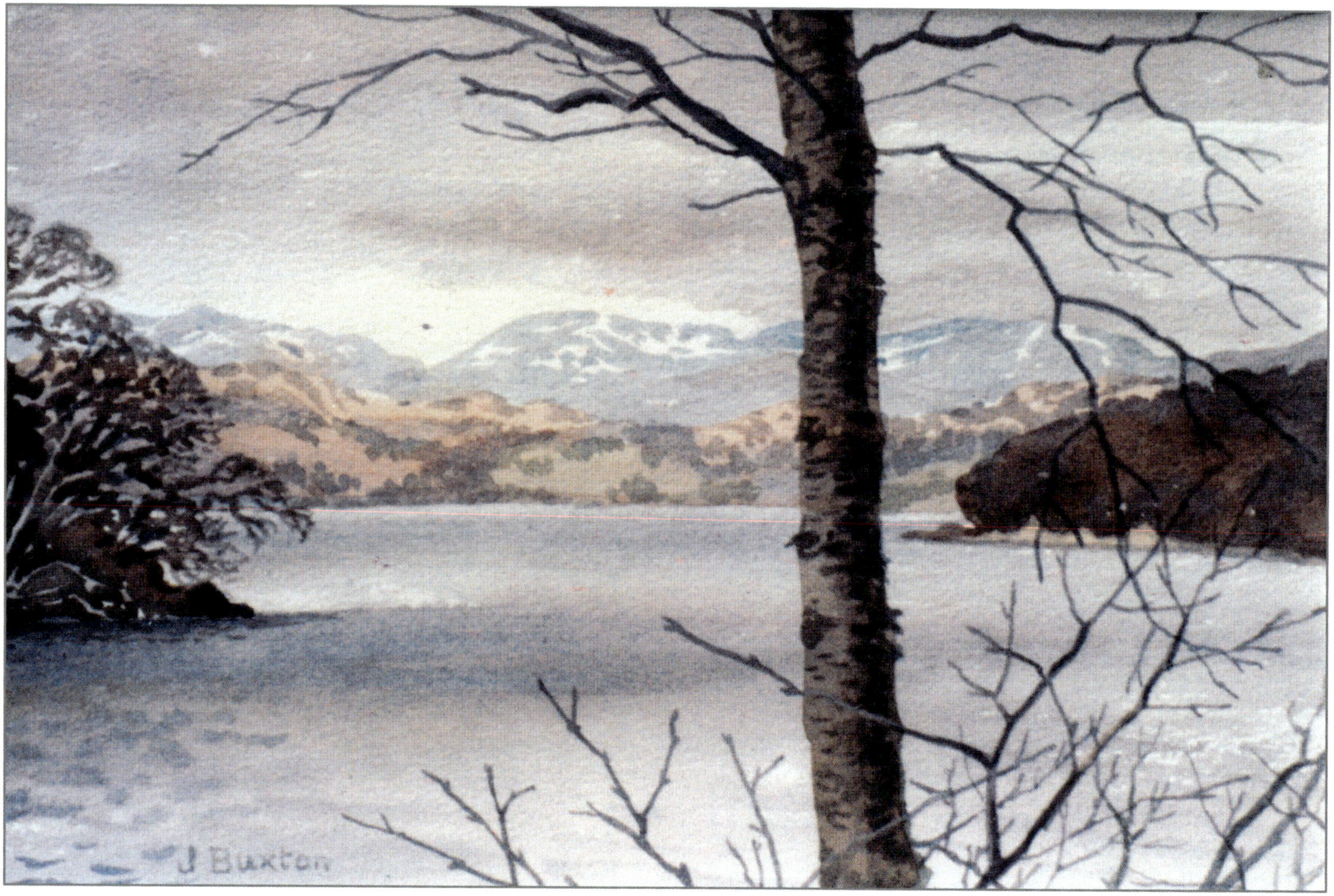

Fairfield from Coniston Water

Duddon Valley

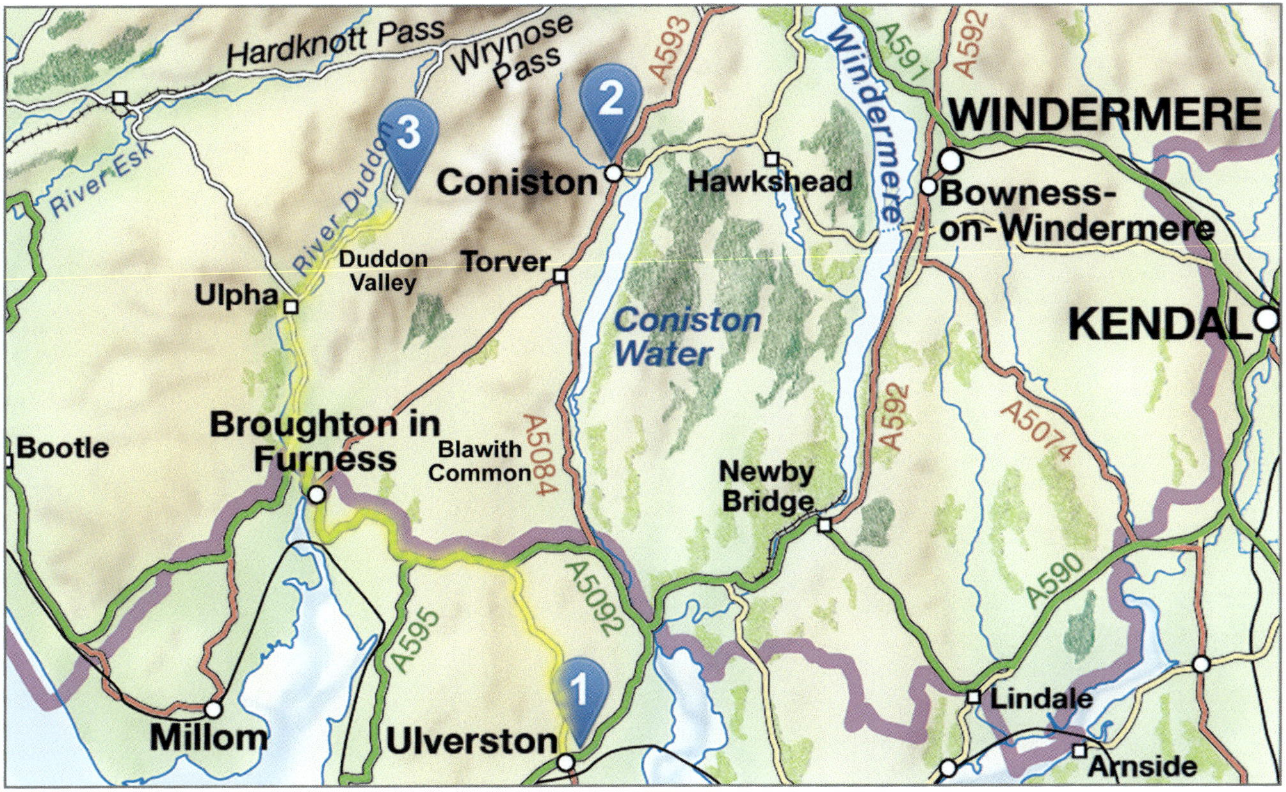

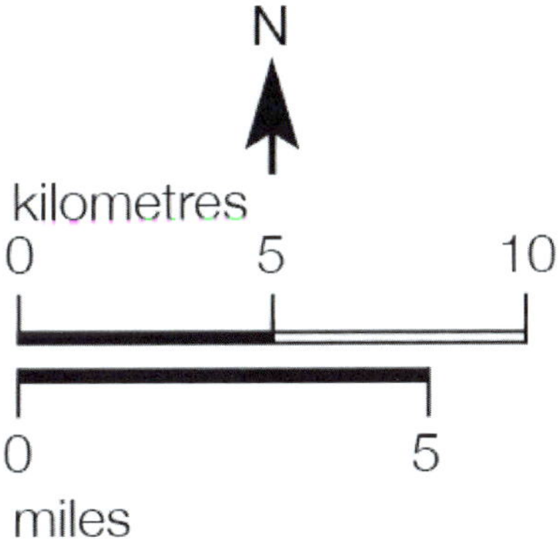

Map Locations

1. Ulverston
2. Coniston
3. Duddon Valley

To the north west of Ulverston lies the market town of Broughton-in-Furness, gateway to the beautiful Duddon Valley and the western fells. Broughton was a favourite stopping-off spot on our trips to Wastwater, with its climbing shop packed with every imaginable rucksack or pair of boots. Broughton has a wide assortment of interesting stores, including lots of options to buy sandwich-making supplies for lunch.

The Duddon Valley, and Caw

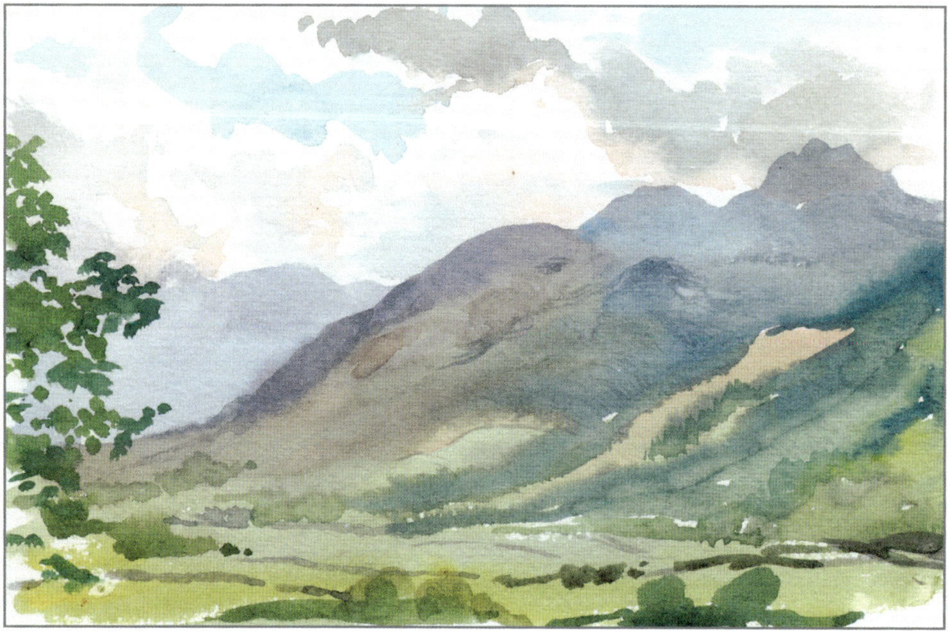

Duddon Valley

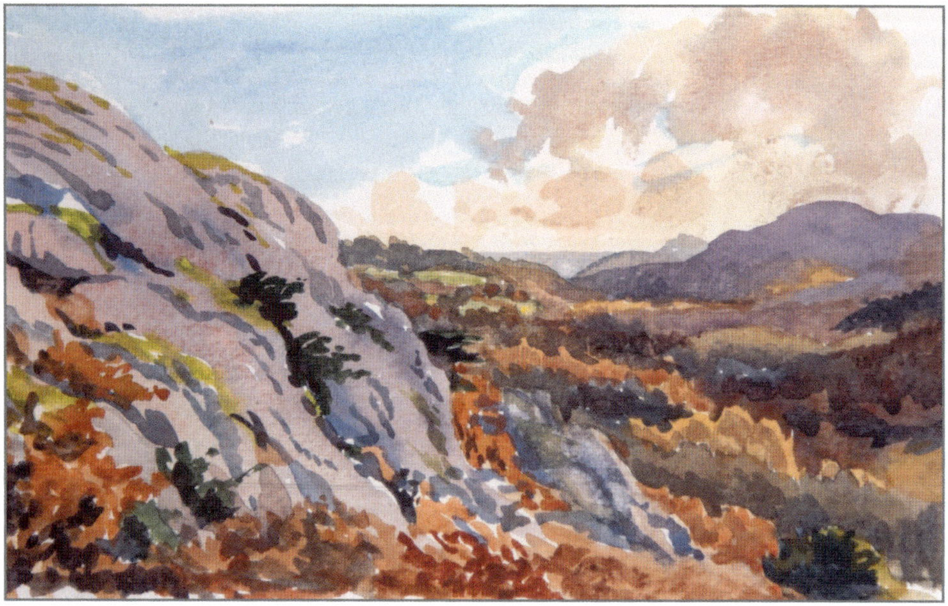

Jennifer painted the Duddon Valley in a variety of seasons though her preference was always for painting the autumn reds rather than the summer greens.

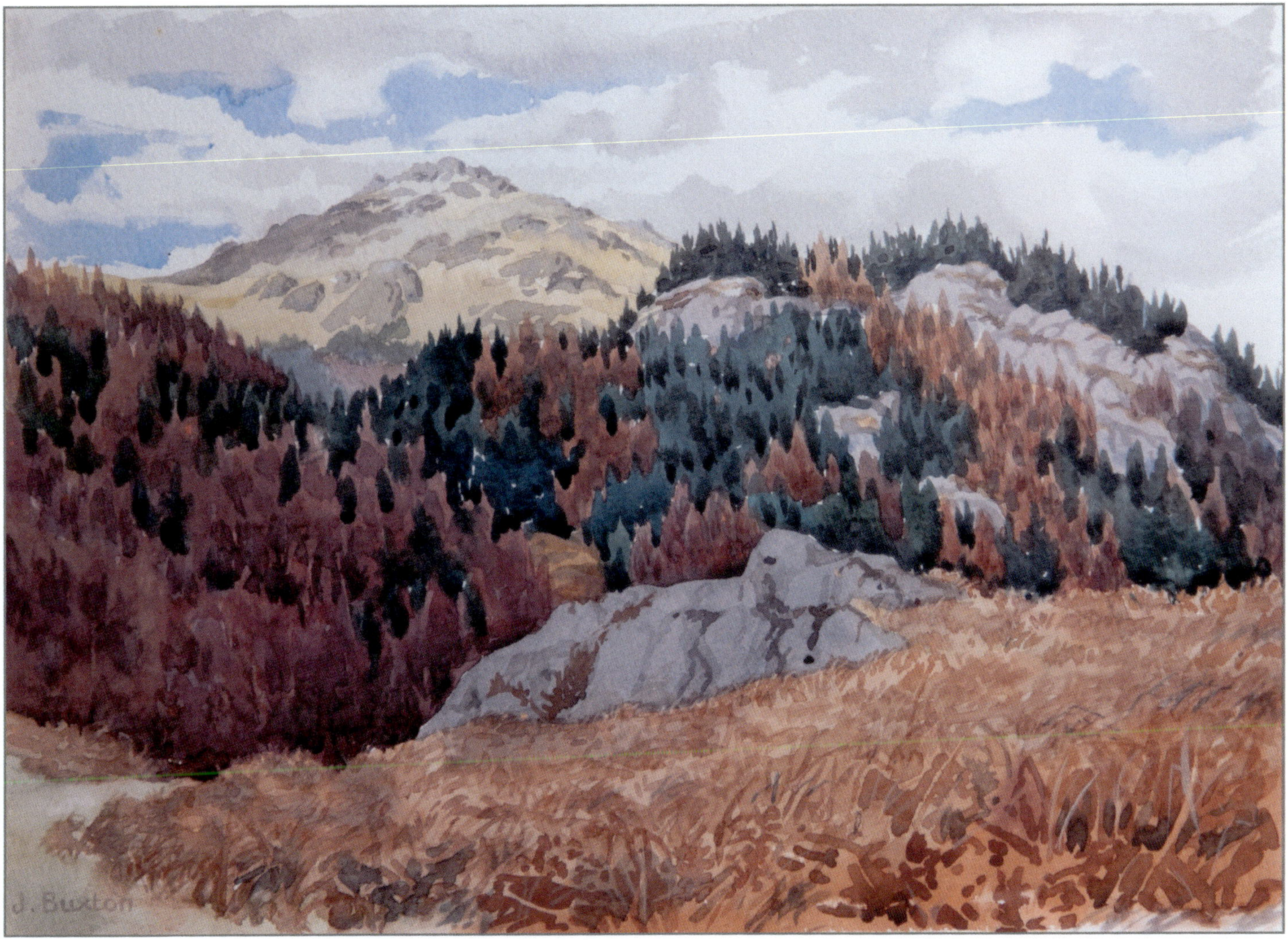

Towards Seathwaite and Caw, Duddon Valley

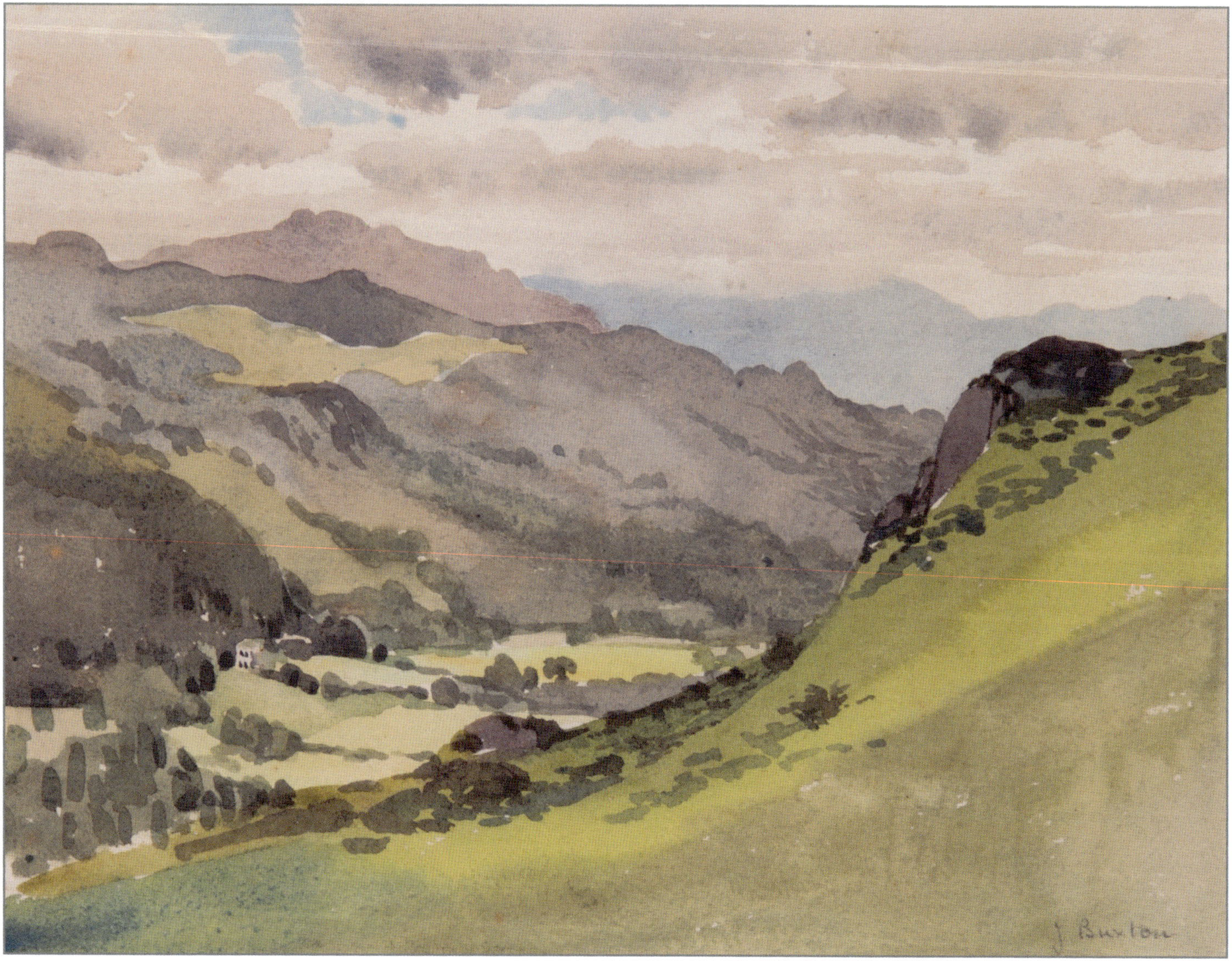

The Duddon Valley, with Green Crag behind

Central Lakes

The road from Coniston passes by the picturesque Tarn Hows on its way to Windermere, one of the best known towns in the Lake District.

The roads around Windermere can be congested with traffic in the summer but Jennifer and I would visit sometimes for the climbing shops in Ambleside and to enjoy lunch or a cream cake at one of the many delightful coffees shops that proliferate in the area.

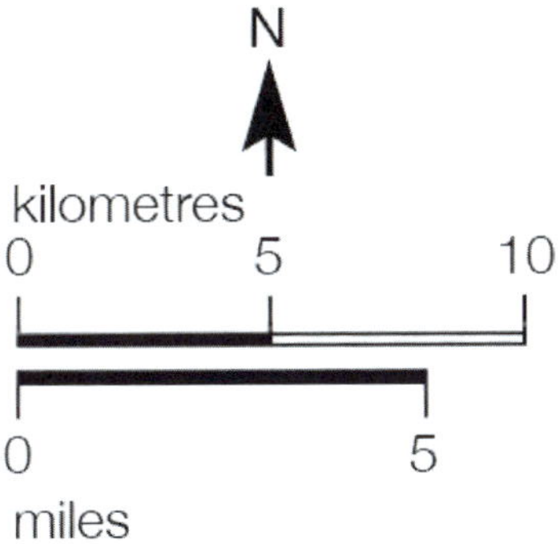

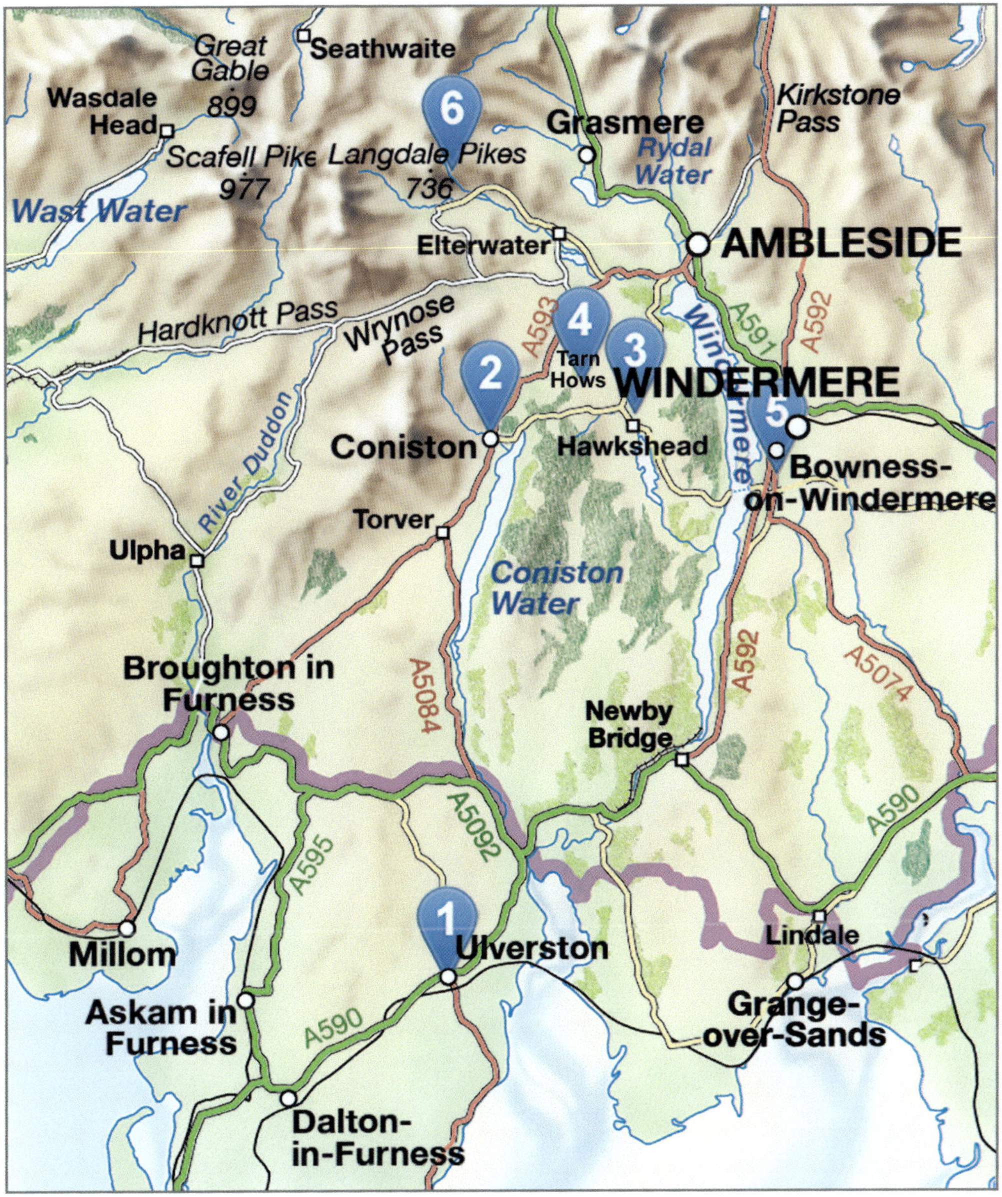

Map Locations

1. Ulverston
2. Coniston
3. Hawkshead
4. Tarn Hows
5. Windermere
6. Langdale Valley

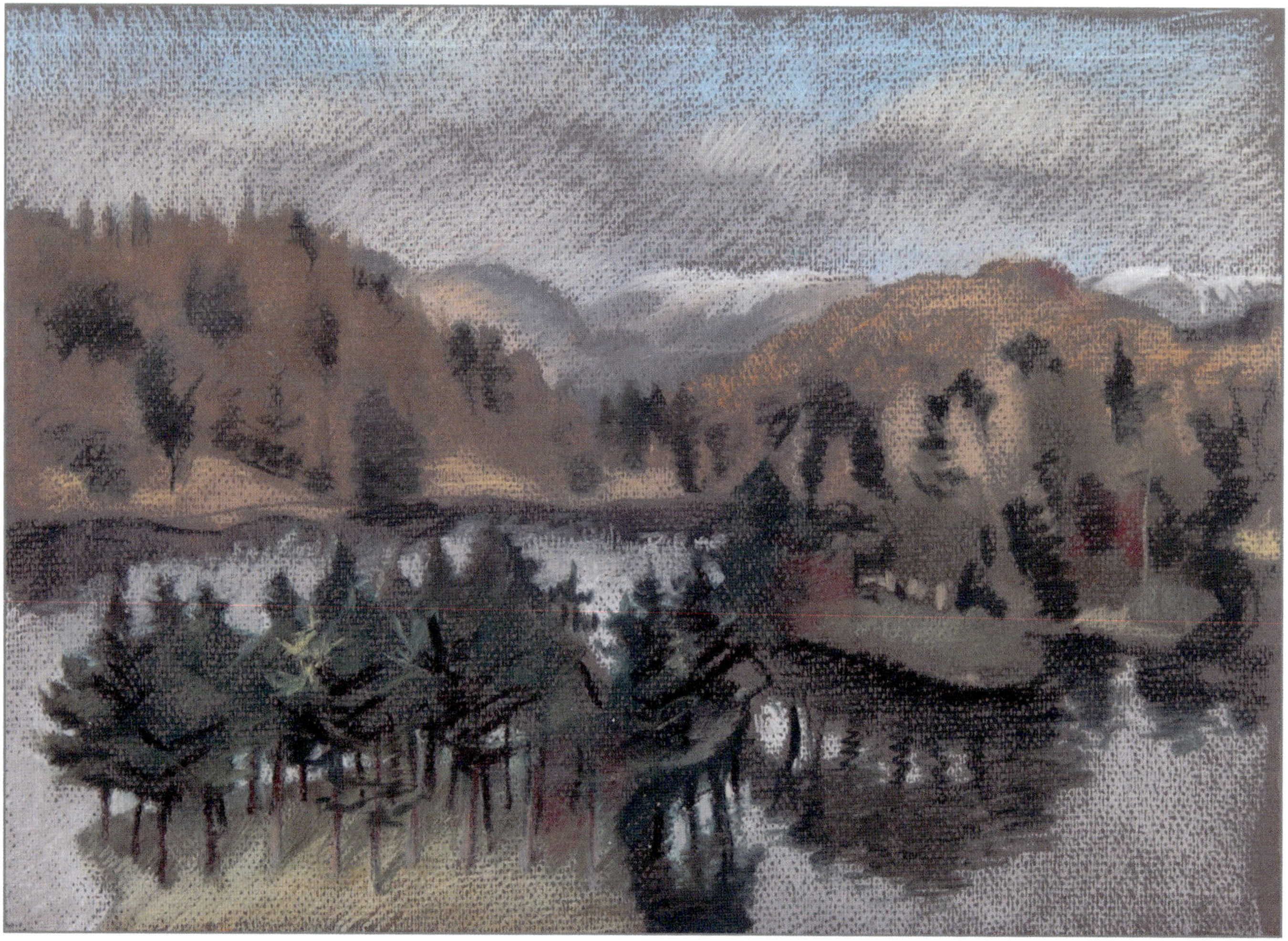

Tarn Hows

Tarn Hows is a popular beauty spot run by the National Trust. It is one of the few Lakeland walks that is paved so you don't need a pair of hiking boots or wellingtons to enjoy it when it's wet out, which it often is.

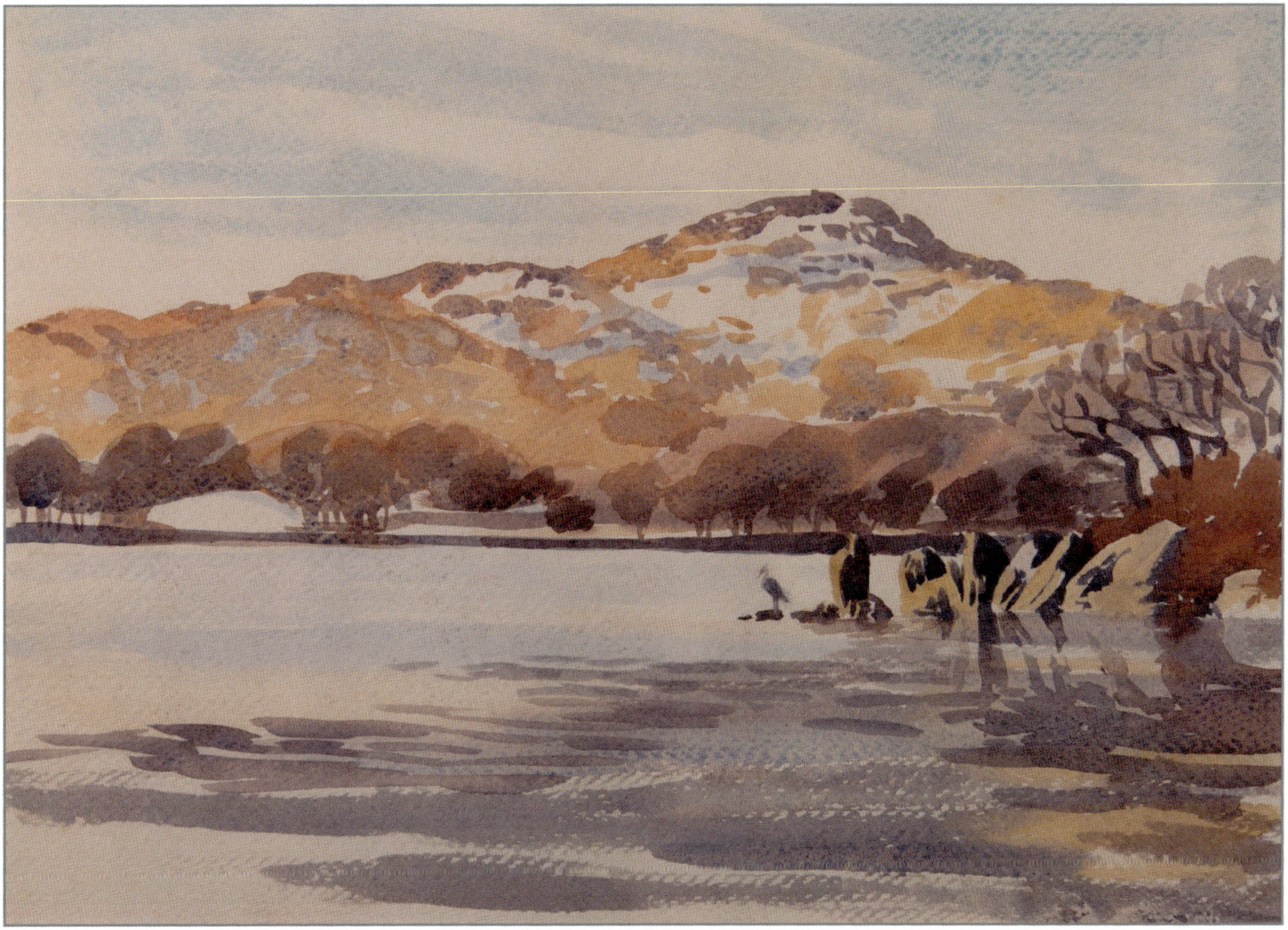

Gummers How, from Lakeside

We stayed in a rental flat at Lakeside for a number of Whitsun holiday breaks when Henry and I were young. There's a wonderful walk up to High Dam and Low Dam above the road along the west side of the lake. The path took us across a wide open field that we used to call Mad Dog Meadow for the effect it had on our two dogs.

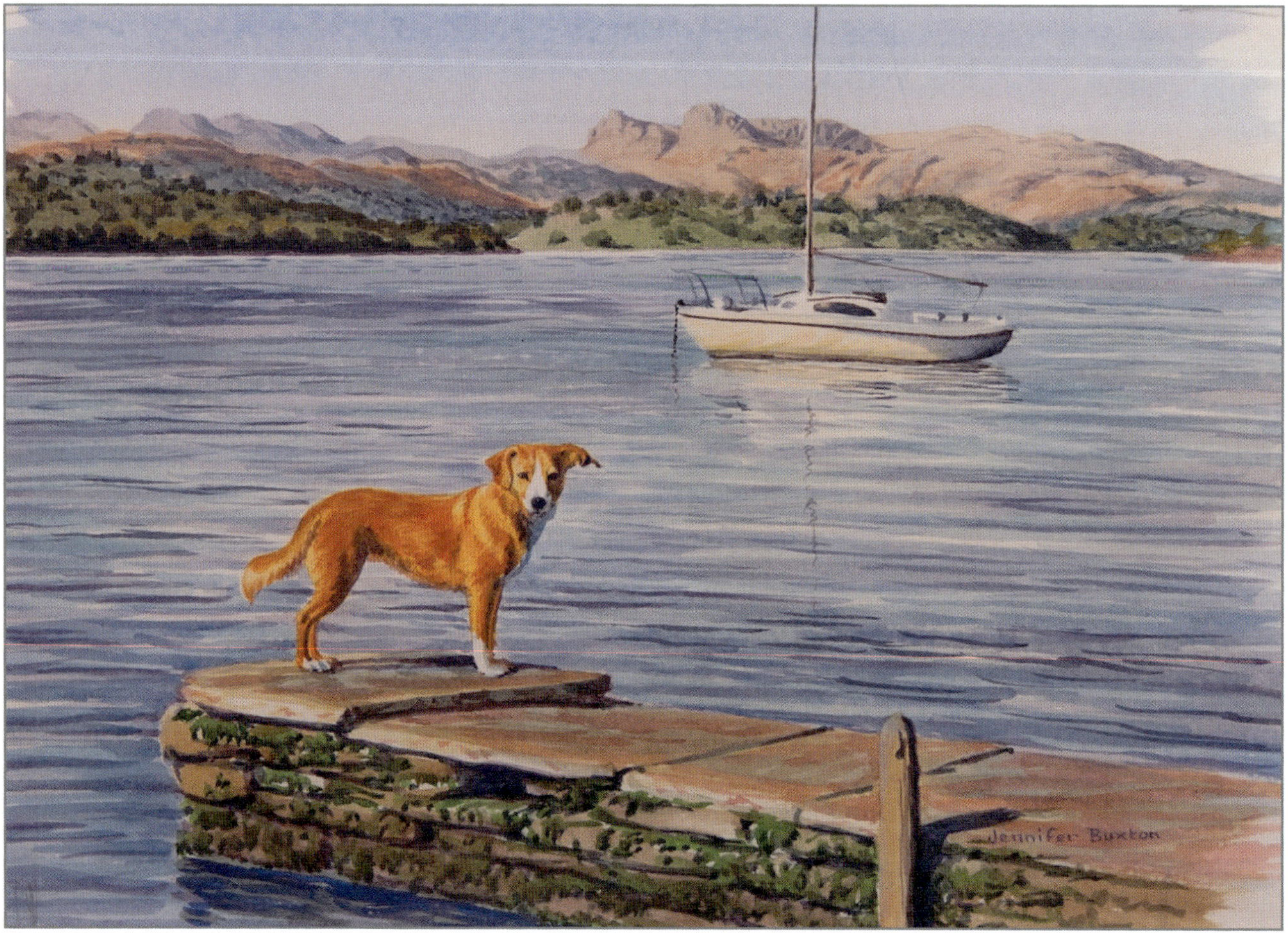

Lake Windermere richly deserves its reputation as a national beauty spot. Access however can be tough, bordered as it is in many places by large houses and private estates. The traffic too can be a test of your patience, and like many locals Vic had little time for caravans and buses. In truth though, the Lakeland roads take some getting used to. Bi-directional roads can feel like there's not enough room even for a single car, and the locals think nothing of passing you whenever they have a chance!

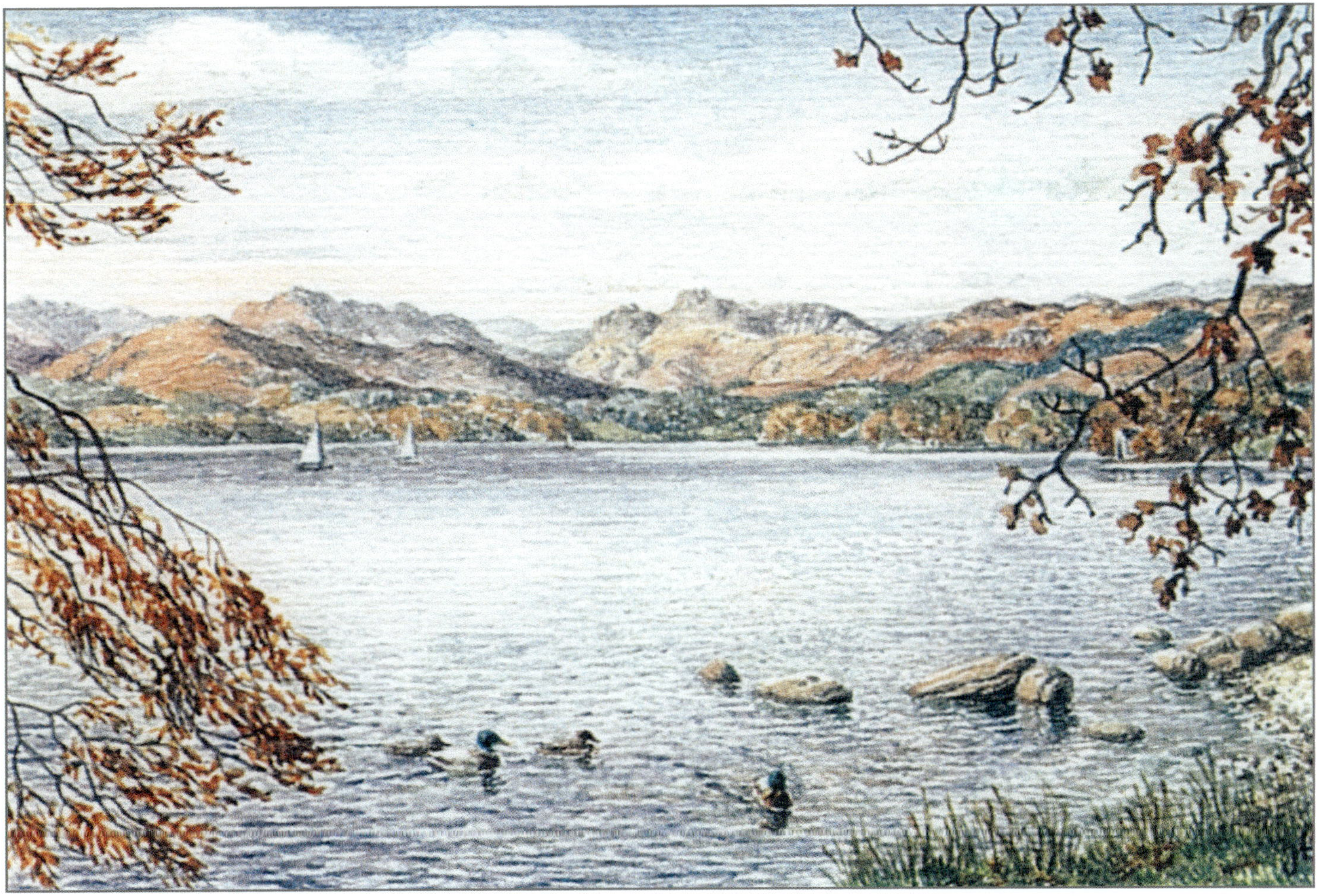

Summer on Lake Windermere, with the Langdale Pikes behind

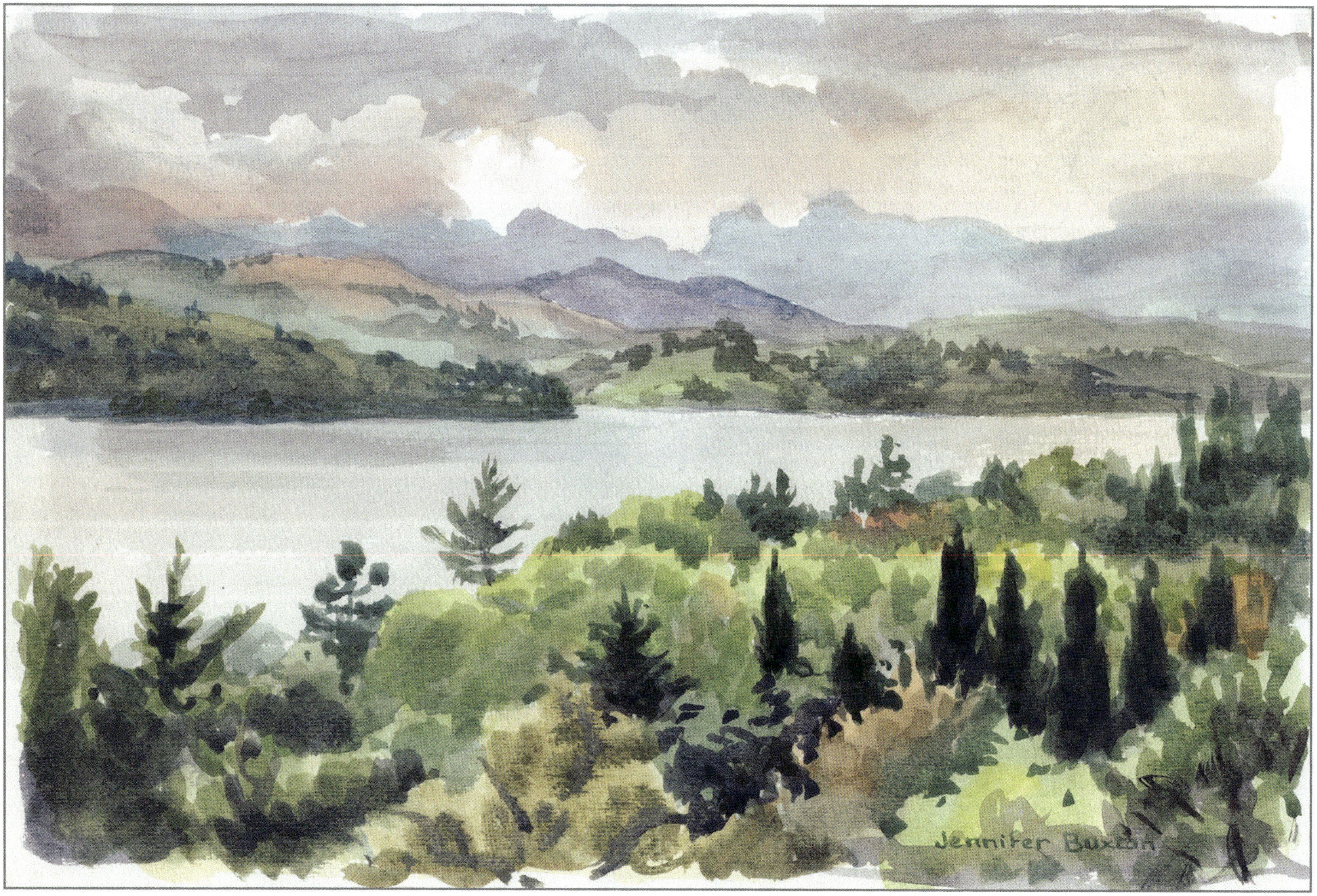

Looking across Lake Windermere to the Langdale Pikes

The Langdale Valley

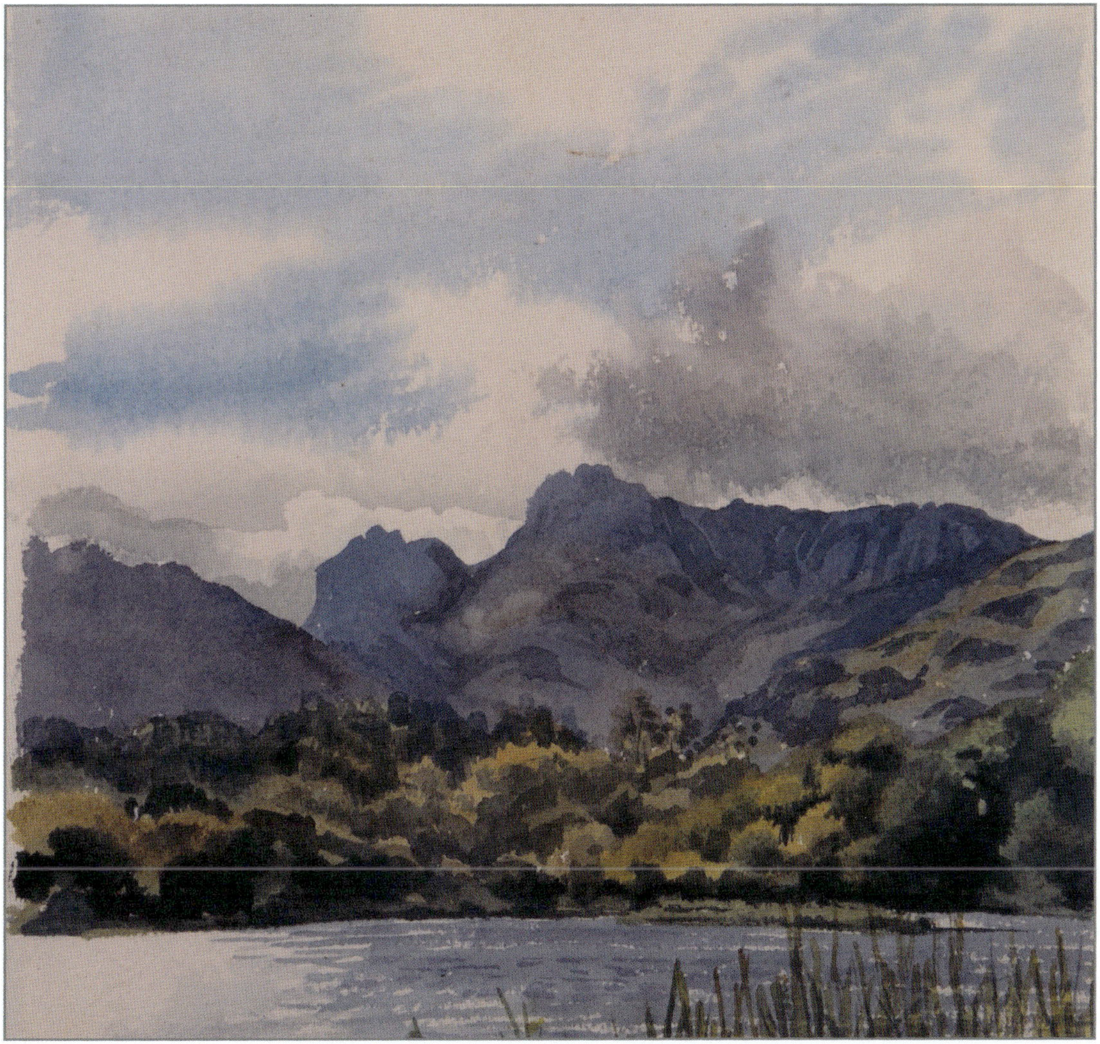

Harrison Stickle from Elterwater

The Langdale Pikes, Bow Fell and Crinkle Crags are some of the iconic fells of the central Lake District. Jennifer painted them often as Vic and Henry loved to walk in the area.

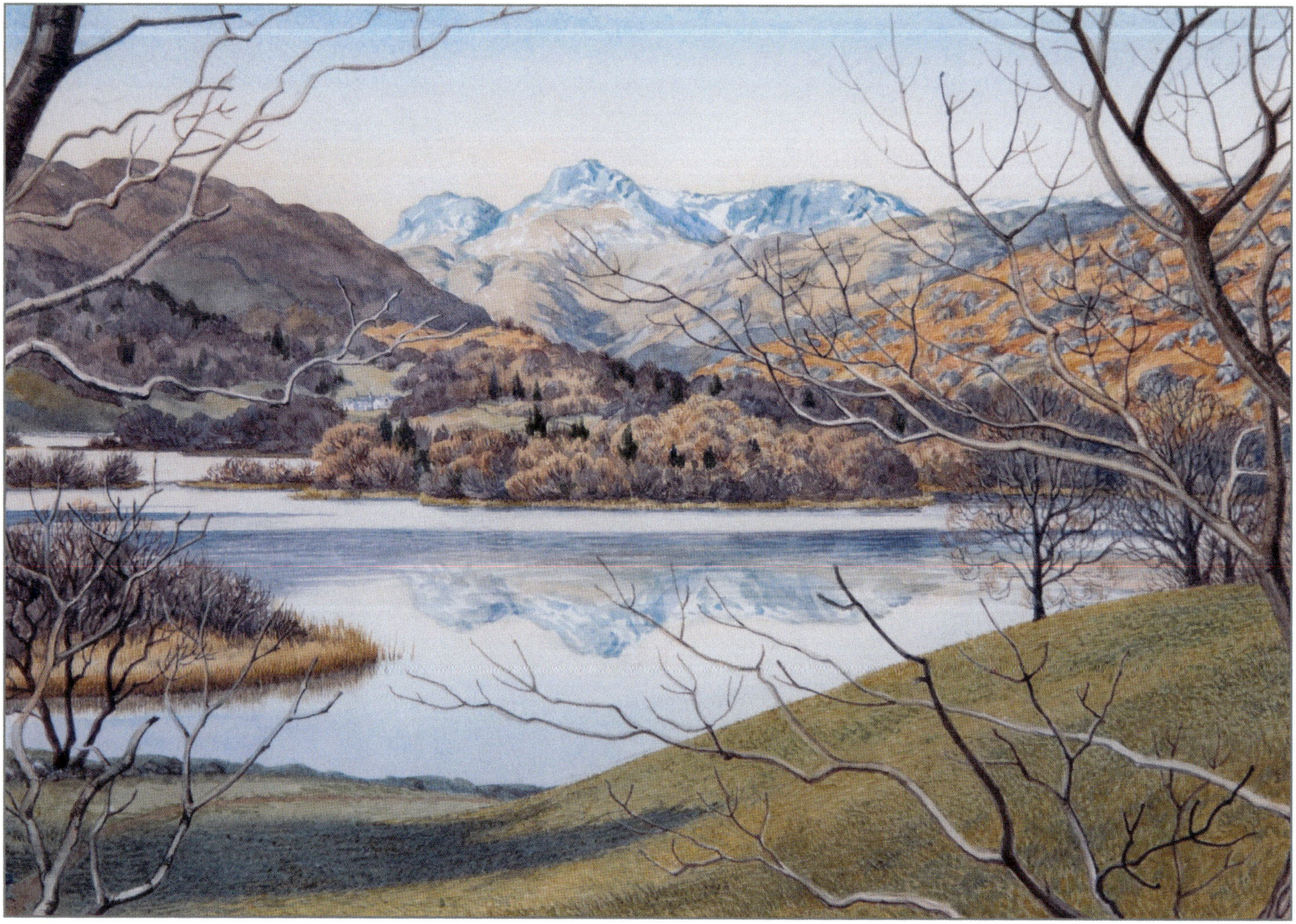

Many of Jennifer's paintings of the area feature Elterwater as it provides a beautiful foreground to the Langdale Pikes. She and I would walk around the lake so that she could paint and I, with undying optimism that was seldom rewarded, would attempt to catch a fish.

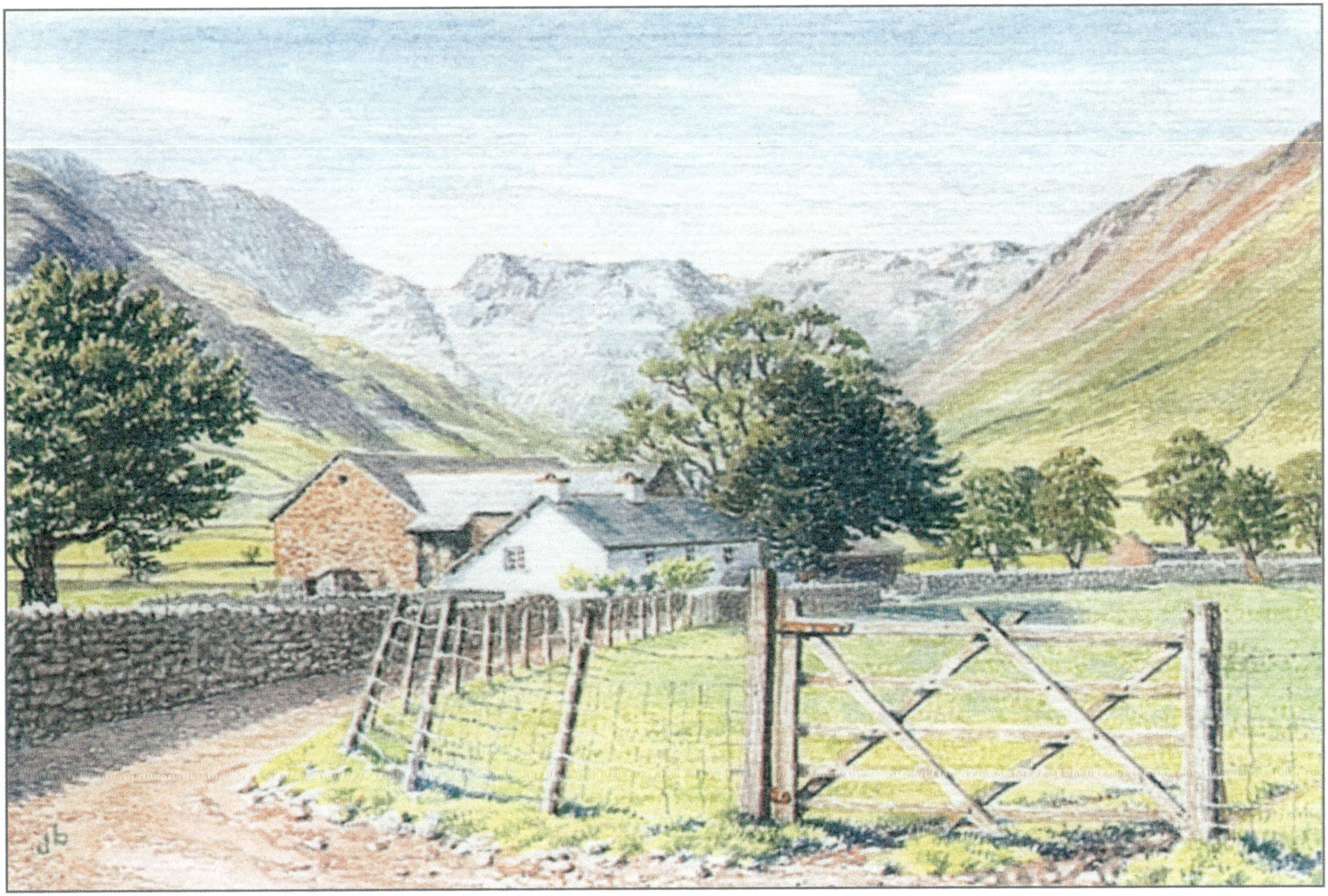

Summer in the Langdale Valley

The Langdale Valley is one of the most beautiful valleys in the Lake District.

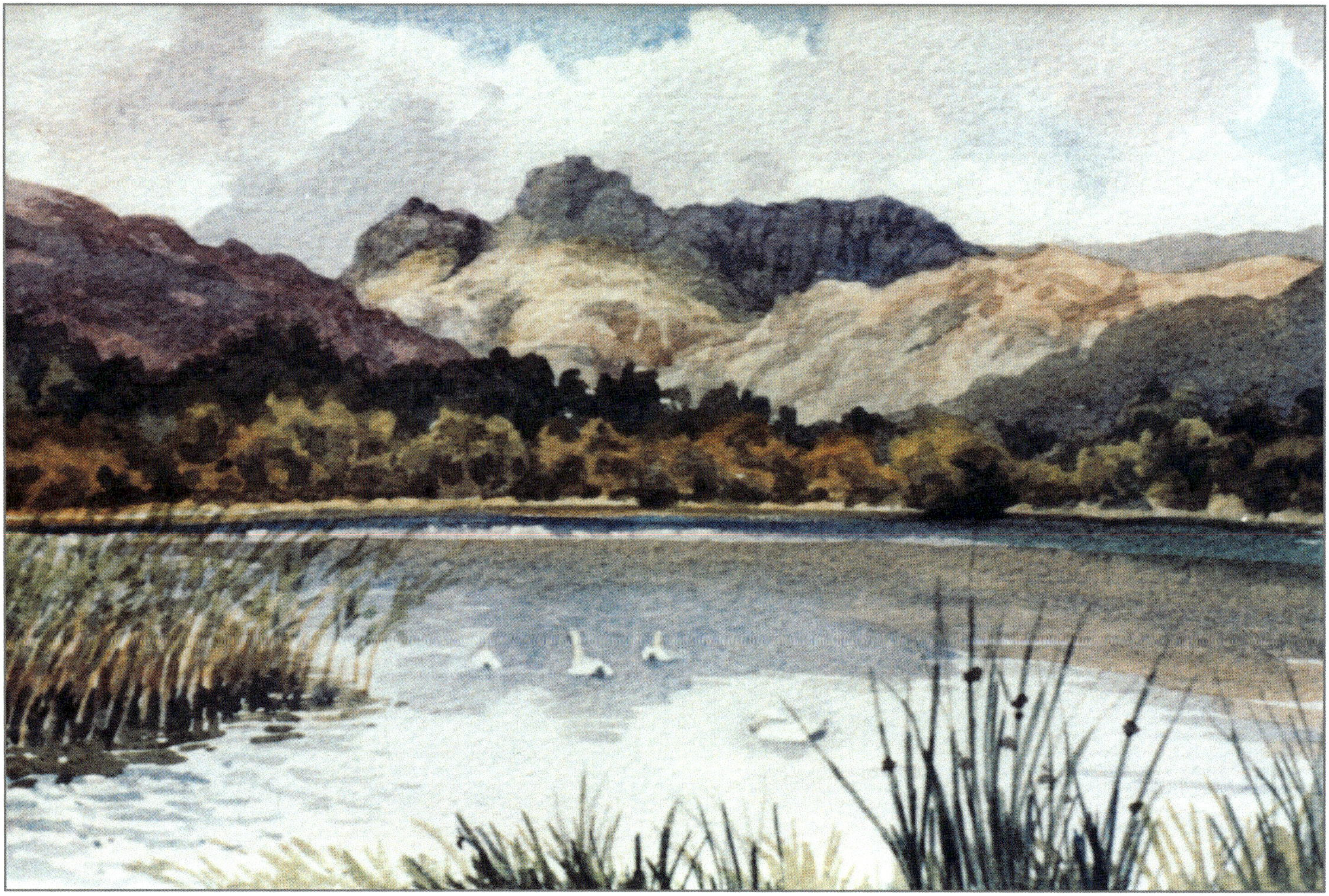

The Langdale Pikes from Elterwater

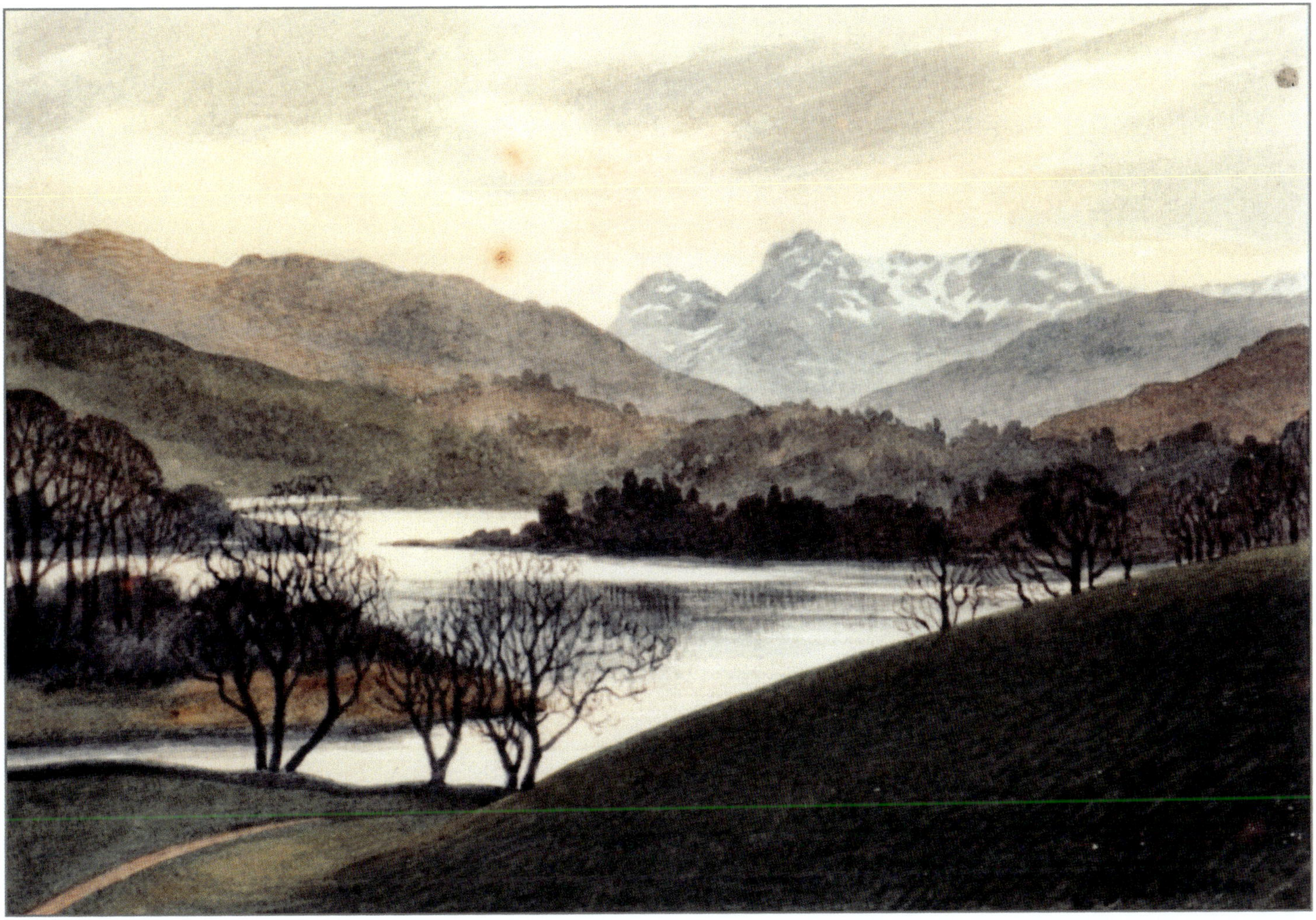

Harrison Stickle is the most recognizable of the Langdale Pikes, but although it looks to be much higher, that's misleading because Pike of Stickle to the left and Pavey Ark to the right are almost as tall. This image is from a photograph and is unfortunately a little worse for wear as we no longer have access to the original.

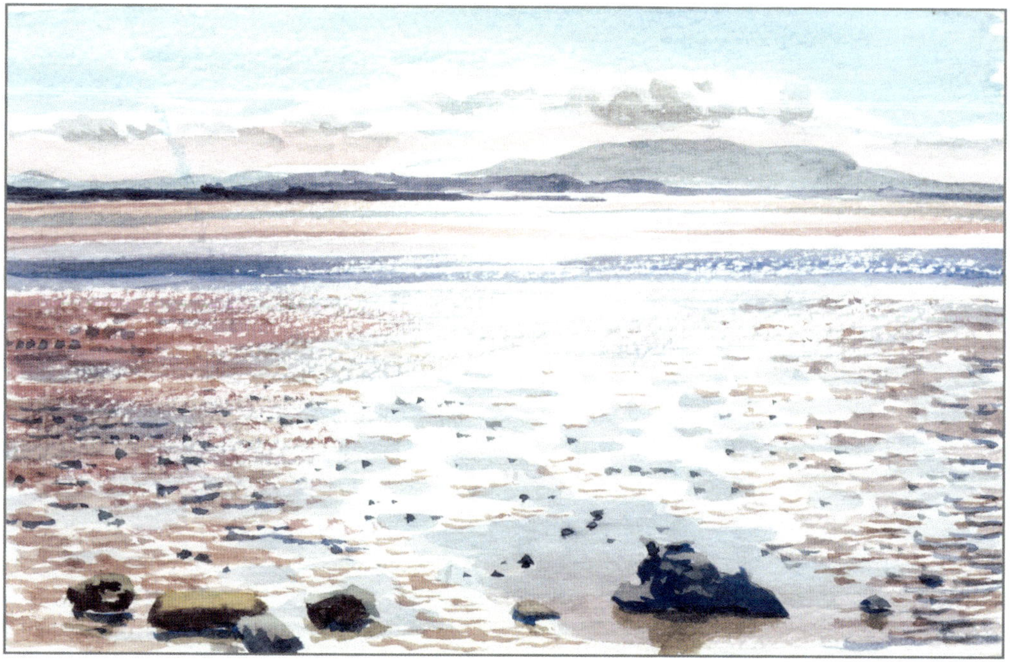

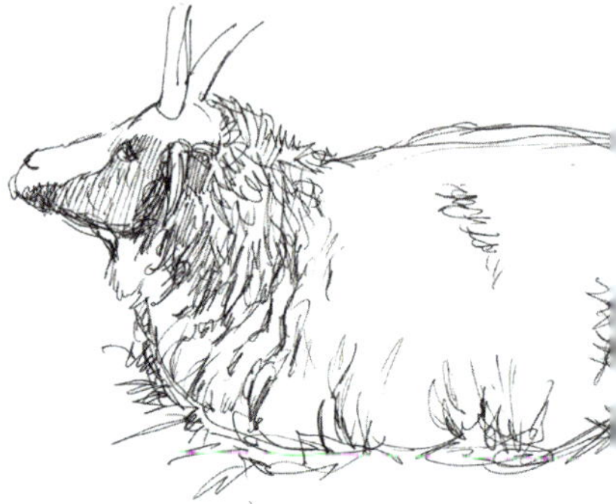

The Shoreline on the way to Broughton-in-Furness, with Black Combe in the background

The road along the coast near Ravenglass passes Muncaster Castle, which is a beautiful spot to break the journey. It is supposedly the most haunted building in the UK, though there's probably a better chance of seeing an owl or a hawk at the Bird Centre they have on site.

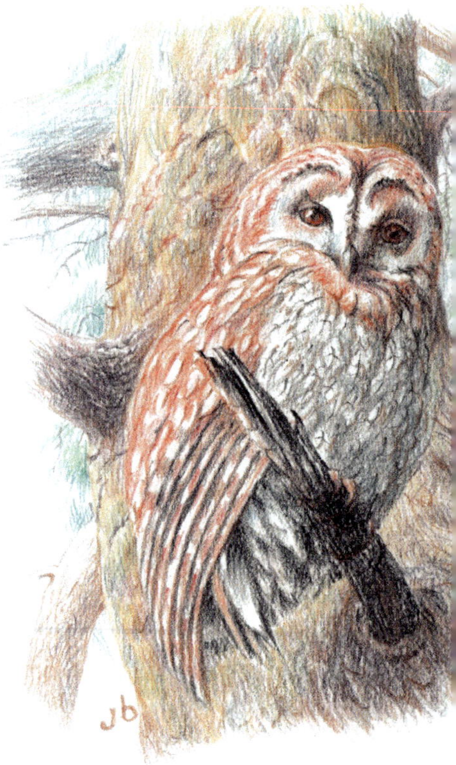

Day Trips to the Western and Northern Lakes

In her later years Jennifer spent much more of her time in the southern lakes and hence most of her paintings and sketches from the further reaches of the park are in private collections and no longer accessible. In this section I chose to present some of the paintings we do still have access to as day trips from her home in the south, in order to illustrate the beauty of the northern and western lakes.

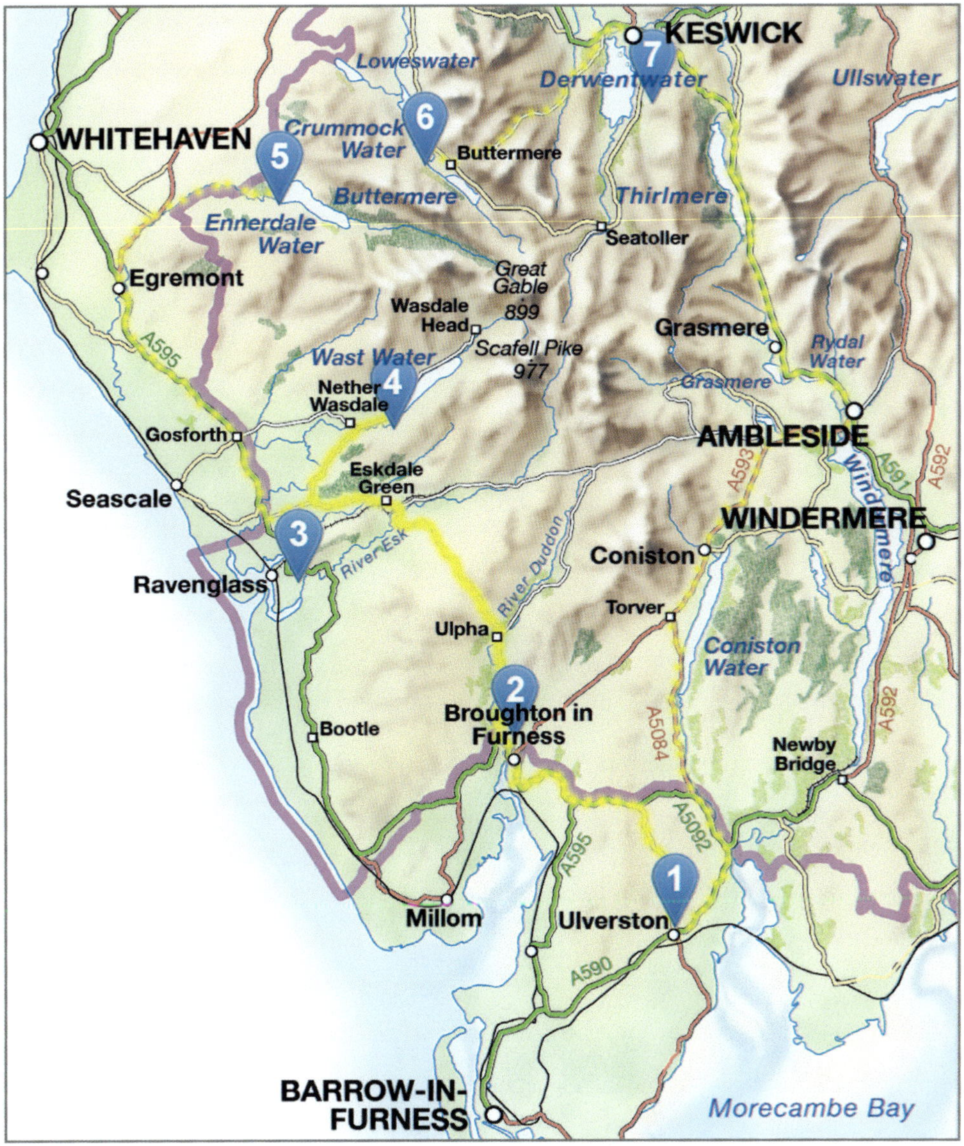

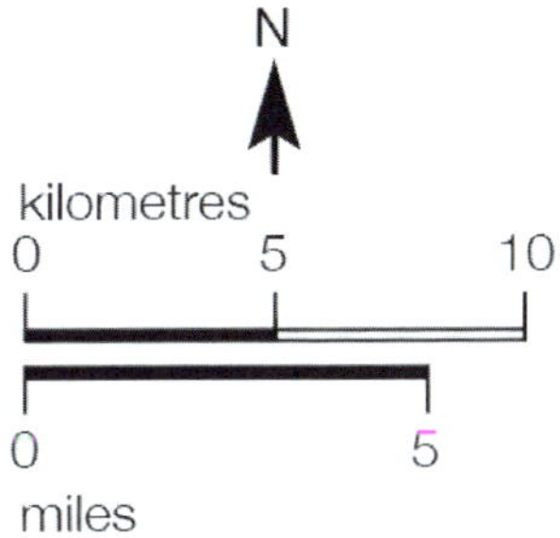

Map Locations

1. Ulverston
2. Broughton
3. Muncaster Castle
4. Wastwater
5. Ennerdale Water
6. Crummock Water
7. Derwentwater

Wastwater

The road north from Broughton-in-Furness to Wasdale Head passes across some rather desolate moorland around Ulpha

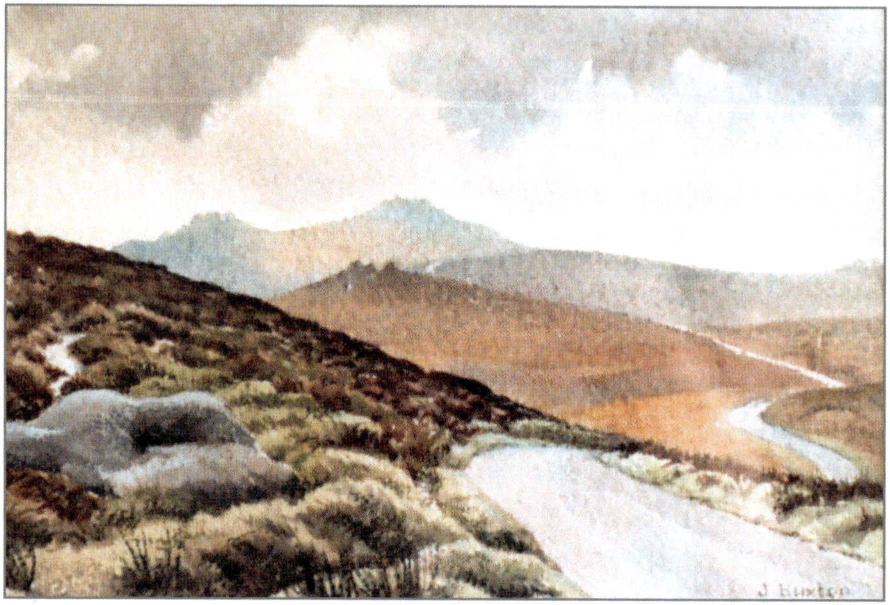

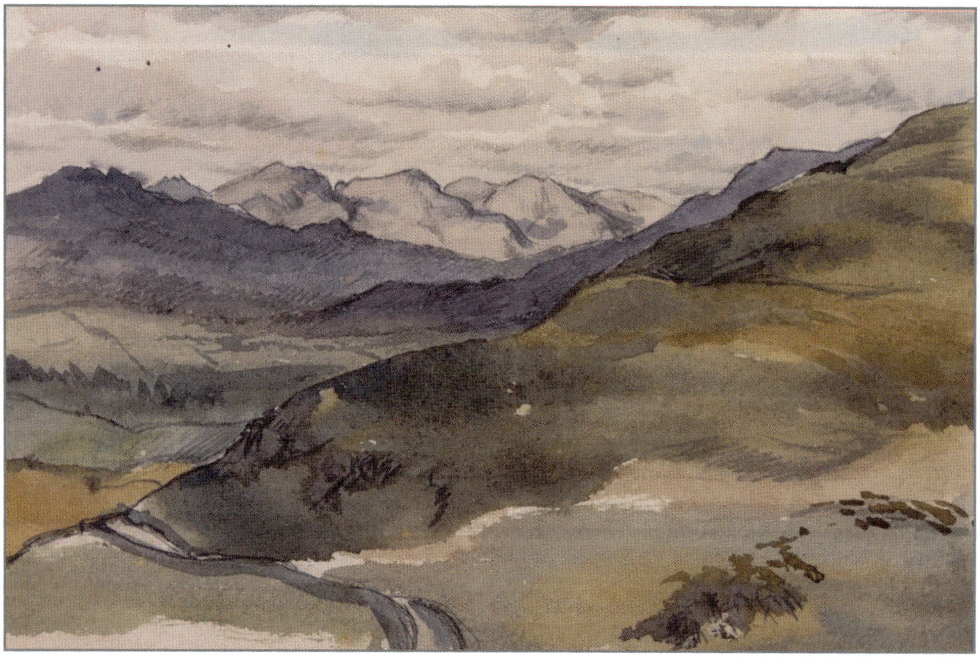

Scafell and Scafell Pike, England's tallest mountains

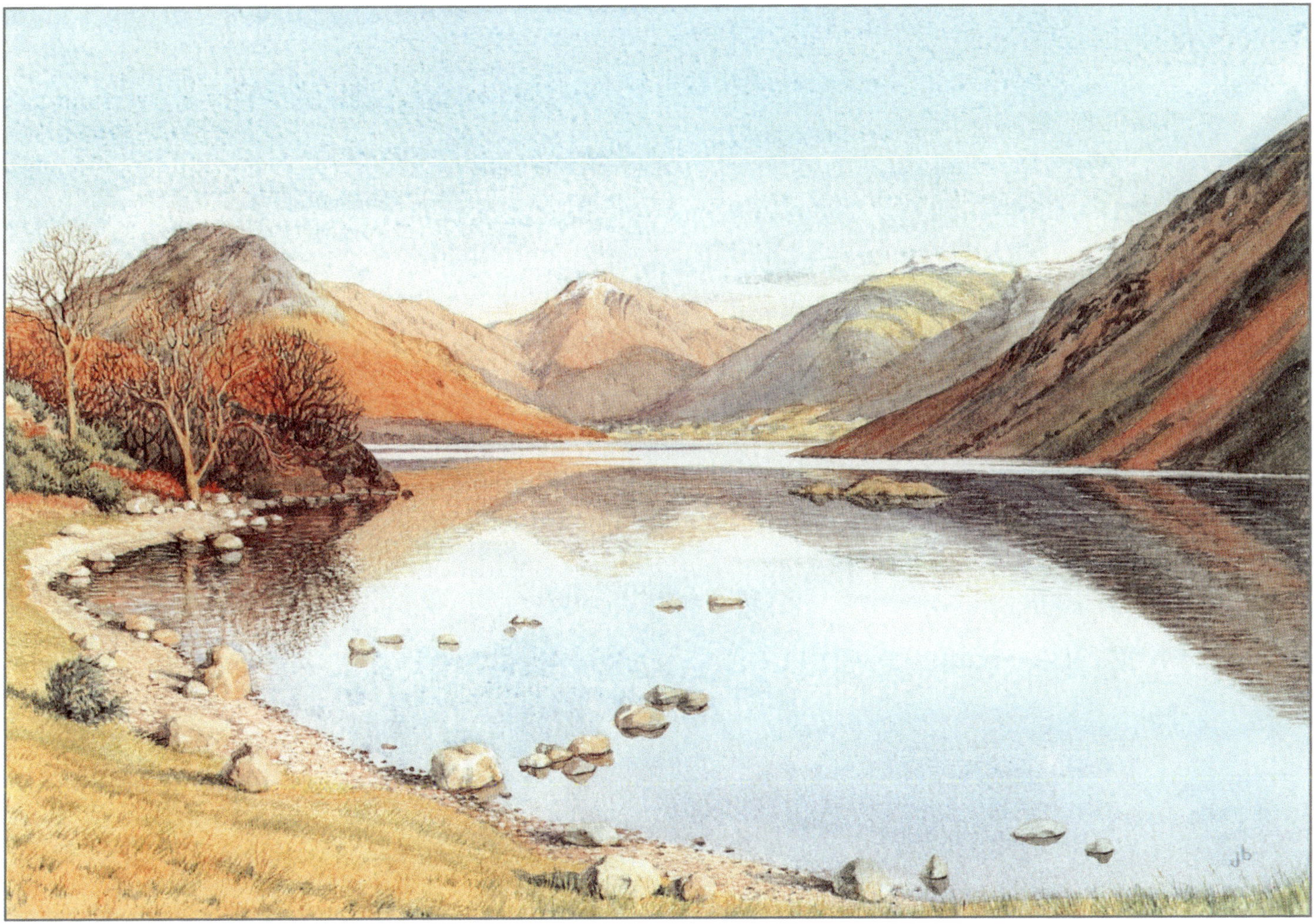

Wastwater, looking north east towards Great Gable. Wastwater is the deepest of the lakes; its mood changes with the weather and the shadows from the high screes to the south.

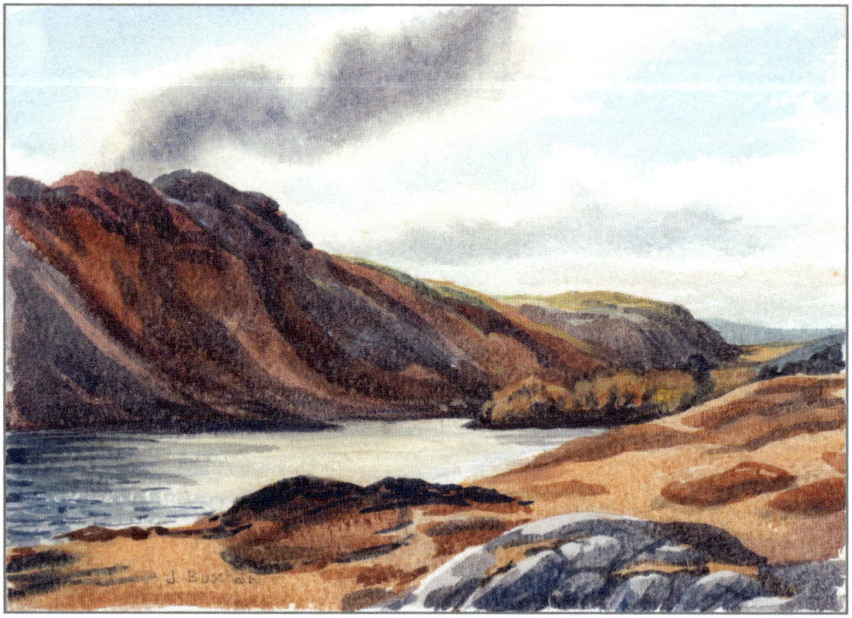

Wastwater -
looking south

Wasdale Head at the northern end of the lake is the access point to some of the Lake District's most impressive fells. Henry and Vic would come here to climb Great Gable, ScaFell and ScaFell Pike, as usual with Jennifer and I opting to stay in the valley by the lake shore.

Wastwater -
looking west

The wind can howl down the length of Wastwater. On one occasion the rubber dingy that Henry and I were paddling in got overturned by the strength of the wind, and I hope the fish got a chance to feast on our lunch before it sank past them into the depths of the lake!

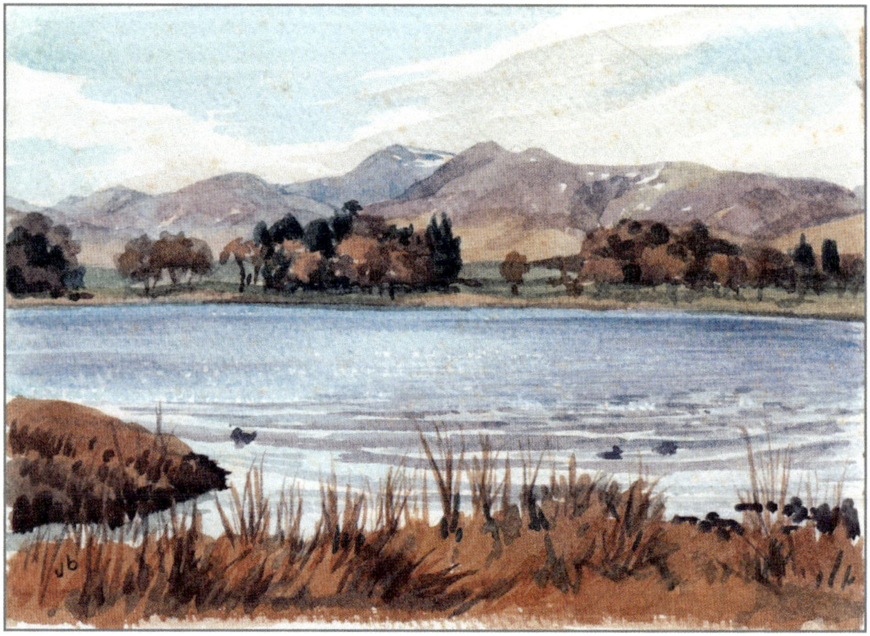

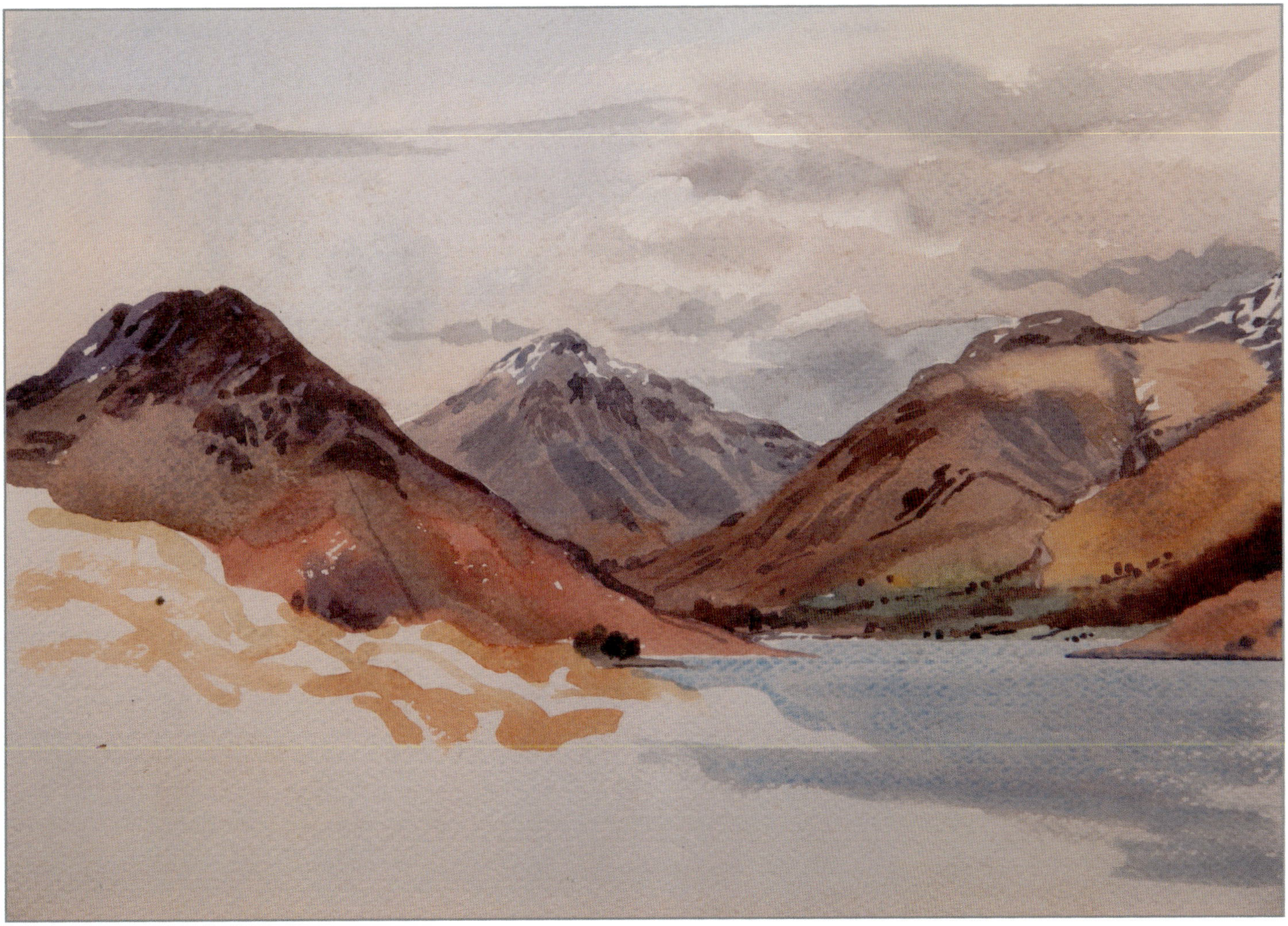

Great Gable at the head of Wastwater

Ennerdale Water

I don't remember visiting Ennerdale Water as a child, which is strange because my book on places to fish in the Lake District made it sound like even I could catch a fish there! I did make several trips to the lake in later years with Jennifer to paint.

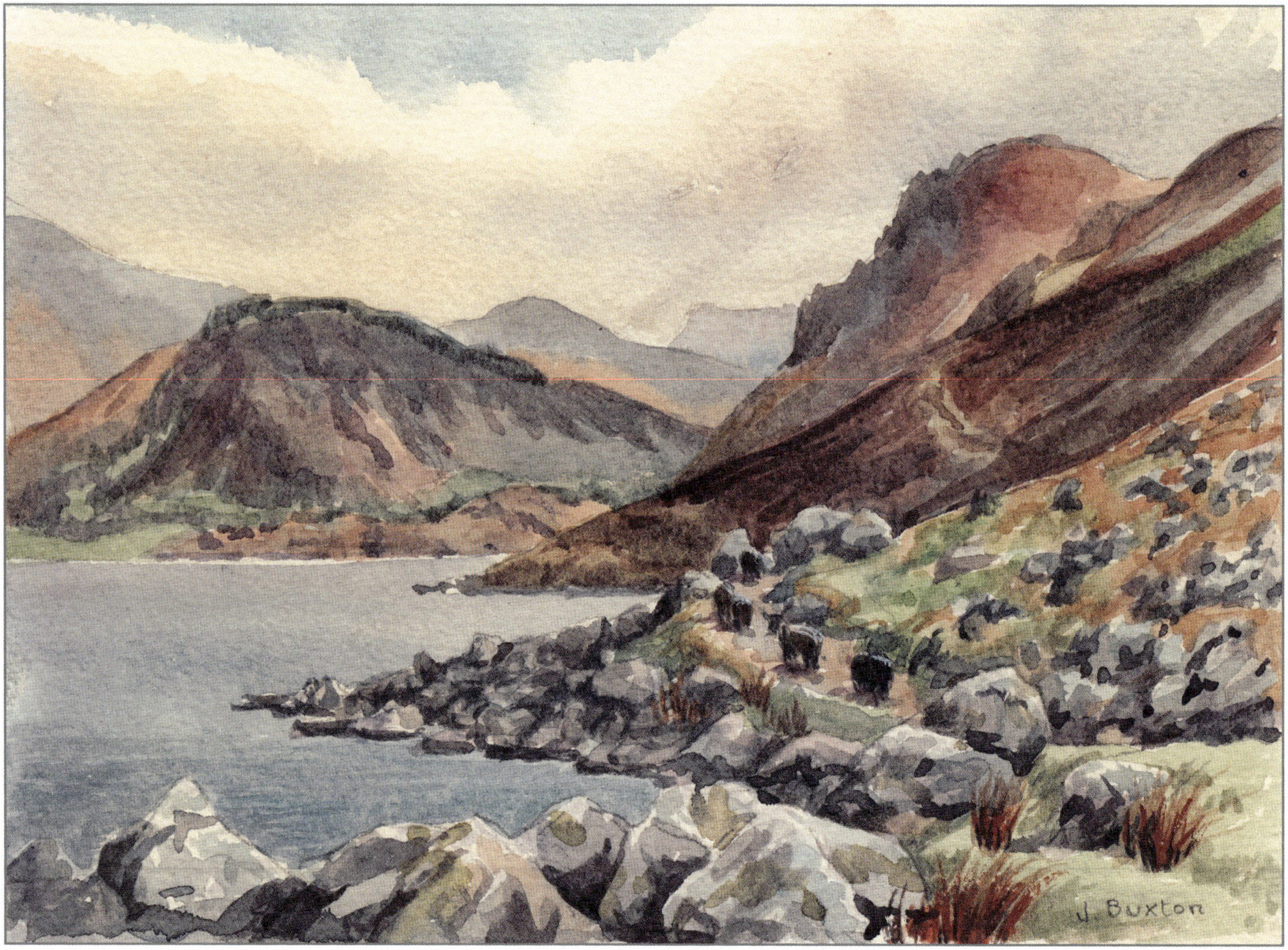

Ennerdale Water

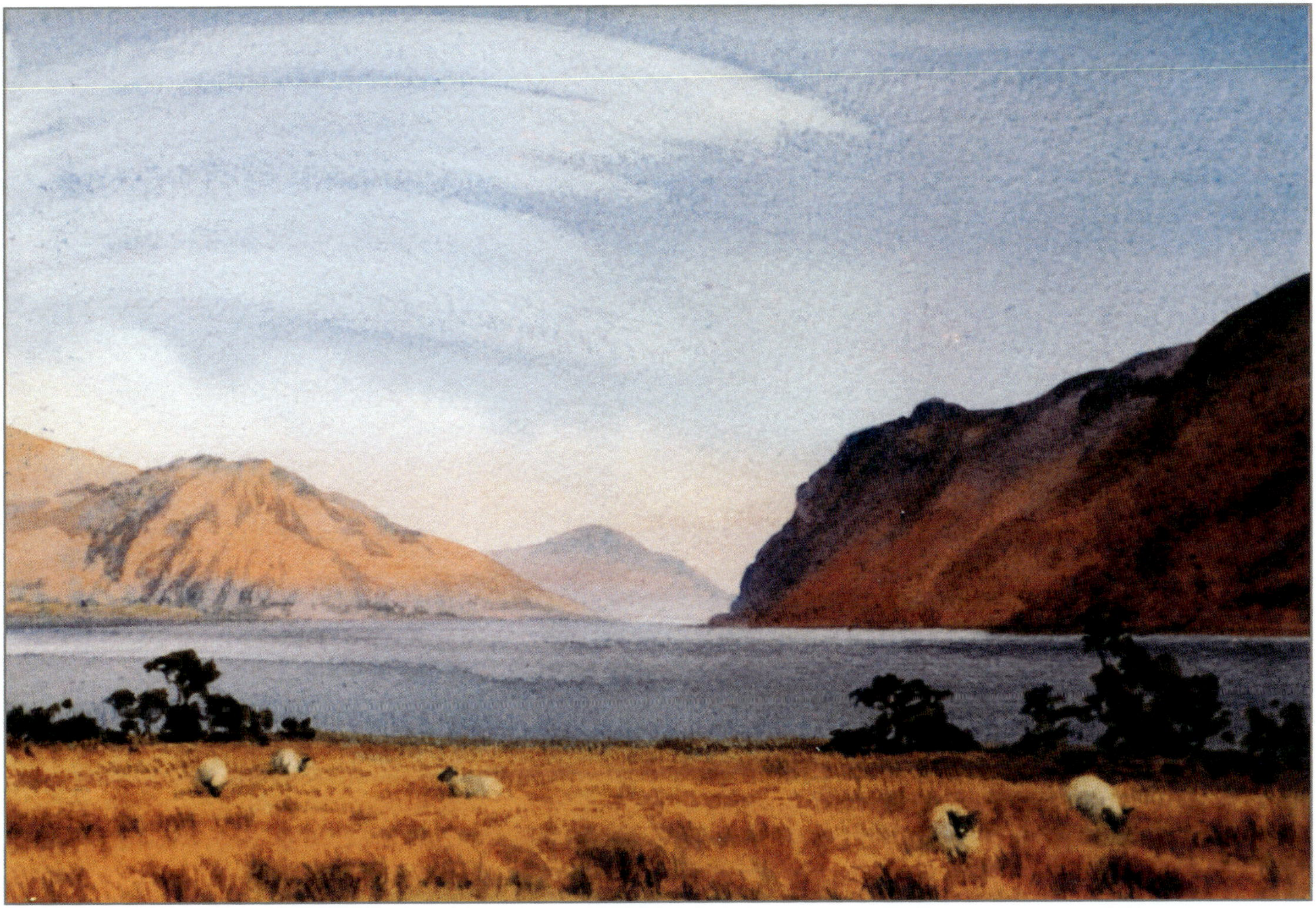

Ennerdale Water from the north west, with Bowness Knott on the left, Anglers' Crag on the right

The Northern Lakes

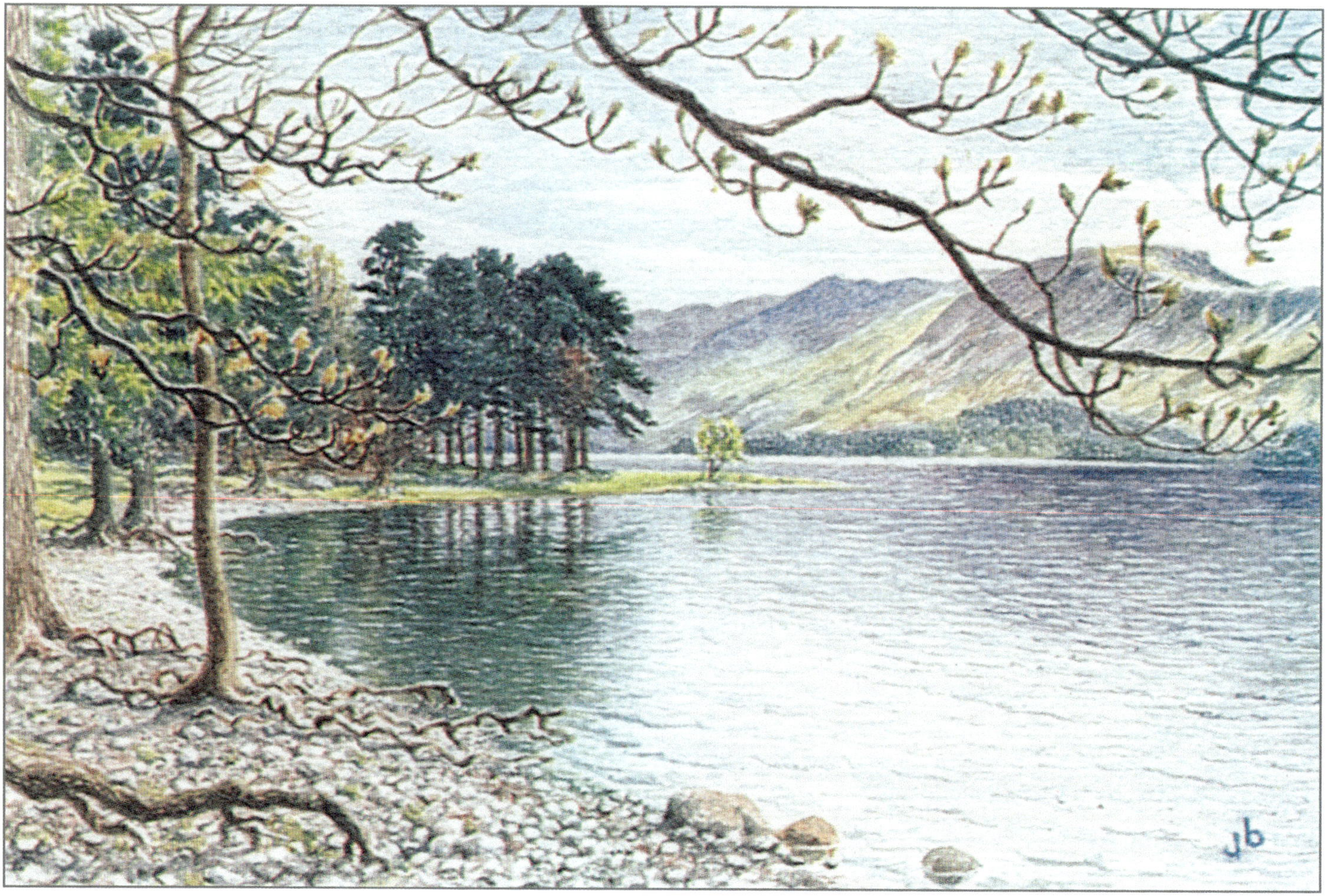

Spring on Derwent Water

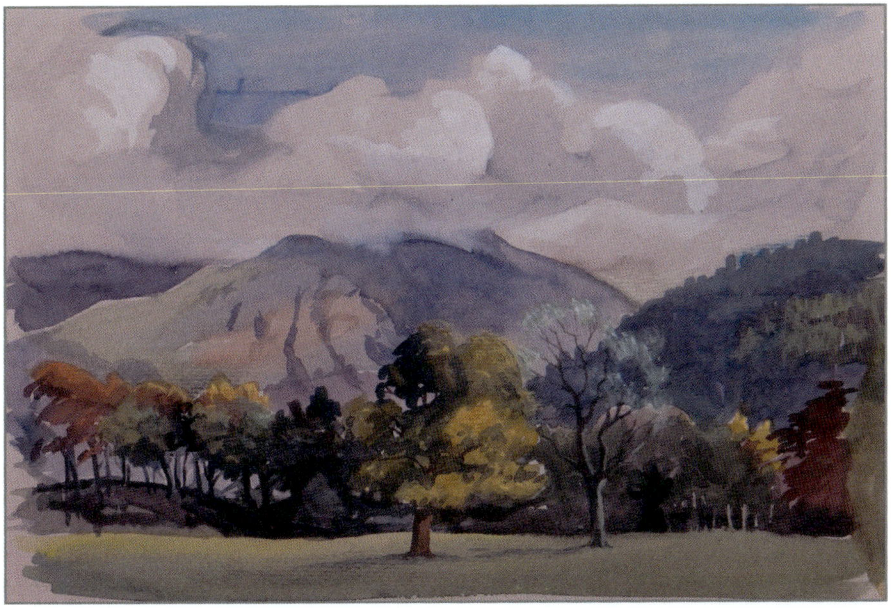

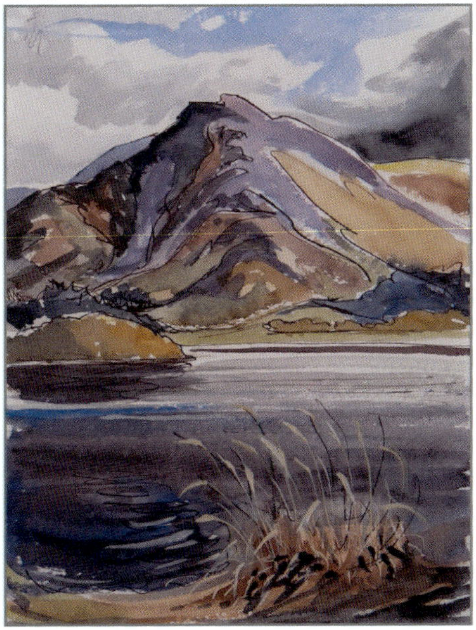

Buttermere

The town of Keswick is the gateway to the Northern lakes: Derwent Water, Bassenthwaite Lake, Buttermere, Crummock Water and Loweswater.

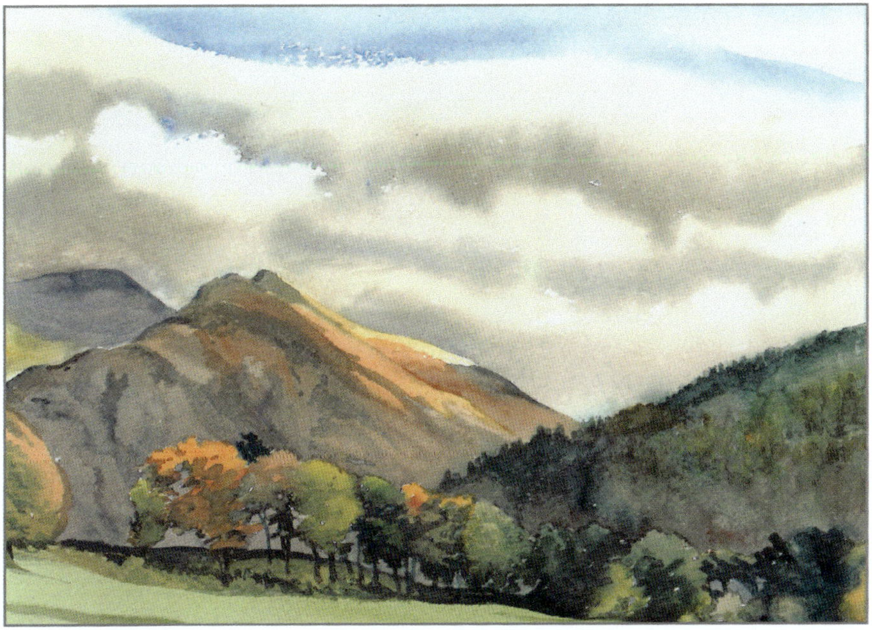

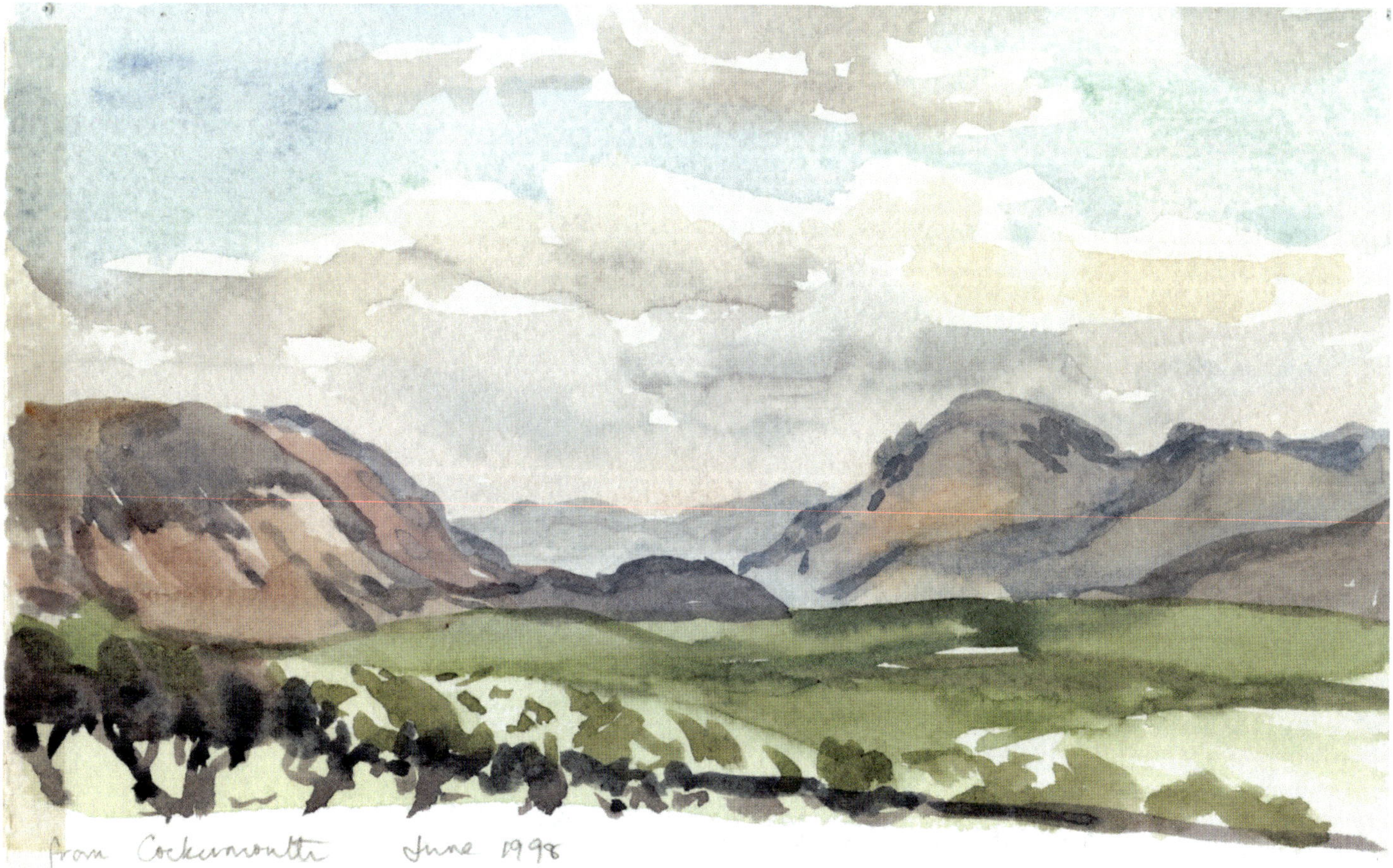

The view from Cockermouth

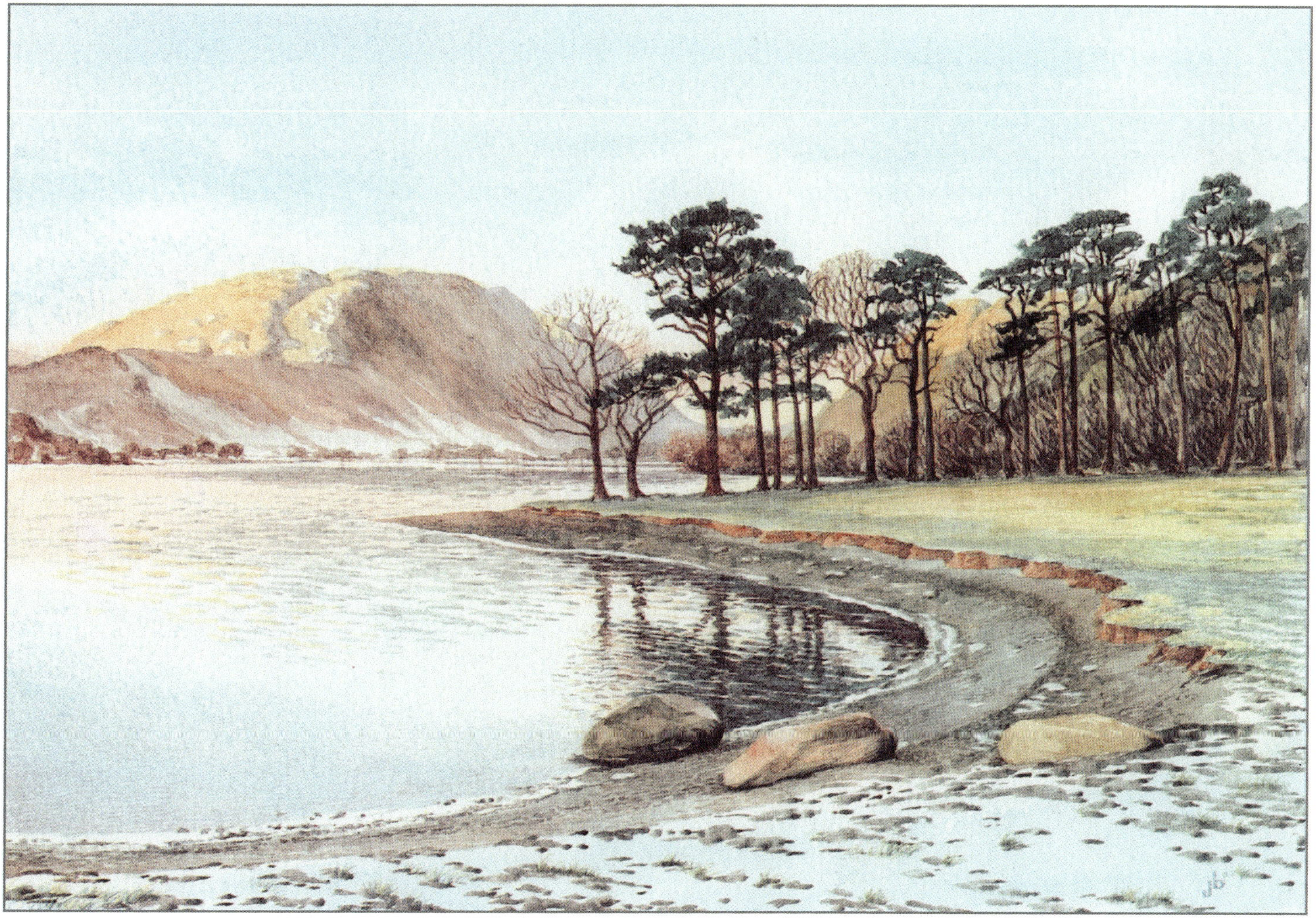

Crummock Water

Lakes and Fells of the English Lake District

The Art of Jennifer Buxton RMS HS

Closing thoughts

While prolific in her painting and sketching, unfortunately Jennifer was not so reliable when it came to recording when and where the painting was created. I have done my best to match paintings to locations, and in this regard I would like to thank my brother Henry who is a much more reliable guide to the Lake District fells than I. In addition, some of the paintings are no longer accessible and I've had to reproduce them from older photographs, in which case the quality of reproduction has sometimes been compromised unfortunately.

A big thank you to various friends who have been of invaluable assistance in bringing this book project to fruition. My editor and wonderful friend Sue, thank you so much, I couldn't have done this without you. And of course to my mother Jennifer, whose love of this area over so many years has left us this rich collection of artwork to enjoy. Jennifer touched so many peoples' lives in a positive way, I wish she could have been with us to see this project completed.

Thank you to Mick Ashworth (www.ashworthmaps.co.uk © Ashworth Maps and Interpretation Ltd) for the excellent maps that allowed us to better explain the locations where Jennifer painted. Additional maps are © OpenStreetMap contributors - www.openstreetmap.org

Tom Buxton, May 2021

Erata

If you feel I have erroneously described a location then by all means please let me know: as with previous books I will correct and make changes as I add more of Jennifer's artwork from private collections to fill the gaps in the record.

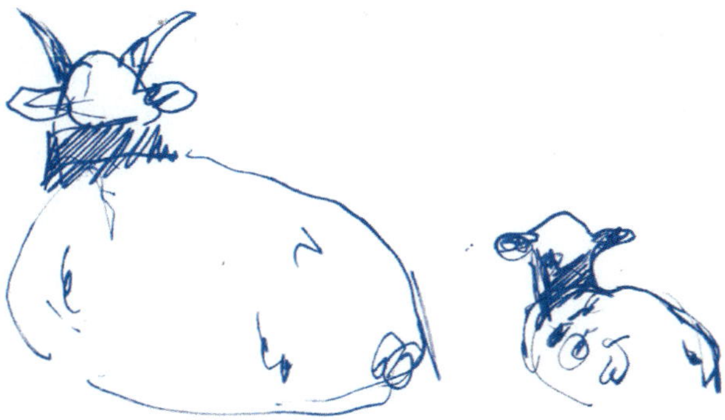

It always amazed me how Jennifer could
give attitude to something even when
it wasn't looking in your direction!

the end

Proceeds from the sale of this book go to support the preservation of the English Lake District

Other titles by Jennifer Buxton

(available from www.JenniferBuxton.uk)

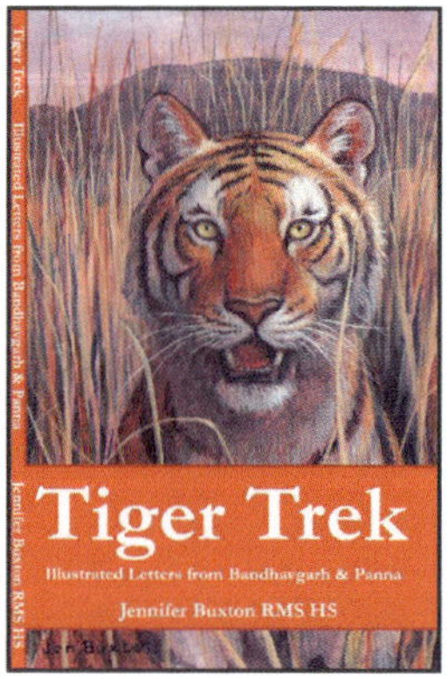

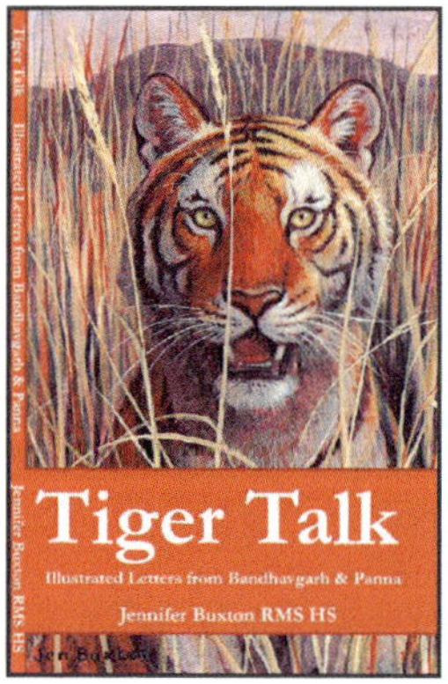

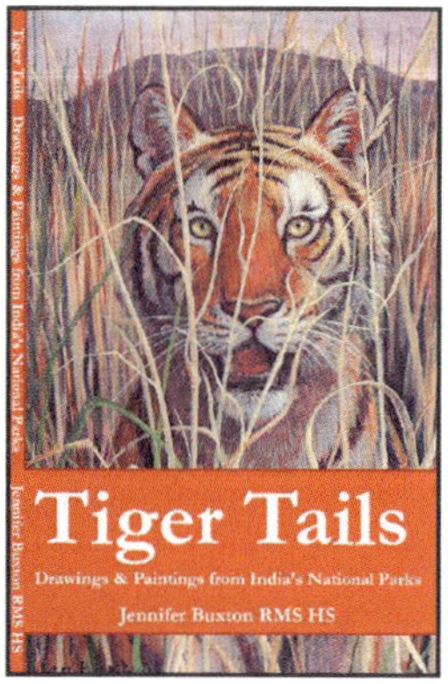

Tiger in the Grass *(2021)*

Tiger Trek and Tiger Talk are based on illustrated letters Jennifer wrote to her godchildren during two of her early visits to see tigers in Bandhavgarh and Panna National Parks in India. Tiger Tails presents a selection of Jennifer's artwork from 18 visits to some of the classic national parks of central and northern India.

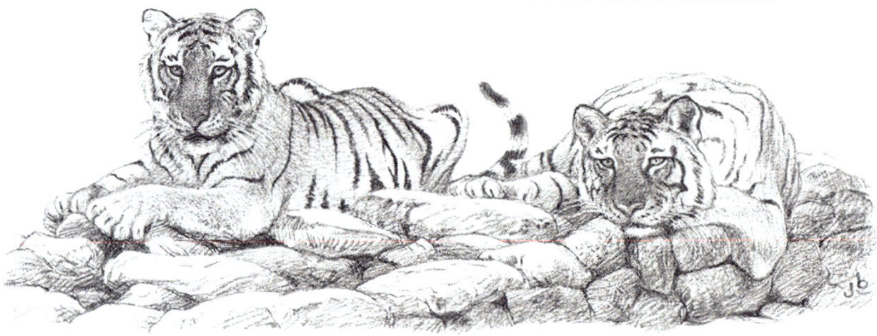

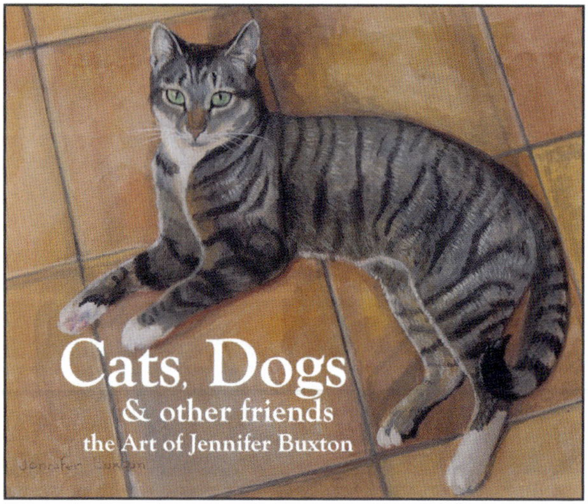

Cats, dogs & other friends *(2022)*

A book of exactly what it says - cats, dogs, horses, sheep, tigers, elephants, birds; possibly a person or two. Jennifer's love of animals and the world they inhabit comes across vividly in this charming book.

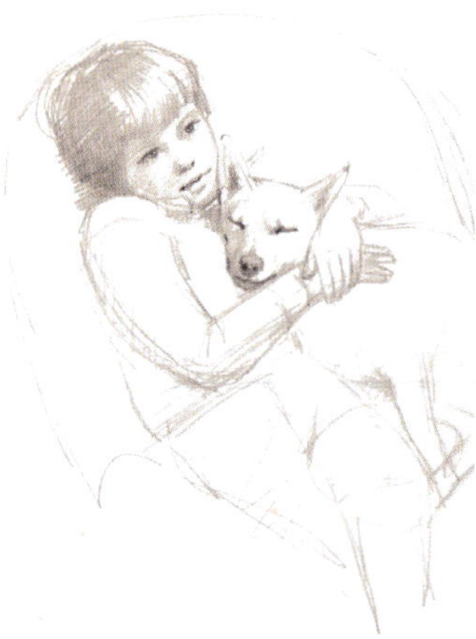

Overlapping footprints in the jungle

Between 2004 and 2014, Jennifer travelled to India over 18 times in search of tigers. The funds she raised through art sales, lectures and donations went directly to conservation and education efforts in and around Panna and Bandhavgarh National Parks.

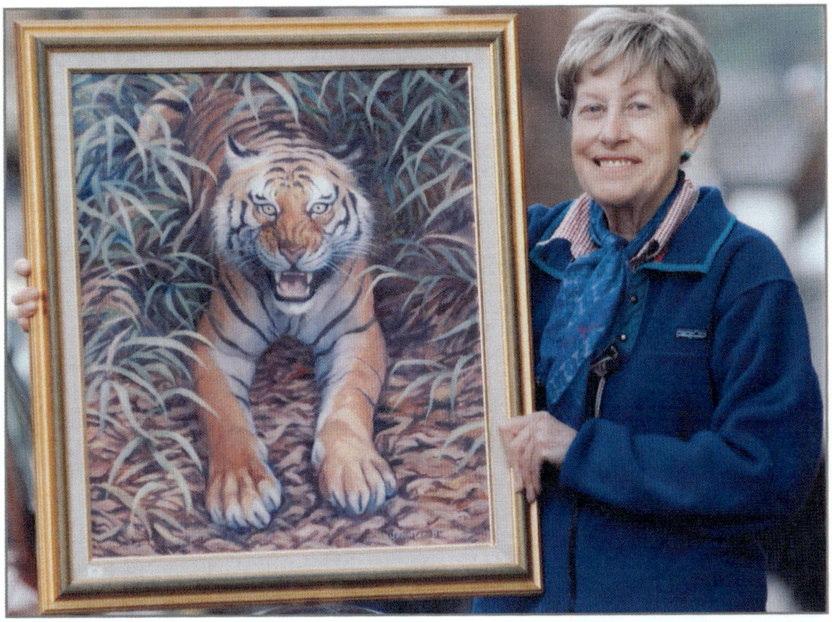

(© Newsquest Cumbria)

Over time, as she got to know some of the local people living around the parks, Jennifer became convinced that the best hope for the tigers' survival lay in initiatives to support their co-existence with humans in this rapidly developing environment. This is the meaning behind her superposition of a human footprint and a tiger's pugmark which we've used as a delimiter in some of her books.

Jennifer supported an initiative to compensate farmers for livestock lost to tigers, and another to purchase travel corridors to allow male tigers to travel between the parks. She also participated in a major project in partnership with local businesses to help villagers on the outskirts of Panna to understand the importance of wild tigers and the national parks to their local economy by rebuilding the Madla village school and promoting lessons for the children on the park and its animals.

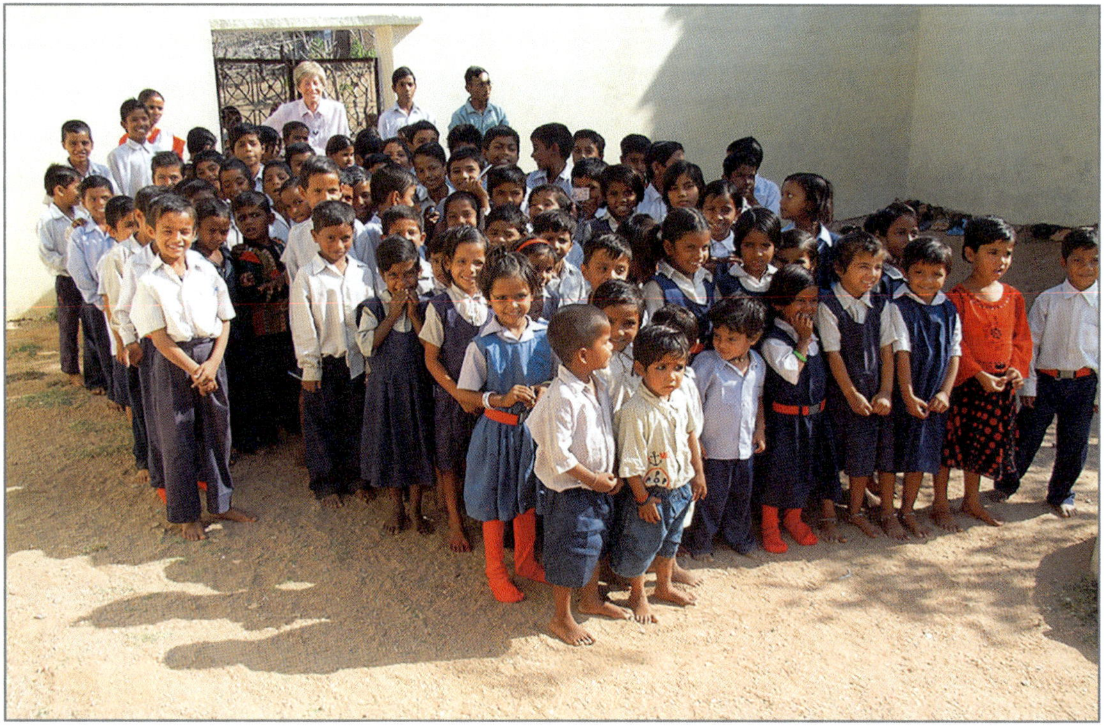

Children in Madla School, November 2006

This initiative helps local children come to appreciate the value of the Panna Tiger Reserve and its animals to themselves, India, and the World.

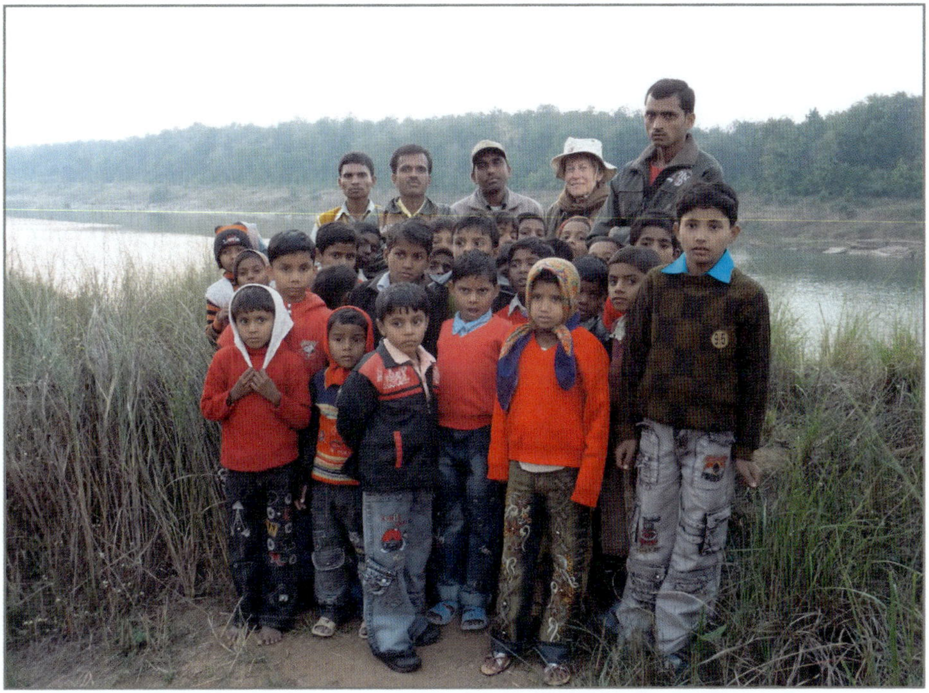

Children from Madla School on a trip
into the Panna Tiger Reserve

Tigers are critically endangered and their survival in the wild is far from assured.

Proceeds from the sale of Jennifer's tiger books go directly to help conservation efforts in and around the tiger reserves of central India.

Thank you for your support

www.JenniferBuxton.UK

a Lifetime of Art

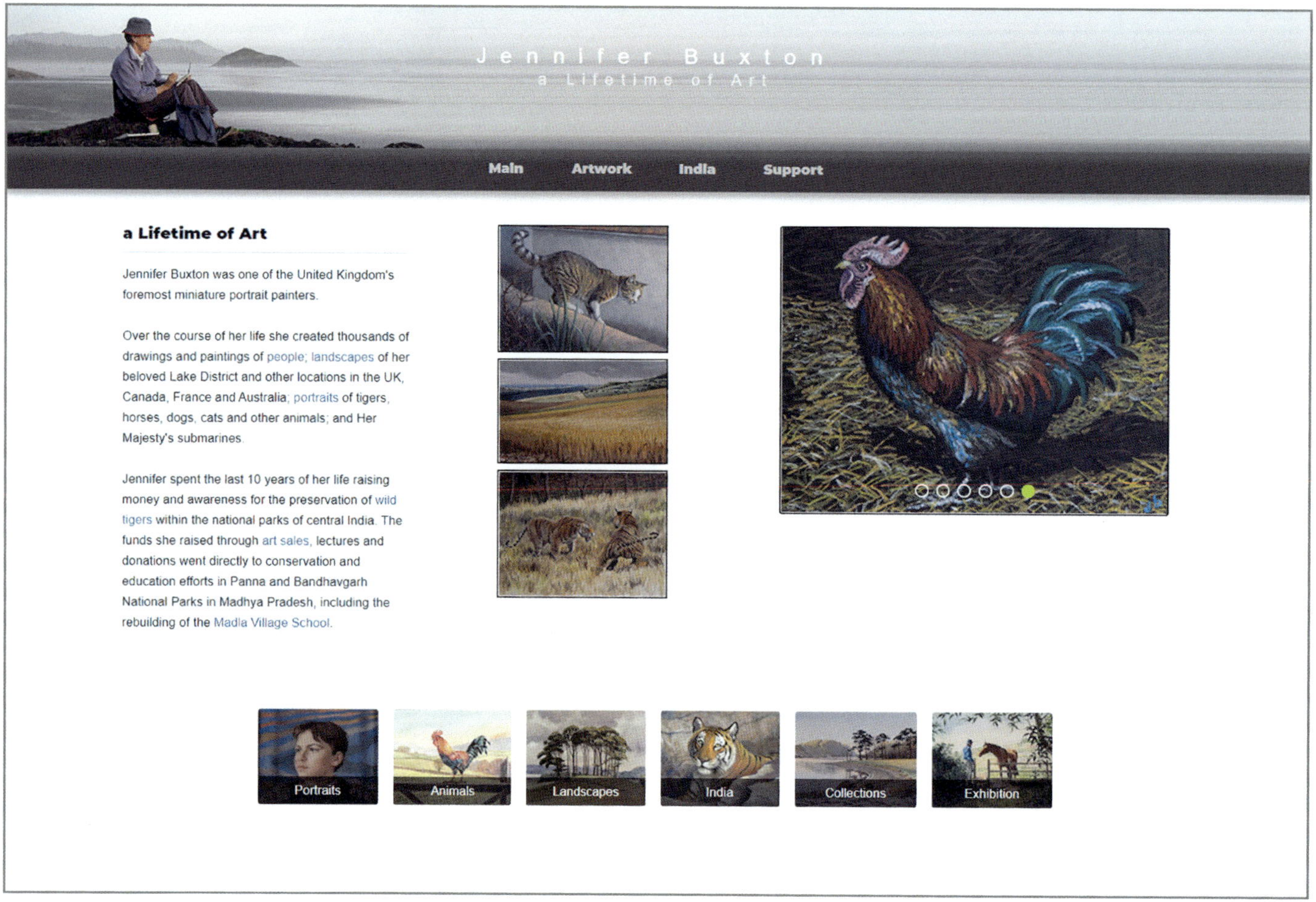

For more information or to see examples of Jennifer's work visit
www.JenniferBuxton.uk

Printed in Poland
by Amazon Fulfillment
Poland Sp. z o.o., Wrocław

81537438R00068